Advance Praise for

The Post-Petroleum Survival Guide and Cookbook

Who knew petrocollapse could be so tasty? Albert Bates has shown us the
way through the coming crisis with candor, humor... and good taste.

— GREGORY GREENE, writer/director, *The End Of Suburbia* and
Escape From Suburbia

This book is like a Swiss army knife. Sharp. Simple. Very practical.
Extremely useful. Full of survival tools, which you may need in the next
five minutes or five years from now. Highly recommended to everyone
from students to politicians to corporate executives.

— DR. VALENTIN YEMELIN, climate scientist,
UN Environment Programme/GRID-Arendal, Norway

An honest look at both the frightening and hopeful post-peak oil scenarios,
Bates provides us with information and inspiration to not only survive
but thrive in an energy-constrained world.

— MEGAN QUINN, outreach director, The Community Solution

With luck, we will never need to know how to throw together an
expedient fallout shelter, but this book tells how, and what to stock it with.
Still, there is no need for delay in starting to deploy the full range of
sustainable living choices that Albert Bates offers. These are indeed
Recipes for Changing Times — very tasty food for thought!

— JOHN PIKE, Director of GlobalSecurity.org,
member of the US Council on Foreign Relations.

This is really the book we've been waiting for — a practical, optimistic
guide to life beyond the peak — to its ingenious, resourceful and
common-sense possibilities as well as to its inevitable challenges.

— ROB HOPKINS, TransitionCulture.org

As we blithely motor up to the top of Peak Oil, thoughts turn to
what lies ahead. To help those who find the plan of driving straight off a cliff
disagreeable, there is an experienced Sherpa by the name of Albert Bates,
pointing out the best ways to negotiate the downward slope. All the
essentials are covered: water, shelter, fuel, food, and, of course,
food preparation: I especially recommend his Borscht.

— DMITRY ORLOV, www.SurvivingPeakOil.com

The Post Petroleum Survival Guide is exactly what we've needed
— a cheery, funny, and supremely useful book about the end of civilization —
that actually tells us what we can do about it and how to prepare. It's amazingly
comprehensive, with pointers on everything from the how and where of growing
food, to conflict resolution. Packed full of great resources and references, this
is the guidebook I'd want to have at my side. I can't wait to send copies to all
my distraught, despairing friends anguishing about the end of the world!

— STARHAWK author of *The Spiral Dance,*
The Fifth Sacred Thing and *The Earth Path.*

In *The Post Petroleum Survival Guide and Cookbook,* Albert Bates
demonstrates with great clarity and panache that if you love this planet,
you must change your life.

— DR. HELEN CALDICOTT, pediatrician and author of
If You Love This Planet: A Plan to Heal the Earth and *The New Nuclear Danger:*
George W. Bush's Military-Industrial Complex

Don't wait for the post-petroleum age— enjoy the benefits these
power-packed, tasty, healthful, economical foods now!

— LOUISE HAGLER, author of *Miso Cookery, Meatless Burgers,* and *Soyfoods Cookery*

One of the planet's leading ecovillage activists offers a smorgasbord of healthy,
sustainable, practical advice for meeting our daily life needs — from potable
water and nutritious food to energy and transportation — as we encounter
the challenges of peak oil and other unprecedented threats. With a direct,
conversational approach, and packed with pithy, memorable insights,
Albert illuminates how to grow local, vigorous, grassroots economies and utilize
low-tech as well as cutting-edge technologies so we can live simply, yet better,
in what he terms both a horrible predicament — and wonderful opportunity.

— DIANA LEAFE CHRISTIAN, author, *Creating a Life Together: Practical Tools*
to Grow Ecovillages and Intentional Communities, and *Finding Community:*
How to Join an Ecovillage or Intentional Community

Albert Bates' *Post Petroleum Survival Guide* is a rich compendium,
a blueprint for moving into a changing energy future. It's a *Whole Earth Catalog*
distilled to the essentials for smaller-energy-footprint living, leavened with
deep wisdom, a wide variety of localizable food recipes, juicy quotes and
reminders to enjoy life as we power down. It will feed body and soul.
Use it to build your community ark.

— JANAIA DONALDSON, producer and host, "Peak Moment" television series

THE POST-PETROLEUM
SURVIVAL GUIDE
and cookbook

} *recipes for changing times*

ALBERT BATES

Cary, this will help see you through to the near term to a much better future.

Albert Bates
2007
Nashville

NEW SOCIETY PUBLISHERS

Cataloging in Publication Data:
A catalog record for this publication is available from the National Library of Canada.

Cover design by Diane McIntosh. Photos: iStock/Photodisc/Getty Images.

Printed in Canada.
First printing October 2006.

Paperback ISBN-13: 978-0-86571-568-4
Paperback ISBN-10: 0-86571-568-8

Inquiries regarding requests to reprint all or part of *The Post-Petroleum Survival Guide and Cookbook* should be addressed to New Society Publishers at the address below.

To order directly from the publishers, please call toll-free (North America) 1-800-567-6772, or order online at www.newsociety.com

Any other inquiries can be directed by mail to:

New Society Publishers
P.O. Box 189, Gabriola Island, BC V0R 1X0, Canada
1-800-567-6772

New Society Publishers' mission is to publish books that contribute in fundamental ways to building an ecologically sustainable and just society, and to do so with the least possible impact on the environment, in a manner that models this vision. We are committed to doing this not just through education, but through action. We are acting on our commitment to the world's remaining ancient forests by phasing out our paper supply from ancient forests worldwide. This book is one step toward ending global deforestation and climate change. It is printed on acid-free paper that is **100% old growth forest-free** (100% post-consumer recycled), processed chlorine free, and printed with vegetable-based, low-VOC inks. For further information, or to browse our full list of books and purchase securely, visit our website at: www.newsociety.com

NEW SOCIETY PUBLISHERS   www.newsociety.com

To Zenzo Kuzakari

I hope that in every
community throughout this country, that
spirit can be fostered which makes a piece of work
worthwhile because you love to do it, regardless of the time
you put into it, and because it is worth everything that you can put
into it to give to the world a really perfect thing.
— Eleanor Roosevelt, 1934

Contents

Foreword

By Richard Heinberg

By the end of the current century everyone will be pursuing a post-petroleum existence. That's not a particularly scary thought — initially, at least — in that it implies both that society will have decades in which to make the transition and that most of us who are alive today won't be around to see whether or not we like the result.

However, oil analysts who study depletion trends say that the changeover may actually be a bit more challenging — and that it may begin so soon that any complacency on our part could seriously hamper our survival prospects. Petroleum geologists and industry experts have made a cogent case that the all-time peak of global oil extraction is likely to occur within the next five years; meanwhile, a recent study ("Peaking of World Oil Production: Impacts, Mitigation and Risk Management") commissioned by the US Department of Energy concludes that we need twenty years of crash-program preparatory work in order to avoid the "unprecedented" economic, social, and political costs that Peak Oil would otherwise entail. Some macro-social analysts (I include myself here) even believe that, unless we do prepare for Peak Oil and respond to its challenge with uncommon levels of cooperation and intelligence, it could trigger a societal collapse of the sort that brought down the ancient Romans, Mayans, and Easter Islanders.

For those who are paying attention to this emerging crisis, the message couldn't be clearer: we have no time to waste. The sooner we begin living in the post-petroleum world the easier the transition will be for us personally, and the more knowledge and skills we will have to contribute to the greater collective efforts that will be needed.

There is a profound and growing need for a Peak Oil Survival Guide. As people initially become aware of the impending global withdrawal symptoms from our addiction to non-renewable, dwindling petroleum they tend to clamor for answers to obvious questions: *How will I get around when gasoline gets really expensive? Where will my food come from when the tractors don't have fuel? How about water? Should I move to a place with better survival prospects?*

I've fielded such queries again and again during the past few years as I've crisscrossed the country talking to groups large and small about the problem of Peak Oil and its ominous implications for our lives. I have therefore contemplated writing a book somewhat like this one on many occasions, but for one reason or another have repeatedly been drawn toward other projects.

It's just as well. Albert Bates has produced a volume with more wit and judicious advice than I could possibly have done; indeed there is probably no one better suited than he to address this topic. Albert has been living a post-petroleum lifestyle since the 1970s, and, as Director of the Ecovillage Training Center at The Farm in Tennessee (a legendary intentional community exploring the frontiers of creative solutions to environmental and social problems), has taught subjects ranging from straw-bale home-building and mycoforestry to Permaculture and urban village design.

In a typical stroke of mad genius, Albert chose to make this a cookbook as well as a survival guide. There is nothing more basic to human life than eating, and Peak Oil will require some serious adjustments in how we feed ourselves. But what good is mere survival if we cannot find enjoyment as we go? Self-sufficiency and relocalization of economic activity will require creativity and humor as well as serious planning and hard work.

The cuisine described herein is not regional, because the book is intended to be universal; nevertheless, as post-petroleum agriculture necessarily becomes more localized, ingredients may become more place-specific. Albert is keenly aware of this paradox, and offers us meals that will thrill our palates wherever we're rooted. In the past-peak future, we may have vastly more time for activities such as cooking and savoring our garden-grown food — one of the silver linings of the transition ahead. Why not become a gourmet chef and turn necessity to artistry?

As Albert Bates gently informs us, Peak Oil survival will not be so much a matter of implementing new high-tech energy sources as one of getting back in touch with the rhythms of the seasons and the lay of the land. Thus we can probably glean more relevant guidance for our future from veterans of rural areas during the Great Depression than from even the most brilliant investment analysts or exotic materials scientists.

Using quotes from sometimes-obscure but always blazingly illuminating sources, Albert sheds light on the nature of money and how Peak Oil will affect our economic lives; on how to secure a source of clean water; on dealing with wastes once the trash trucks fall silent and the flush toilets stop flushing; on heating our homes, cooking our food, and reading books at night without hastening global warming in the process.

This is clear, practical information that could save your life and those of your family and community members. It is the sort of information that desperately needs to be collected and distributed *now* — while the printing presses and delivery trucks are still up and running.

Cookbooks are handy things; that's why they sell so well. The best ones offer clear instructions and mouth-watering photos of the finished products. It is a bit of a challenge to paint the post-Peak Oil world in inviting terms, but Albert Bates has met that challenge. His cookbook is both lucid in its directions and appealing in its outcomes. Amidst all the dozens of books on Peak Oil (the ranks of which are growing by the month), this is one that is both truly original and fun read.

Here is information that's helpful to have on the home bookshelf, and that's also good to access and apply proactively *before* the obvious need arises.

Start living a post-petroleum lifestyle now and avoid the rush.

Richard Heinberg
August 13, 2006

Richard Heinberg is a journalist, editor, lecturer and the author of six previous books, including The Party's Over: Oil, War and the Fate of Industrial Societies *and* Powerdown: Options and Actions for a Post Carbon World, *and most recently,* The Oil Depletion Protocol: A Plan to Avert Oil Wars, Terrorism and Economic Collapse. *A member of the core faculty at New College of California School of Sustainability, and a research fellow with the Post Carbon Institute, he is widely acknowledged as one of the world's most foremost Peak Oil educators.*

Acknowledgments

For ideas and encouragement along the way: Albert Bartlett, Albert Gore Jr., Amory B. Lovins, Andy Langford, Chris and Judith Plant, Colin Campbell, Dan Miner, Davie Phillips, Declan and Margrit Kennedy, Diana Leafe Christian, Dmitry Orlov, Don Pitzer, Doug Cobb, Faith Morgan, Felicity Hill, Frank Michael, Gregory Greene, Herman Daly, Ianto Evans, James Howard Kunstler, James Lovelock, Jan Bang, Jan Lundberg, Jared Diamond, John Ikerd, Judy Wicks, Julian Darley, Lester Brown, Liora Adler, Maria Ros, Mark Robinowitz, Marshall Rosenberg, Mary Olson, Matt Savinar, Matt Simmons, Megan Quinn, Michael Ruppert, Pat Murphy, Peter Bane, Richard and Janet Heinberg, Rob Hopkins, Robert Gilman, Ross Gelbspan, Scott Horton, and Yaacov Oved. For help with research: Agnieszka Komach, Andrew Brown, Charles Hall, Charles Komanoff, Colin Campbell, David Blume, Joseph Tainter, Kerry Emanuel, L. Hunter Lovins, Mauricio De la Puente Martínez de Castro, Michael Sligh, Motarilavoa Hilda Lini, Peter Kinfield, Ronald Nigh, Sandor Katz, Steve Sawyer, Tree Bresson and Valentin Yemelin. For recipe advice: Kippy Nigh, Mark Schoene, and Sharon Wells. For cutting-room collaboration: Audrey McClellan, Kathy Hill, and Gayla Groom.

Author's Preface

There is an irony about depleting a finite resource: the better
you are at doing the job, the sooner it ends.

— Colin Campbell, 2005

Reading every new Peak Oil book that comes out can be very depressing. Ask me. I've been doing it now for several years. There is a kind of morbid fascination, watching the world spin out of control as we sit, transfixed, observing. And it is somehow comforting to read the comments of fellow observers. We all see the future barreling down on us, and we are all motionless, hypnotized.

We are like spectators at a bullfight, watching a noble animal die. At the same time, it isn't like anyone in the audience is exempt. We are all in the position of the bull. We can see the sword in the matador's hand, we can feel the blood dripping from our wounds, but still we charge ahead, egged on by the shouts of the crowd.

At some point I just want to throw up my hands and say, "Enough already!" I get it. This particular bull wants nothing more than to turn away and go back to the cows in the pasture.

But I'm trapped. We are all trapped.

Most of us were simply born into this situation and had nothing to do with creating it. At the same time, most of us are guilty of burning fossil energy and doing nothing to replenish the supply. We are all guilty of global warming. We are all pushing other species into extinction. We are all depleting soils to make food and using up natural resources at unsustainable rates. Every one of us is to blame.

But honestly, blame is useless. Complaining is useless. We need a way out. So I wrote this book.

What is it about? It's about changing how we live. It's about stopping overconsumption by stopping overproduction. It's about doing less while living better. It's about an attitude change.

I had hoped to explore a central theme of living life at a different pace, having fun and getting by while deindustrializing our overextended, frenetic lifestyles. As though I was living out some kind of archetypal writer's fantasy, I found a secluded desert island and holed up in a grass shack, drinking tequila with surfers and beach bums while I wrote about the lifestyles of surfers and beach bums.

Some early readers of the manuscript thought I needed to explain the problem more. Yawn. As if reading about peak oil wasn't bad enough, they wanted me to actually write about it.

While I did include some of my own thoughts about the problem, I decided it would be better to let my fellow hypnotized observers do that part, so I sprinkled the book liberally with their pithy quotations. Most are pretty pessimistic. I hope they don't sour anyone's appetite for the food.

It took some explaining to get the publisher to understand why this should also be a cookbook. In my opinion it should also have been a coloring book, but I couldn't sell that. The point is to make a real downer of a subject more fun and to practice community, which is (not to spoil the ending for you) the ultimate solution. We're going to solve this problem over a nice meal and perhaps a glass of fine wine.

There are usually three broad scenarios that depict the world after global oil and gas production starts its downward slide. The first is a soft landing, with government and market wisdom reacting to fill the gaps in industrial economies with newer and better alternatives. The second is a fast slide, in which a combination of government missteps and corporate blunders cause a stuttering inconsistency of essential services, perhaps triggering an economic recession that gradually deepens as major structural changes are forced upon every sector of society. The third is a hard landing after falling off the cliff, with a sudden market collapse, the default of national currencies, starvation, loss of familiar habitats, and ultimately a die-off of as much as two-thirds of the human population of the Earth.

In the stark terms of Dmitry Orlov, who witnessed the collapse of the Soviet empire in the early 1990s:

The temporary bounty of fossil fuels has allowed a lot of the former peasants to live like nobles for a time — residing in mansions, moving about in carriages, and having people serve them. Once these sources of energy are depleted, many of these former peasants will be forced to revert back. They will once more have to live in huts, travel on foot, wield their ancestral scythes and sickles to provide their sustenance, and do their own chores.

I have to confess that I am more optimistic than Mr. Orlov. I lean toward the soft landing, or maybe a middle course that leads us to curb the rapacious appetites that have been so destructive of the natural world upon which we all depend. It isn't that I think governments will get smarter in time to make a real difference, although that could still happen, but I think people will educate themselves and will have time and resources enough to make their own transitions to appropriate lifestyle patterns, regardless of the ineptitude of their leaders. This book is intended to help make the Great Change not only easy, but also enjoyable. I actually see the coming transition as a good thing. After reading this book, I hope you will too.

Albert K. Bates
March 2006

Crude Awakening

*Initially
it will be denied. There will
be much lying and obfuscation. Then
prices will rise and demand will fall. The rich
will outbid the poor for available supplies. The system will initially appear to rebalance. The dash for gas
will become more frenzied. People will realize nuclear power
stations take up to ten years to build. People will also realize
wind, waves, solar and other renewables are all pretty marginal and
take a lot of energy to construct. There will be a dash for more fuel-
efficient vehicles and equipment. The poor will not be able to afford the
investment or the fuel. Exploration and exploitation of oil and gas will
become completely frenzied. More and more countries will decide to reserve
oil and later gas supplies for their own people. Air quality will be ignored as
coal production and consumption expand once more. Once the decline really
gets under way, liquids production will fall relentlessly by five percent per
year. Energy prices will rise remorselessly. Inflation will become endemic.
Resource conflicts will break out.*

— Association for the Study of Peak Oil
Newsletter, March 2002

It is not surprising that we are so fond of oil. It is the primary fuel for transportation, a key source of heat, and a critical component of virtually millions of products — from clothing to construction materials, pharmaceuticals to fertilizers. But given that the supply is

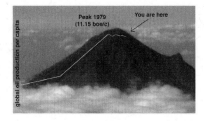

finite, there are two inescapable facts about oil and other fossil-based fuels: the available resource will eventually be depleted; and, along the way, demand will outstrip production.

"Peak oil" refers to the tipping point — that point in time when the absolute peak in production is reached, when there will never again be as much oil and gas flowing into the global economy as there is at that moment. It is not to be confused with running out of petroleum — the world will probably never reach that point because of how difficult and costly it is to find and extract. Peak oil is only the top of the hill. It might be a plateau that lasts ten years. We may be there now.

Every effort will be made to sustain the production peak. There will be dramatic improvements in technology, exhaustive exploration, and price incentives. However, as we have seen from the examples of the United States after 1971, Russia after 1975, and the European Union after 2000, none of those will matter. From the summit of peak oil, every road leads downward.

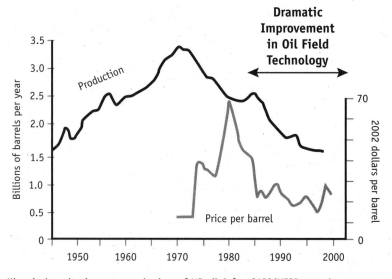

Historical production rates and prices of US oil (after SAIC/MISI, 2005).

Might As Well Face It

In early 2006 the president of the United States, a former oil man, warned his nation that its people were dangerously addicted to oil. That was the word he used. Addicted.

And it's true. Petroleum has become an addiction, not just for the United States, but for all globalized technological nations. Which is to say, nearly everybody. Like all addictions, our oil habit follows an easily charted pattern:

- We develop a tolerance for the craved object (needing increased amounts to achieve the same effect).
- We experience withdrawal symptoms.
- We take the craved object in larger amounts than was intended or over a longer period of time than was intended.
- We have a persistent desire to decrease the amount of the craved object we consume, but are unable to consume less.
- We spend a great deal of time and money in an attempt to acquire the craved object.
- We continue to use the craved object, even though we know it is causing recurring physical, social, or psychological problems.

Most psychologists, when presented with a patient showing these symptoms, would design a structured recovery program to bolster the patient's resolve and motivation to return to normal life without the addiction and would begin a schedule of treatment activities in a favorable setting.

Addiction treatment assumes a patient is rational and able to think and talk about problems. This is where the metaphor begins to unravel. Governments have different psychological makeups than individuals. Rationality is not a word that is easily applied.

Governments are the product of their constituencies' collective desires. It matters little whether they are democracies, socialist states, oligarchies, military dictatorships, or something else entirely. Each answers to some core constituency that ultimately calls the shots.

Looking around the world, we see that the core constituencies of all the industrial countries, regardless of the form of their governments, are consumers. To consumers, the function of government is to provide the conditions for ever-improving levels of human comfort and material wealth. Consumers are infinitely voracious.

For reasons that petroleum economist Marion King Hubbert foresaw in the mid-1940s, any expectation of constant expansion in consumables is a delusion. Consumers are doomed to have their dreams dashed by the very nature of nature. Governments are therefore in the impossible position of

Sit down and be quiet.
You are drunk, and this is the
edge of the roof.
— Rumi

You are getting sleepy... sleeeepppy...

having to pursue goals for their constituents that cannot be achieved. This creates a kind of institutionalized schizophrenia.

Hubbert urged that we turn toward a steady-state, rather than growth-oriented, form of economics. Coming in the Red Scare period, his ideas were regarded by elected schizophrenics as nothing short of a communist threat.

So let's forget about talking to the schizophrenics. This book is about taking charge as individuals, families, neighborhoods, and small communities to meet basic human needs, rather than expecting larger entities — provinces, states, nations, federations, and the like — to suddenly begin behaving sanely.

> For the world as a whole, oil companies are expected to keep finding and developing enough oil to offset our seventy-one million plus barrels a day of oil depletion, but also to meet new demand. By some estimates there will be an average of two per cent annual growth in global oil demand over the years ahead along with, conservatively, a three per cent natural decline in production from existing reserves. That means by 2010 we will need on the order of an additional fifty million barrels a day. So where is the oil going to come from? Governments and the national oil companies are obviously controlling about ninety per cent of the assets. Oil remains fundamentally a government business. While many regions of the world offer great oil opportunities, the Middle East, with two thirds of the world's oil and the lowest cost, is still where the prize ultimately lies ....

> — Dick Cheney (as CEO of Halliburton), 1999

Reaching the Summit

Throughout this book I will be talking a lot about China. That's because China is like a great big dragon that lives in your house and most of the time just sleeps. China has been sleeping since about the time of the Ming Dynasty, 500 years ago. Napoleon noticed it sleeping over there in the corner and remarked that we are all better off while it sleeps. Well, China just woke up. And it's hungry.

China's economy has grown by an extraordinary 9.5 percent per year over the past 20 years. In 2005, China consumed 26 percent of the world's crude steel, 32 percent of its rice, 37 percent of its cotton, and 47 percent of its cement. It could be the world's biggest manufacturer of cars by 2015.

China is today producing one car for every 600 people. To better imagine that, think of the US in 1910, when the population was 92 million and it consumed 181,000 new cars per year or one per 500 people. By 1920, US car consumption had grown tenfold, to 1.9 million per year, or one new car per 60 Usanians. In the United States today, the average number of people in a household (1.8) was recently passed by the average number of cars (1.9). China is now on the same trajectory, with an anticipated 300 million cars on Chinese roads by 2010, about one-third of all the cars in the world. Given that the US's 210 million gasoline-powered cars and light trucks use 9 million barrels of oil per day, it is easy to see how what is happening in China might affect world petroleum demand. That's before we mention India, whose population is on track to exceed China's and whose own car-building craze is just getting underway.

Many countries have instituted modest attempts at curtailing oil dependence over the years. While China was kicking all the bicycles off the streets in Beijing, Germany's National Plan on Bicycles, begun in 2002, devoted the Deutschmark equivalent of $100 million over ten years in hopes of making a 30 percent car-to-bike conversion by 2012. Germany also initiated an ambitious program to switch truck transport to canal and river barges, convert coal and nuclear electrical generation to wind and other renewables, and otherwise wean itself off petroleum dependence at the earliest possible date.

Other industrial nations have pinned their hopes on nuclear energy, but nuclear energy, never completely distinguishable from nuclear weaponry, presents a unique challenge in terms of safety and security, and no one has a real solution for those problems yet. If a solution has not been found after more than half a century of huge investments, it is unlikely any will emerge as our ability to make such research investments shrinks.

Tar sands, oil shales, deep-ocean, advanced oil and gas, enhanced recovery, methane hydrates, gas-to-liquid, and other methods of prolonging the petroleum epoch will be ballyhooed, but any one of those new technologies will carry a much higher price than do present-day gushers of light, sweet crude. Solar-derived hydrogen, methane, biodiesel, ethanol, and other substitutes will all have a niche in the future, but none of them pack the cheap BTU punch and surplus production that petroleum junkies are used to.

In combination, all these strategies may eventually give us the energy that petroleum provides today, but it won't happen quickly. Too many parts of industrial society were built to run on fossil savings, not solar income, and redesigning and rebuilding will take time. Constructing infrastructure requires energy, and that means taking energy from production of fuel (where it is in great demand) and investing it in the built environment

COLD-PRESSED OIL

The practice of pressing nuts and seeds to extract oil goes back to the most ancient civilizations for which we have records. Unrefined oils have always been the cornerstone of a healthy diet. Cold-pressed oils are rich in nutrients and have an array of taste, color, viscosity, temperature tolerance, and aroma. All of this has been sabotaged by industrial oil refineries that make bland, colorless, and flat-tasting clear oils, including some that are detrimental to health. Here are some guidelines for buying good healthy oils:

- Buy "first cold pressed" from a reliable producer, not a refinery.
- Buy certified organic if possible.
- Always buy in dark (green, brown, or blue) glass or ceramic bottles or tins, not in clear glass or plastic bottles.
- Oils should taste delicious: fresh, clean, rich — trust your taste.

If you can't find cold-pressed oils from your area, talk to the growers in farmers' markets. You might encourage them to start producing this essential local food.

The Nuclear Bargain

The hundreds of billions of dollars poured into nuclear industry subsidies by the industrial countries, much of it under a shroud of secrecy, have distorted the cost of nuclear energy. The US Energy Information Agency (EIA) estimates the subsidies alone are now up to $42 per barrel of oil equivalent. EIA did not include in this estimate the front-end subsidy for liability insurance (the US, UK, France, and others have made their nuclear plants exempt from the costs of accidents) or the back-end, not inconsiderable, costs of decommissioning and perpetual waste storage, which will be carried disproportionately on the shoulders of government treasuries and future generations of taxpayers.

Neither do most calculations of nuclear costs factor in cancers, birth defects, and the early deaths of millions of innocents living downwind and downstream of some part of the fuel cycle, or the potentially irreparable damage to human and other beings' genetic heritage.

One can say with appropriate horror that it would be more humane to burn children in electricity-generating furnaces than to cause them the significantly greater amount of suffering and death per gigawatt of nuclear energy.

When these off-the-books charges are tallied, nuclear power not only costs far more than all other forms of energy; it also does not come remotely close to producing as much energy as it consumes.

This is especially poignant because while all these billions of dollars and lives are wasted chasing the atomic power fantasy, there is enough orphaned offshore wind power to completely replace nuclear power in Europe, enough in Texas and the Dakotas alone to replace nuclear sources in North America, and all those wind farms can pay for themselves in as little as three years.

One can say with appropriate horror that it would be more humane to burn children in electricity-generating furnaces than to cause them the significantly greater amount of suffering and death per gigawatt of nuclear energy.

of new factories and exotic equipment. No matter how you slice it, our near-term future will likely see a much lower global energy economy than we currently take for granted.

Resistance is futile. Why not enjoy the slide? This book is meant to help us addicts stop agonizing about our problem and start finding the least painful way to kick the habit.

Fossilgate

Most industrial nations are aware they have a problem but are not willing to endure pain to solve it. Some will try to maintain their own position at the expense of others by dint of military might. They could be unpleasantly surprised by the resistance they encounter (which they may term "insurgencies" or "terrorism") and the combined opposition of the remaining states.

It is the same as when an addict, in the throes of withdrawal and desperate for another fix, bullies his friends, then tries to steal from them, then goes and robs a store. Only with a head addled by the drug can he believe that he won't be shot by the storekeeper.

The choice is not whether to decline, but how to decline: with grace or with violence. At some point, global energy systems, political systems, and economic systems will all have to be fundamentally revamped because the assumptions they are based on have all changed.

M. King Hubbert predicted this in 1949. Having weathered the Great Depression of the 1930s, Hubbert warned that energy constraints will eventually hit global financial markets and bring a new kind of recession from which normal recovery will be impossible. Our constantly expanding industrial-growth model will be gone forever. A constantly contracting post-petroleum model will replace it until some kind of ecological and economic equilibrium is reached.

Those hit hardest will be those who have the most expensive and wasteful daily habits. Many recently coming to the party thrown by fossil fuels will find it easier to leave than those who are drunk and still partying. Countries that still have an agricultural economy and the natural resources to sustain their population may get off more lightly. The rest are facing a hangover they can barely imagine.

Politicians will, of course, delay the inevitable. No one ever gets elected, or remains in office, by promising to deliver less. Delay will predictably turn what could have been a glide path into a cliff, which modern global economies will reach while still going at full speed — and maybe even accelerating.

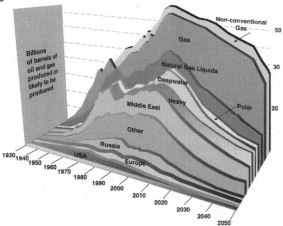

Historical rise and projected decline of production in oil and gas by decade. (Association for the Study of Peak Oil, 2006.)

APPETIZERS

GRASSHOPPER QUESADILLAS

Serves 6

Guacamole
2 cloves garlic
1 large or 2 medium jalapeño peppers
1 small onion
1 large or 2 small tomatoes
1 sprig of fresh or ¼ cup dried cilantro
2 large or 6 small avocados
1 lime
Pinch salt

Quesadillas
2 cups (about 100) grasshoppers (the younger the better)
3 cloves garlic
1 large onion
1 lemon
Pinch salt
12 tortillas
½ cup chili sauce

Guacamole
Mince garlic, jalapeño, onion, and tomatoes and finely chop cilantro. Coarsely mash avocados, squeeze in lime juice, combine other ingredients, and add salt to taste.

Quesadillas
Soak the grasshoppers in clean water for 24 hours. Boil them, then let dry. Fry in a pan with garlic, onion, lemon, and salt. Roll up in tortillas with chili sauce and guacamole. Substitutions include locusts, crickets, wild mushrooms, squash blossoms, huitlacoche (corn smut), and colorines (the flowers of the colorine tree, boiled first in salty water), sautéed.

Difficulty

We almost certainly face a "discontinuity" if we attempt to extend our oil-use habits beyond the production peak. As Richard Heinberg documents in *The Party's Over,* discontinuity will likely resemble the collapse that follows ecological overshoot; i.e., we'll revert to a lower order — of population, tools, agriculture, travel, governments.

Psychological precursors to this change will be a growing sense of foreboding all over the world, heightened stress, panic reactions, chaotic mob behavior, dread, and denial. The next ten years should be very exciting.

Expecting the Unexpected

Preparing for peak oil can be relatively easy, since the preparation is 75 percent mental, 15 percent physical, and 10 percent fiscal. Don't be flabbergasted at what to do. Quit asking should I buy solar? Should I buy an axe? Should I buy a gun? The answers are no, no, and no .... This feeling of a need to buy stuff is in fact the very reason why we have this predicament. We over-consume. The preparation problem is not addressed by buying more stuff; it's addressed by mentally and physically getting used to the idea of getting by on less stuff.

— Chris Lisle, 2005

Sometimes it is comforting to recall that life before Colonel Drake discovered that well in Titusville, Pennsylvania, was not without creature comforts. Blacksmiths under spreading chestnut trees worked on steam-electric "horseless carriages." Trains and horse-drawn wagons brought fresh food from outlying farms. The most daring folks even tottered around on the penny-farthing bicycle. Many of the jobs people had then were not so different from jobs today. Some would be greatly enhanced by the tools we have developed in the past century.

In many other ways, the world is a very different place. The first big change is global warming. Our burgeoning population has added significant amounts of greenhouse gases to the air, and we know from the fossil record that every time atmospheric carbon has risen, so have global temperatures. We have now nearly doubled CO_2 concentrations that existed at the start of the industrial era, and reliable science suggests it will take thousands, possibly millions, of years for natural processes to bring us back to pre-industrial equilibrium. In the near term — the next century or two — the world is going to get warmer. Much warmer.

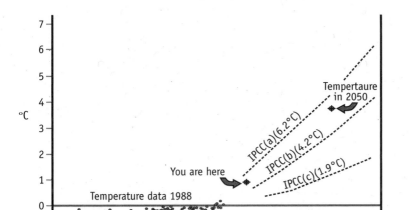

Actual and predicted global temperature change (after Lovelock 2006, IPCC 1990).
The Intergovernmental Panel on Climate Change (IPCC) published its First Scientific
Assessment *in 1990, which contained three scenarios for rate of temperature increase*
worldwide. Most recent data puts temperature somewhere between the upper two sce-
narios. The next assessment is due in 2007.

The areas first noticeably affected by this warming will likely be in
the mid-continental regions, where drier soil conditions will prevail,
droughts will occur more frequently, and desertification will be a serious
threat. Next will be coastal areas, where sea-level rise, increased rainfall,
and storm activity will submerge entire islands and permanently alter the
shape of continents. These changes will be most profound at the higher
latitudes, but no part of the Earth will be spared completely.

In the latter half of the 20th century, animal, insect, and plant populations migrated from the equator toward the poles at an average rate
of about four miles per decade. Lately, global warming has been leaving
them in its dust. From 1970 to 2000, the regions in which a given average
temperature prevails ("isotherms") have been moving poleward at a rate
of about 35 miles per decade. That pace is expected to step up to 70 miles
per decade in the years to come. This speed, and barriers like urban sprawl,
highways, deforestation, and industrial agriculture, spell extinction for less
mobile species and, ultimately, for any ecosystems that depended on them.

As some places grow warm enough to begin forming new deserts,
other places may actually get colder, a result of shifts in ocean steering
currents (like the Gulf Stream) and winds aloft. We now know that over

APPETIZERS

ROASTED CHESTNUTS

The planting of a few Japanese chestnuts *(C. crenata)* in or near New York City shortly before 1904 was one of the most tragic mistakes in history. The Asian fungus carried on those plantings destroyed 4 billion American chestnut trees *(Castanea dentata)* in North America, along with all the wildlife that depended on them. Blight-resistant trees are being planted, but most American chestnuts are not large enough to produce nuts. When you get chestnuts in the store, chances are they are Chinese.

Fresh American or Chinese chestnuts
2 Tbsp cold-pressed oil

With a sharp knife make a small slit on the flat side of each chestnut, piercing skin and shell. Oil the bottom of a cast-iron skillet, add chestnuts, cover pan, and place over medium-low heat to roast. Stir from time to time or shake pan. After 20 or 25 minutes, test one for doneness. Both inner and outer skin should peel off easily. It will taste sweet and nutty, not starchy. Be careful not to burn chestnuts. Cool before cracking open.

Difficulty

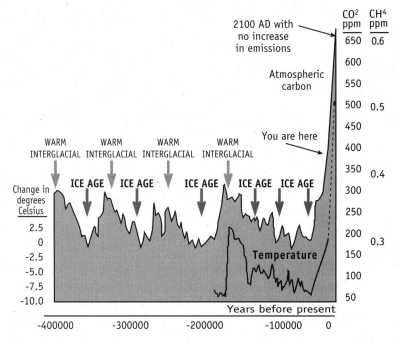

Atmospheric carbon and temperature change over 160,000 years.

the past ten years, the amount of warm water reaching Greenland from the Caribbean has diminished, most likely due to the effects of melting ice in the northern latitudes and the slowing of the Atlantic Conveyor. If the condition continues, it could cause a new, rapid-onset ice age for parts of Europe, even as polar ice melts and the rest of the world heats up.

If you have ever sat quietly on a winter day and watched snow and ice melt, then many of these patterns will be familiar. The ice gets wetter on the surface, and that wetness makes it shine, but it is also more transparent, which means the sun's rays penetrate deeper. Wet ice is also darker and so absorbs more sunlight, which makes it melt faster. As accumulations thaw, they crack apart, and those cracks become conduits for meltwater. Below the surface — sometimes seen, often unseen — the water is making and enlarging channels for itself, pulled by gravity and pushed by the pressure of the ice behind. Air bubbles flow in this water like tiny sledgehammers, smashing new channels and enlarging older ones.

At summer tent camps in Greenland's interior, ice-penetrating radar is mapping a maze of drainage crevices, tunnels, and cracks below the surface that are completely invisible to the human eye. The process is not invisible to our senses of hearing and touch, though. As Greenland's 12 glaciers thaw and their sweat dribbles into the sea, the bedrock sighs and stretches like someone arousing from a gentle sleep. Unburdened, it tries to stand up straight again. We mere humans feel and hear this as Richter 5 earthquakes. In 2005 the total number of ice-quakes in Greenland was three times the average ten years earlier, with five times more in summer than in winter.

Half a world away, in the Antarctic, warm oceans are melting the offshore ice shelves that form a barrier between the continental ice sheets and seawater. A few decades ago, the shelves extended 5,200 square miles farther than they do today. As these shelves melt, the land sheets discharge more icebergs and then, diminished in depth and eroded from their own water underneath, melt faster. Meltwater that started as trickles in the hot sun forms broad unseen rivers that move the great sheets oceanward.

In the past, deep underground, these rivers could encounter such thick coastal shelves that they would refreeze, slowing the loss of ice. When the Larson B Ice Sheet broke apart and slid off West Antarctica in 2002, it added an area the size of Rhode Island to the ocean. It also unplugged many hidden dams in the meltwater rivers extending up under the West Antarctic Ice Sheet. Since the Larsen collapse, the West Antarctic has a snowball's chance in hell of holding its shape.

The volume of icebergs leaving West Antarctica's coasts doubled between 1995 and 2005 and is expected to double again by 2015, to 100 cubic miles per year. Greenland's ice mass is diminishing at nearly twice that rate.

If either Greenland's glaciers or the West Antarctic Ice Sheet were to slide away completely, global seas would rise by 15 to 20 feet, re-sculpting coastlines worldwide. While worst-case estimates for sea-level rise from such august bodies as the Intergovernmental Panel on Climate Change have suggested such increases might take a century, the meltwater roller skates under the West Antarctic Sheet and the earthquakes caused by the unweighting of the Greenland land mass could precipitate giant masses of ice sliding into the ocean in the short span of a single summer.

Gargantuan icebergs crashing into the ocean on that scale could unleash a torrent of tsunamis traveling the Earth at jet-aircraft speed. When the waves finally subside, the oceans will not have receded. Sea level could remain elevated for 20,000 years, perhaps longer. If the East Antarctic Ice Sheet were to melt as well, seas would rise as much as 200 feet.

If I were a town planner in Rotterdam, Tokyo, Cancun, Bangkok, New York, or Miami, I would not be working on waterfront parks and beaches.

ALUMINUM AND TEFLON

Although aluminum is the most abundant metallic element in the Earth's crust, it has no known beneficial function in living organisms, and can be toxic if consumed in excessive amounts. The following are some common sources of aluminum that you should avoid:

- Antiperspirants and underarm deodorants
- Aluminum cookware (especially dangerous if used to cook acid foods such as tomatoes)
- Beverages from aluminum cans
- Municipal drinking water, which often has aluminum compounds added
- Baking powders
- Bleached flour
- Processed cheese
- Some table salts
- Some antacids

Teflon® is the nonstick coating on many pots and pans and on spatulas and spoons made to use with them. It imparts perfluorooctanoic acid to your food, and that substance has been linked to cancer and birth defects. Avoid Teflon.

I recommend cooking with ironware whenever possible. Most of my recipes call for a cast-iron skillet. Cast iron is inexpensive, lasts for generations, conserves heating fuel, brings out the taste in food, and adds trace amounts of iron, which the body needs to make blood.

APPETIZERS

QUINTANA CHILTOMATE SALSA AND FRESH TORTILLA CHIPS

Makes about 2 cups

2 cups fresh masa or 3 cups masa flour
2 medium-large round, very ripe tomatoes or 8 ripe cherry tomatoes
Choice of chilés: 1 habanero, 2 large jalapeños, 4 serranos, or 1 manzano pepper, fresh with veins and seeds removed
3 garlic cloves, unpeeled
½ tsp sea salt
½ small onion, finely chopped
1½ tsp cider vinegar or sour orange juice
2 Tbsp fresh-squeezed lime juice
⅓ cup loosely packed chopped cilantro

Masa

If you can't find fresh masa in the market, you can buy Maseca, Minsa, or masa harina corn flour and mix with water to form a firm dough. Knead until very stiff. Pack into plum-size balls and turn out tortillas using a traditional press, or roll flat and round on a floured surface with a rolling pin.

Corn tortilla chips

Place the flattened ball of masa (as thin as you like to have it) on the hottest part of the griddle and turn it *as soon as you can manage it.* Bake the second side in a slightly cooler part of the griddle until the top of the tortilla appears cooked (dry), which takes about a minute or more. Only then do you turn the tortilla over for the last time. If it is laid down from one side to the

I would be thinking about very large and long dikes about now. Or maybe about moving low-lying populations to higher ground.

The kinship between ocean and ice is very old and very essential. It is yet another means by which Nature sequestered carbon to soothe our fevered planet when it drifted too close to the sun. Ice at the poles reflects sunlight into space, and that also keeps us cool. The role ice-chilled saltwater plays in propelling our deep ocean conveyors is well known. What is less known is what happens when it is no longer there. It seems quite likely we, or our children, are about to find out.

Soiling Our Nest

> *President Clinton met this evening with the chief executives of General Motors, Ford Motor and Chrysler to promote his trade policies, but received instead an earful of complaints about the Administration's interest in limiting emissions of gases that may contribute to global warming.*
>
> — *The New York Times,* October 3, 1997

Global warming is not the only ticking time bomb. For 50 years, the nuclear industry has routinely been receiving permits to dump radioactive wastes into the air and water even though British, French, Dutch, Russian, and other governments are well aware of the lethal consequences to future generations. The US Nuclear Regulatory Commission expects 1.7 million non-accidental cancer and genetic deaths in the *world* population from current US-based plants alone.

At least the nuclear industry has watchdog agencies, even if their historic role has been more like that of lapdogs. The level of regulation in the chemical and pharmaceutical industries is far more lackadaisical. Thousands of chemical and pharmaceutical dumpsites are leaching toxic compounds into the environment without anyone seeming to notice. Rivers, oceans, and atmosphere have been treated as a vast open sewer, and the damage to human and ecosystem health is only beginning.

The new nano-bio sciences are rife with life-extinguishing risk on a planetary scale. When we crossed nature's bright red line and began to splice DNA for ourselves, we unleashed forces that may be slow to reveal themselves but are potentially more lethal to our species than any other thing we have done. The slow process of selective breeding within species is a normal biological constraint for good reason; it protects all life from recombinant genes that are unsuccessful, ecologically destructive, or dangerous. Self-recombining laboratory-made DNA, which we now witness escaping cornfields in Mexico and salmon hatcheries in the Atlantic, presents a hazard to all living creatures that can scarcely be measured.

It was only a matter of time before the miracles of modern chemistry were weaponized. The wars of the 20th century showed combatants' increasing willingness to employ even the most lethal pathogens in the service of their causes. Today those formulae are finding their way back into use and being augmented by new generations of engineered toxins. Nearly universal access to information, usually through the Internet, has accelerated these developments and placed extremely dangerous substances into extremely irresponsible hands.

So this is where we find ourselves. We have spent the past hundred or so years at a huge party thrown by petroleum. Our host has spared no expense and has lavished wonderful gifts upon us, and we are surely grateful. Some of the gifts we have used wisely and some we have wasted. The party has been going on for so long that most people, although tired, have the sense that it's a permanent thing — that we can go home and go to bed and come back again tomorrow and it will still be here.

Wrong.

It's nearly over now. The band is packing up. Tomorrow we have the big cleanup.

The Viridian camp sees a shiny green
future awaiting us in the post-oil world, old-school oil guys
like T. Boone Pickens see an exploration and drilling bonanza, energy
industry investors like Matt Simmons and Henry Groppe see soaring energy
prices, gold bugs see rampant inflation and soaring gold prices, ferals and
hippies see a return to living closer to nature, socialists see the revival of
Marxism, conspiracy theorists see government/elite conspiracies and the rise of
the New World Order, primitivists see the collapse of industrial civilization and
human die-off, libertarians see an opportunity for the market to bring new
energy sources and technologies to us, fascists see an opportunity for a return
to authoritarianism and some of the uglier approaches to population control
used by their ilk in the past, economists see supply and demand issues being
resolved by energy prices, military-industrial complex members see the need to
militarily dominate the energy-rich regions of the planet, end-times Christian
fundamentalists see another symptom of the impending Rapture and survival-
ists see an opportunity to say "I told you so" and finally get to use the skills
and tools they've spent their lives practicing for.
Big Gav, peakenergy.blogspot.com, 2005

Salsa and chips cont.

other in a sweeping motion, it should puff up with a big air pocket inside. Slide it to the edge of the griddle and let it continue to cook for another minute, no more. The pocket will lose its air. Quarter into chips, layer thinly on a dry cookie sheet, and keep warm in oven until ready to serve.

Salsa

Heat dry griddle or heavy skillet. Roast the tomatoes in the skillet, turning frequently until blistered and blackened. This can also be done on a cooking grate over an open fire. Cool tomatoes, then place them in a well-crumpled paper bag and rub the bag from the outside, removing blackened skins in the process. Do not rub so hard as to lose juices from the tomatoes. Roast the peppers and unpeeled garlic; cool and repeat the paper-bag process to deskin them. In a large mortar, use the pestle to crush and grind the peppers, garlic, and ¼ tsp of the salt to a coarse paste. Grind in the tomatoes, transferring the mixture to a bowl as needed. (If you don't have a mortar, grind the peppers, garlic, and salt in a food processor or blender, add the tomatoes, and pulse to a coarse paste.) Transfer to a serving bowl and mix in chopped onion, vinegar, and lemon juice. Add water as needed (2 to 4 Tbsp) to obtain a spoonable consistency. It will take a few hours for the vinegar and citric juice to penetrate the onion, so allow time to mellow before serving, or cover and refrigerate for a day. Add cilantro just before serving. Serve with toasted chips.

Difficulty

Rebuild Civilization

*I was in New York in the 30's. I had a
box seat at the depression. I can assure you it was a
very educational experience. We shut the country down because
of monetary reasons. We had manpower and abundant raw materials.
Yet we shut the country down. We're doing the same kind of thing now but
with a different material outlook. We are not in the position we were in 1929–30
with regard to the future. Then the physical system was ready to roll. This time
it's not. We are in a crisis in the evolution of human society. It's unique to both
human and geologic history. It has never happened before and it can't possibly
happen again. You can only use oil once. You can only use metals once. Soon
all the oil is going to be burned and all the metals mined and scattered.*

— M. King Hubbert, 1983

*The Second Half of the Age of Oil will
be characterized by a decline in the supply of oil,
and all that depends upon it, including eventually financial
capital. That speaks of a second Great Depression and the End of
Economics as presently understood. It is an unprecedented discontinuity
of historic proportions, as never before has a resource as critical as oil
become scarce without sight of a better substitute. All countries and all
communities face the consequences of this new situation.*

— Colin Campbell, 2004

The Great Change

t is not an overstatement to say that reaching the point of peak
production of oil and gas will change everything. The change will

15

APPETIZERS

DEVILED TOFU

"Post-petroleum cuisine" sounds awful. I'd prefer to use a label like "Great Change Cooking." What distinguishes this new style from what came before is a much wider range of substitutions to adapt recipes to local ingredients, the possibility that kitchen appliances like blenders and food processors may be unavailable (or unable to be powered), and the likelihood that there will be more time available for both preparing food and enjoying it. In presenting these recipes, I have chosen to use hand tools in preference to power tools, to suggest a range of variation in ingredients, and to try to imagine what might be available locally in most places.

Tofu shops are an inherently local enterprise, with more than 10,000 in any major city in Japan today. Soymilk, soy mayonnaise, and many other soy products are likely to be in abundance, not merely because of the emergence of this local business all over the world, but also because soybeans fix nitrogen in the soil and so will become essential in organic crop rotation when nitrogen fertilizers (derived from natural gas) are increasingly scarce and expensive. In this recipe, you will want your tofu to be very firm, rather than soft or silky.

Serves 6 (about 12 "egg" halves)

1½ pounds firm tofu
1¾ tsp sea salt
2 tsp rice vinegar
2 tsp lemon juice
2 cups water
½ cup soy mayonnaise

be profound and pervasive. No part of the world's economies will be left untouched.

Over the past many decades, a number of small institutions have been laboring to lay the groundwork for this change. Most people have never heard of them, but they include the Centre for Alternative Technology in Wales, the Nordic Folkecentre for Renewable Energy in Denmark, the National Center for Appropriate Technology in the United States, the Global Ecovillage Network, and many more, large and small, governmental and non-governmental. These institutions, always at the fringe of society, are about to move to the mainstream.

Some of the new infrastructure we will see going up around us will be modest variations on familiar themes: hydrogen filling stations, fields of wind turbines, and giant ethanol plants. Other parts will be completely unexpected. One change will be the way people use money.

Here is the problem in a nutshell. Both the developed world and the developing world have piled up mountains of debt. Mostly they are indebted to each other. The US is indebted to Japan, Japan is indebted to China, China is indebted to the Middle East. It has always been assumed that the world economy would continue to expand, so any credit extended would earn interest. That could be about to change.

What would happen if instead of continuously growing in order to show a steady profit, the global economy had to continuously shrink to reflect the depletion of one-time natural resources, notably fossil fuels? Stock markets, buoyed by a tide of profits that can no longer rise, would crash. Banks, which must earn interest on loans, could no longer do so and would fail. The price of houses, especially the large, inefficient ones located in places where you need a car to obtain groceries, built and maintained by mortgage loans from banks, would implode. The piles of paper and magnetically stored electrons that have held people's confidence as the measure of their wealth could be worth zero. Thousands of companies could go bankrupt, with millions left unemployed. "Once-affluent cities with street cafés will have queues at soup kitchens and armies of beggars," warns British environmentalist Jeremy Leggett.

But it doesn't have to happen.

Follow the Money

I have a friend, A. Goodheart Brown, who lives in the Appalachian mountains of North Carolina and is a great storyteller. Without taking the time a great storyteller would take, let me share one of Goodheart's stories.

Once there was an island with a mild climate and a stable population. There were taro, mangoes, breadfruit, and coconuts aplenty. Near one village on the eastern coast of the island, the ocean brought fish in great quantities. Another village, on the north coast, was known for its fine coconut wine, called "tuba." It was common for the north villagers to trade their wine for the fresh fish catch of the east villagers.

Because of the success of their wine, the north village found itself with a surplus of fish, which tended to spoil, so it built a large facility to make dried fish sticks, and soon, because of their usefulness as a common tender, the fish sticks became the accepted currency of the island.

The leader of the north village was a very shrewd businesswoman and was always thinking of ways to improve. She suggested that rather than leaving fish sticks in homes to spoil, the village should keep the fish sticks in a special warehouse where they would stay dry. To anyone who deposited their fish sticks, she would issue a paper credit. In this way, the island got its first paper currency. Since the east village caught the fish, they soon found themselves with a lot of paper money, so the north village offered to build a special vault under the fish stick warehouse where, for a small fee, they would provide space to the east village to store its money.

Soon the leader of the north village grew tired of walking up and down the steps to the vault every day and decided it would be much easier if she simply kept accounts in a ledger and gave the islanders checkbooks. A fireproof safe was built in her office to store the ledger, and once a month she sent her customers statements.

In this way the island prospered until one day the current changed and the fish disappeared. At about the same time, a devastating fire destroyed the fish stick warehouse. "Oh, woe is me," said the east village leader. "Our money is gone. We are poor again."

The north village leader said, "Don't worry. We don't even need to rebuild. The money is in the vault, the ledger is safe, and your accounts are intact. Your checks are still good for tuba, even if there are no longer fish sticks backing it up. We will redeem your money by selling you tuba." And the people all accepted this, all over the island. It isn't what backs money up that gives it value; it is what you can buy. Confidence in the currency is its real value.

One day the north village leader was looking at one of the old paper credits and a smile came to her face. "Pay to the bearer on demand one fish stick," it read. Why should we be storing all these IOUs, she

Deviled Tofu cont.

½ tsp dry mustard
⅛ tsp pepper
¾ tsp turmeric
Dash of paprika
Small sprig of parsley
8 cherry tomatoes, sliced in half

"EGGS"

Drain and rinse tofu. Using a small paring knife, cut tofu into squares — 4 for a pound, 2 for a half pound — and shave the squares into an oval, imitating the shape of a hard-boiled egg; then slice them in half. With a small spoon, carefully scoop out the centers of each of the ovals to form a cavity. Reserve tofu scraps. Combine 1 tsp salt, ½ tsp vinegar, ½ tsp lemon juice, and 2 cups water in a large baking dish. Marinate all the prepared ovals in the salt water while preparing the filling.

Filling

Crumble tofu scraps into a medium mixing bowl. Add remaining ingredients except the paprika, parsley and cherry tomatoes, and blend thoroughly.

Serving

Drain "eggs" on paper towel or a brown paper bag and stuff with filling. Sprinkle the tops with paprika and arrange with parsley and cherry tomatoes.

Difficulty

APPETIZERS

PEAR ANTIPASTO

Balsamic vinegar is made in Modena, Italy, from the must of white Trebbiano grapes and aged in a series of barrels of different woods to produce its rich, sweet taste. It is widely available now, but may be less so in years to come, so is worth considering as a storage item. A little goes a long way.
Serves 6

3 ripe Anjou, Comice, or local pears
⅓ cup fresh lemon or other citrus juice
3 to 4 ounces local hard or vegan cheese, unsliced or grated
1 Tbsp balsamic vinegar

Halve and core the pears, leaving their skins intact. Pare each half into thin slivers. Spray with lemon juice to keep from turning brown. Place 4 or 5 slices of pears and ½ ounce of cheese on each salad plate. Moisten cheese with a few drops of balsamic vinegar and serve.

Difficulty

wondered. And that night she carried all the money out onto the beach and burned it.

Somehow the leader of the east village got word of this and became alarmed. He went to the north village leader and demanded to see his money. She showed him the ledger book. "No," he said, "I want to see my money!" She explained that it would take two weeks to print more money, so he promised to return in two weeks for his money. In two weeks he came back and withdrew it all. But then, two weeks later, he returned and asked to deposit it again. His faith in the banking system had been restored.

That night the leader of the north village took all the money out to the beach and burned it again.

Money is not our medium of exchange because it is money. It is money because it is our medium of exchange. As Forrest Gump might say, "Money is as money does."

Eventually the north village created a bank and floated its money against international currencies. It also issued credit cards and installed an automatic teller machine. People could earn interest on their savings. They could take out loans to buy new fishing boats and build houses.

One day the manager of the tuba company came to the bank and asked for a loan. While they were talking, a bank vice-president asked the company manager if he would be interested in selling options for some future contracts for his wine. As the vice-president explained it, if the harvest was good, then there would be lots of coconuts and the wine would be worth less. If the harvest were poor, such as after a storm, there would be fewer coconuts, but the wine would be worth more. The bank would offer to buy wine in advance of the harvest at a fixed price, and the wine company would pay a small fee for the contract. This was called an option. The clerk would then spread his risk by selling parts of his contract to other islanders. This was called a hedge.

Eventually the bank found it could do a brisk business in options and hedges. It made more money on its money. There was even a stock exchange to trade coconut futures, papaya options, and bamboo hedges. All was happy and well until one day ...

You can fill in the ending. Maybe a storm came and washed away the bank, including the ledger book. Maybe the dollar, which the currency was indexed to, collapsed. The people discovered that the wealth they had on paper was not worth as much as a fish they could eat or a bottle of coconut wine.

Of course there were also lots of problems that came with the money system. All was not happy and well for everyone. People borrowed, but not everyone could repay. What became of those people? Were they thrown in jail (and what is a jail? they may have asked) or allowed to declare bankruptcy? The bank needed to make a profit in order to pay interest on deposits, so it had to be assured of a constant return. The need for constant profit applied to all the businesses and people that took loans, so there was gradual inflation of prices and wages.

Understanding Capitalism

> *We can isolate the values of [US] American*
> *society that have been responsible for its greatest triumphs*
> *and know that we will cling to them no matter what. They are, in one*
> *rough mixture, capitalism, individualism, nationalism, technophilia, and*
> *humanism (as the dominance of humans over nature). There is no chance*
> *whatever, no matter how grave and obvious the threat, that as a society*
> *that we will abandon those. Hence no chance to escape the collapse ....*
> — Kirkpatrick Sale, 2005

Capitalism dominates the global economic system at this moment. With the collapse of the 80-year Russian experiment in state-managed socialism, right-wing neo-cons trumpeted the victory of capitalism *über alles* at the end of the 20th century. Even the enormous Chinese economy began to deploy capitalism as a development tool in its new enterprise zones. But what, exactly, is capitalism?

Both socialism and capitalism draw upon the accumulated wealth of the past to finance the growth of social infrastructure that will be needed in the future. In socialist systems, including communism, a central authority (although it might be regionally dispersed into smaller nodes of authority and democratically chosen) decides what expenditures will produce the greatest good and allocates resources to them. Socialist and capitalist systems raise money pretty much the same way everywhere: by taxing the income and profits of individuals and enterprises. In some systems the state simplifies the taxation process by owning all or part of the enterprise and by managing all or part of the care and feeding of the population.

Capitalism is rooted in private ownership and private decision making about how resources are allocated. The system works well because it

Sweeteners	
Sweetener	**Substitution Ratio to one cup sugar**
Confectioners' sugar	1¾ cup
Brown sugar	1 cup firmly packed
Turbinado sugar	1 cup
Maple syrup	¾ cup
Honey	¾ cup
Barley malt & rice syrup	¾ cup
Molasses	1¼ cup
Stevia	¼ teaspoon
Saccarine (Sweet and Low®)	1 teaspoon
Aspartame (Equal®, Nutrisweet®)	1 teaspoon
Sucralose (Splenda®)	2 teaspoons

You can read about alternative currencies, complementary currencies, local exchange trading systems, and other ideas for constructing our future economy on our website (thegreatchange.com) or visit complementarycurrency.org.

is driven by a profit motive — that is to say, by greed, which seems to be an emotion that almost all humans feel, although in most of the world's religions it is looked upon as a *bad* thing. The tenets of capitalism used to justify greed are that those who spend wisely do well; wherever unmet needs exist, there are profitable opportunities; talent and skill are rewarded; and, properly applied, a little wealth can generate more wealth.

Ethical Constraints

It is worth enlarging upon this last point, that wealth generates more wealth. In Islam, the Prophet Mohammed forbade his followers to lend money for interest. There is no such prohibition in Christianity, although charging usurious rates of interest is considered immoral, and Christians like to tell the story of Jesus tossing the money-changers out of the temple.

Jesus is said to have told his followers, "To those who have, more shall be given, but for those who have nothing, even what they thought they had shall be taken away." Many Christians construe this to mean that there are winners and losers in life and that it is okay for the wealthy to get wealthier, even super-rich. Jesus probably meant nothing of the kind but was making a statement about spiritual growth.

As to material wealth, Jesus reportedly said, "It would be easier for a rope to pass through the eye of a needle than for a rich man to enter the Kingdom of God," although monks in the Middle Ages, whose knowledge of Aramaic was less than perfect, mistranslated "rope," which was made of camel's hair in antiquity, with the ancient Aramaic homonym meaning "camel," giving us the modern Bible that speaks of a camel passing through the needle's eye, a much more graphic image.

Neither was Siddhartha Gautama, the Buddha, a stranger to this discussion. In general terms, Buddhism regards industry and acquisitive habits as valuable attributes that direct our higher natures away from indolence and sloth. The danger that lurks below industriousness is desire and attachment, typically with regard to worldly possessions, and Buddha instructed his followers that desire is best avoided and that all suffering derives from attachment.

Alternatives to Money

In her landmark book *Interest and Inflation-Free Money: Creating an Exchange Medium that Works for Everybody and Protects the Earth* (1987), Margrit Kennedy challenged the whole idea that we have to have a money system based on constant growth. Nothing grows endlessly. Nature is a

Religious Teachings on Consumption

Indigenous: Mi'kmaq chief, North America: Miserable as we seem in thy eyes, we consider ourselves ... much happier than thou in this, that we are very content with the little that we have.

Judaism: Isaiah 55:2: Why do you spend your money for that which is not bread, and your labor for that which does not satisfy?

Christianity: 1 John 3.17: How does God's love abide in anyone who has the world's goods and sees a brother or sister in need and yet refuses to help?

Islam: Qu'ran 7.31: Eat and drink, but waste not by excess; verily He loves not the excessive.

Taoism: Tao Te Ching, 33: He who knows he has enough is rich.

Hinduism: Acarangasutra 2.114-19: On gaining the desired object, one should not feel elated. On not receiving the desired object, one should not feel dejected. In case of obtaining anything in excess, one should not hoard it. One should abstain from acquisitiveness.

Confucianism: Confucius, XI.15: Excess and deficiency are equally at fault.

Buddhism: Buddhadasa Bhikkhu: The lessons nature teaches us lead to a new birth beyond suffering caused by our acquisitive self-preoccupation.

Bahá'í Faith: The Bahá'í Statement on Nature: The major threats to our world environment ... are manifestations of a world-encompassing sickness of the human spirit, a sickness that is marked by an overemphasis on material things and a self-centeredness that inhibits our ability to work together as a global community.

Meher Baba: Discourses, 391: Man seeks worldly objects of pleasure and tries to avoid things that bring pain, without realizing that he cannot have the one and eschew the other. As long as there is attachment to worldly objects of pleasure, he must perpetually invite upon himself the suffering of not having them — and the suffering of losing them after having got them.

From the Center for a New American Dream, "Quotes and Teachings of World Religions on Care of the Earth and Responsible Consumption," at www.newdream.org/faith; Meher Baba's *Discourses, 7th ed.;* and "Buddhism and Ecology: Challenge and Promise" are at environment.harvard.edu/religion/religion/buddhism.

wave. If we have a large expansion, we need a large contraction to balance it. If we are talking about global economies, these large contractions can be seriously damaging. So Kennedy came up with some ideas for economies that are steady-state. They don't use interest. They are simply based on the fair exchange of value for value.

One example of a non-inflationary money system is the Local Exchange Trading System, or LETS, created by Michael Linton in British Columbia's Comox Valley in 1983. In less than ten years, Linton's experiment grew to handle some $10 billion in annual trades in 450 systems in North

APPETIZERS

MUSHROOM QUESADILLAS

Makes 12 to 15 quesadillas

8 chiles de arbol or other dried hot peppers, deseeded
6 garlic cloves, roughly chopped
12 chanterelle, 6 medium shiitake, or local wild mushrooms
¼ cup olive oil
1 tsp Mexican oregano
1 tsp shoyu
1 tsp nutritional yeast
12 to 15 flour tortillas
¼ cup grated queso fresco (Oaxaca is best), mozzarella, or soft vegan cheese

Stem the peppers and remove the seeds and veins. Mince the garlic. Dice the mushrooms and peppers. Heat olive oil in a large iron skillet over strong heat and add oregano, garlic, peppers, and mushrooms. Sauté until brown, sprinkling with shoyu and nutritional yeast at the end. Remove from skillet and spoon into tortillas, sprinkle grated cheese on top, fold, and return to the greasy skillet to lightly brown. Cover before serving.

Difficulty

America and had begun local systems in Australia, New Zealand, the UK, Germany, and elsewhere.

How does it work? Everyone has an account, but instead of money transferring from one bank to another, all exchanges take place within a single system. Each new account starts at zero and thereafter may hold a positive or a negative balance. Those with negative balances have, quite simply, created the money that is in the positive accounts. As money is essentially a promise by someone to give goods or services to another, local money is actually the commitment of people in the community to the community.

Money like this, which you issue yourself, is sometimes called "complementary currency." In Ithaca, New York, it is called "hours." In Nimbin, New South Wales, it is called "bunyips." It is estimated that up to one-third of the exchanges in Manchester, England, involve "bobbins." In the city of Poix in Ariège, France, a bimonthly farmers' market trades exclusively with "grains de sel." In Japan they use *Hureai Kippu* (or "caring relationship tickets"), denominated in hours of service, to compensate providers of daily care to the handicapped, sick, and elderly. A variation on this is "time dollars" (timedollar.org), which are a tax-exempt kind of currency that empower people to convert their personal time into purchasing power by helping others and their community.

The local accounting service maintains a system of accounts for its users. Administrative costs are recovered, in the internal currency, from each account according to the cost of the service. The system operates on a not-for-profit basis.

If someone catches a fish and wants to exchange it, he or she can let the exchange system partners know how many units in the local currency he or she will accept for that fish. This is called an offer. If someone wants to have fish for dinner, they can go to the fisher, negotiate the price, and tender an acceptance. The "buyer" issues credit from their exchange system account, which is debited. The "seller" receives the credit into their account. At the end of every transaction, all of the credits and debits in all of the accounts in the system balance.

In the mid-1980s, Self-Help Association for a Regional Economy (SHARE), a micro-credit program in the southern Berkshire Mountains, developed a program for a local currency denominated in units of cordwood to be called "Berkshares." While Berkshares were still on the drawing table, a delicatessen owner, Frank Tortoriello, learned his rent had been doubled. He couldn't find a bank to lend him relocation funds, so he approached SHARE for a loan to finance a move to a new location.

SHARE suggested Mr. Tortoriello issue "deli dollars" to finance the move. For eight US dollars, an investor received ten deli dollars, which were redeemable in merchandise after six months had passed. Deli customers bought $5,000 worth of notes in the first 30 days of issue, financing both the move and renovation costs. Berkshire Farm Preserve Notes, Monterey General Store Notes, and other self-help notes were quick to follow.

Below the radar
beams of officialdom a quiet monetary
revolution is afoot. The centuries-old monopoly of
national currencies as medium of exchange is already ending.
For example, airline frequent flyer miles are a private corporate cur-
rency in the making. More than a quarter of global trade is conducted in
barter, i.e. using no currency at all (for instance, Pepsi Cola has been repa-
triating its profits out of Russia in the form of vodka). At the other end of the
spectrum, private citizens are reshaping their own futures by issuing comple-
mentary currencies without any reference to a national central bank. This has
recently been proliferating within almost two thousand different communi-
ties in a dozen countries around the world.

— Bernard A. Lietaer, 1999

Freiwirtschaft

During the global recession of 1932, the small Austrian town of Wörgl issued 32,000 "Free Schillings" (interest-free Schillings) protected by a deposit of normal Austrian Schillings in a local bank. They put a "rest fee" on the money that amounted to 1 percent per month. The fee had to be paid by the person who held the note at the end of the month, and a tax stamp was then glued to the note. Without the current stamp, the note was worthless. This caused everyone who received the note to spend it before they spent their standard Schillings so they would not have to pay the fees at the end of the month. It was a game of musical chairs, and at the end of each month the music sped up, people spent Free Schillings like crazy, and the Wörgl economy boomed.

While ordinary Schillings circulated an average 21 times in the course of a year, Free Schillings circulated 463 times, and the notes created goods and services worth 14,816,000 Schillings. While most of the countries in Europe suffered dire shortages, setting the stage for ethnic persecution, extreme nationalism and ambitious war, Wörgl reduced its unemployment by 25 percent, and the town government used the money it raised in tax

UNDERSTANDING SOY SAUCE

Shoyu is the traditional fermented condiment of Japan, made with equal parts soybeans and wheat. Tamari refers to a shoyu containing little or no wheat. Soy sauce is made in a process involving chemical hydrolysis of proteins, pioneered in 1886 by Maggi in Switzerland and later industrialized in China and Japan. Braggs Amino Acids are also the product of a chemical reaction of hydrolyzed protein and hydrochloric acid. I recommend naturally fermented shoyu as the most healthful and least fossil-fuel dependent.

APPETIZERS

TEMPEH GRAVLAX

Finding yourself in a warm climate with no mechanical means for refrigeration can present a serious challenge to even the most ingenious cook. Traditionally, people gathered and stored ice in winter (in sawdust-covered blocks in large insulated or underground buildings) or constructed "swamp coolers" to chill the air around perishables. Given advances in materials and technology over the past 50 years, it seems likely that compact solar refrigeration and ice-making devices will soon become widely available, and some may operate without any electricity requirement. In the meantime, solar-electric and (bio) gas-powered refrigerators are a sound investment.

Serves 6 to 8

1 Tbsp caraway seeds
2 tsp aniseed
5 juniper berries
1 dry or canned chipotle pepper, deseeded and deveined
1 cup white or yellow fine cornmeal
2 Tbsp nutritional yeast
½ tsp stevia powder or comparable sweetener
3 Tbsp finely chopped fresh dill
1 pound tempeh
½ cup aquavit, brandy, eau de vie, or Damiana
2 Tbsp balsamic vinegar
3 Tbsp shoyu

Crush the caraway seeds, aniseed, juniper berries, and chipotle using a mortar and pestle and combine with cornmeal, nutritional yeast,

stamps for public works. It built bridges and improved roads. When 300 other towns began to adopt the Wörgl system, the Austrian central bank stepped in and declared it illegal. The case went to the Austrian Supreme Court and Wörgl, Austria — and the world economy — lost.

> As local groups and communities
> created their own local scrip currencies and exchange sys-
> tems, they learned about economists' deepest secret: money and
> information are equivalent — and neither is scarce! As money morphed
> from stone tablets, metal coins, gold and paper to electronic blips of pure
> information — the economic theories of scarcity and competition began to be
> bypassed by electronic sharing and community cooperation .... Today, rapid
> social learning about the politics of money and how it functions is revealing
> this key mythology underlying our current societies and its transmission belt:
> that faulty economic source code still replicating today's unsustainable
> poverty gaps, energy crisis, and resource depletion.
>
> — Hazel Henderson, 2006

Local currencies have been common throughout history, although they tend to proliferate whenever a community perceives a need to protect its internal economy from outside disturbances such as war or depression, or when the national currency collapses and people are forced to devise their own alternatives.

In reality, money is a measurement, not a thing. It is an agreement between people to use something common for all exchanges. For most people, this agreement has been in place since before they were born and is taken for granted.

It is called into question now because polarization between haves and have-nots is reaching historically unprecedented levels. Fewer than 450 billionaires worldwide control more wealth than 4.5 billion other people. Of the 6.4 billion people on Earth at the start of 2006, 3.7 billion were malnourished. Most proposals for reform adopt a socialist idea of taking from the haves to give to the have-nots. In contrast, complementary currencies enable people to create new wealth. Instead of overturning the old world order, they make a small change that gives a fair shake to everyone.

Consider the transformation of Curitiba, Brazil, which achieved European living standards in one generation while being recognized by the United Nations as the "most ecological city in the world." This occurred in large part because Curitiba issued its own local currency and kept its economy vibrant, even when the economy of Brazil was stagnant.

Complementary currencies like "bobbins" and "grains de sel" are under local control and need not fluctuate or have artificial scarcities like those created by central national banks. They also generate very different behavior among the people using them. Participants report important non-economic benefits such as the development of new friendships, deeper ties in the community, a sense of purpose, a feeling of being valued, and a general fostering of cooperation instead of competition.

> *Already the world economy may*
> *be largely an article of faith. It's like a thing*
> *projected out over the precipice by the collective belief*
> *of everyone. After the 1987 stock market crash, Ronald*
> *Reagan — the most powerful man in the world — in an amazing,*
> *naïve insight, said, "There won't be an economic*
> *collapse as long as people believe there won't." People can bring the whole*
> *house of cards down just by losing faith. That underlies the inherent unpre-*
> *dictability of things. It's not just when does this resource run out, or when is*
> *there enough destruction of this to stop that process. It's to do with the people*
> *to some extent prefiguring what is actually happening through their aware-*
> *ness and their unconscious. They start to withdraw, individually and*
> *collectively, their support for systems. Arguably, historians might end up*
> *looking back, post energy descent, and argue whether it all could have*
> *continued if people had kept the faith.*
>
> — David Holmgren, 2005

Holding on to Wealth

There is a lot of advice floating around today about buying gold and silver — do I get coins? Bullion? Is land still a good investment?

People should not speculate or acquire lots of things that are relatively useless from a practical standpoint. If everyone in Europe and North America starts hoarding gold and silver, it will become too expensive for people in South America and Africa to get their dental cavities filled. Don't buy things you can't eat or use immediately to make an honest living. If you are serious about growing food, then investing in some nice farmland makes sense. Investing in home solar-electric, wind, or micro-hydro systems also makes sense.

Tempeh Gravlax cont.

stevia, and dill in a 6-inch or larger bowl. Slice the tempeh into 1-inch by 5-inch filets. Bread the filets with the spice and cornmeal mixture. Pour aquavit, vinegar, and shoyu into a skillet and warm on medium heat. Add tempeh and gently steam for 15 minutes. Remove tempeh to a bowl and immerse in remaining pan liquids. Cover and refrigerate for 3 to 4 days, turning every 12 hours and basting the tempeh with the brine. Add additional aquavit if tempeh seems too dry. Serve with mustard, pickles, horseradish, and dark rye bread.

Difficulty

APPETIZERS

SUSHI NORI

Traditional sushi chefs roll their eyes when someone mentions California rolls, but the upsurge in interest in sushi throughout the world is directly related to the willingness of restaurants to experiment with substitutions of popular ingredients like cream cheese or brown rice for authentic Japanese foods. California rolls anticipated Great Change cooking.

6 to 8 rolls

2 cups sushi, risotto, or short-grain white or brown rice
2¼ cups water
3 Tbsp rice vinegar
2 Tbsp mirin or Shaoxing cooking wine (Substitutes: Sake or dry sherry)
1 Tbsp sugar or equivalent sweetener
1 tsp sea salt
6 to 8 sheets nori
1 medium carrot, sliced in thin strips
1 daikon radish, sliced in long strips
½ small jicama, sliced in long strips

Shoyu

3 Tbsp olive or other local cold-pressed oil
Dash of powdered kelp
1 large shiitake mushroom, stemmed and sliced in long strips
2 fingers enoke mushroom
¼ pound tempeh, sliced in long strips
1 small avocado, sliced in long strips
⅓ cucumber, peeled and sliced in long strips
¼ pound cream cheese or vegan counterpart
Wasabi paste
Pickled ginger

Sushi Rice

Rinse rice until the water runs clear and drain in a colander or on a tray.

If you have your life savings in a bank, they're probably not going to do you as much good as they would if you invested them in preparing your children to have greater self-reliance or helping one of your neighbors start a business. Invest in your neighborhood, your community, and your region.

Alternatively, there are many small-scale ethical lending institutions coming into being, organizations like the Permaculture Credit Union. By putting your savings into institutions like these, you can be confident that the money is being lent to build a more ecologically stable and socially equitable future. It also saves you the effort of managing your investments in your neighbors and community because the credit union does that.

In this chapter we have been looking at what holds economies together and how to rebuild them from the grassroots when they start to unravel. But "civilization" is not just about economic relations. Commerce may have a lot to do with the evolution of complex societies, but so do social relationships, religion, art, language, tools, food, and climate.

If we think of ourselves as *Homo petroleo,* a new human species that has evolved in just one century by harnessing the tremendous advantages of fossil fuels, then we should also consider that our new species is facing rapid extinction if we do not re-evolve, or devolve, even more rapidly. All those relationships that brought us to this point are changing now. The change is comprehensive — it sweeps across all aspects of our lives, and it touches each of us. The change is fast — not even a century this time, maybe even less than a decade.

Step one of the journey is building a protective platform that is stable in this sea of change. We can call it civilization, because it is a social platform more than anything else. It is fundamentally a mutual interdependency: all of us in the lifeboat must both protect all the others and rely on the protection of the others if any of us is to survive. It begins by building camaraderie among the like-minded, those of us with a common vision, and it extends outward to draw in the rest as the tempest of history tosses us.

The steps that follow are all about helping each other put our houses in order and get back to the basics: learning how to save water, make soil, grow food and store it, build an efficient home and heat and light it, retain a measure of mobility, and create a sustainable livelihood. Civilization thus rebuilt gets back to community again — how to get along with each other and how to reorganize at larger and larger scales. Amidst all that, there is the process of adapting to the new way of the world — after petroleum.

No one is saying this change will be easy. In the right frame of mind, though, it can be a lot of fun. It can be the right thing for the planet and for all of us riding together through space.

*I think it is likely, a hundred years
from now, that* Homo sapiens *will be living in
small communities, supplying most of their needs from
the surrounding farmland, rather like medieval Europe. The one
advantage they will have though is knowledge. It took thousands of
years before the Norfolk Four Course crop-rotation system was discovered
in 18th century England. That is now available to anyone near a library,
bookshop, or Internet connection. While the medieval villager looked upon a
windmill as something to grind corn or raise water, we could look upon it as a
means to generate electricity .... With light and heat available in the evenings
and centuries of learning in books, there would be time to contemplate the
future, consider solutions and possibly progress in ways not imagined now.
The villages of the future would be an interesting subject for a science
fiction novel. For our great-grandchildren, it will be science fact.*

— Paul Thompson, 2005

Sushi Nori cont.

Place the drained rice in a rice steamer, a crock pot, or a pot with a tight-fitting lid and add 2 cups water. Cover and boil over medium heat for about 2 minutes; reduce heat and simmer for another 5 minutes. Reduce heat to low and cook for about 15 minutes or until water has been absorbed. Remove from heat, remove lid, and place a towel over pot. Replace lid and let stand for 10 to 15 minutes.

While the rice cooks, combine vinegar, mirin, sweetener, salt, and ¼ cup water in a saucepan. Heat over low flame 1 minute while stirring. Do not boil. Set aside to cool until you can comfortably touch the bottom of the pot with your hand. Empty rice into a *hangiri* or other nonmetallic platter and spread it evenly over the bottom with a *shamoji* or large wooden spoon. Run the *shamoji* through the rice in slicing motions to separate the grains. While doing this, slowly add vinegar mixture. Add only as much as is necessary; the rice should not be mushy. If you have help, fan the rice with an *uchiwa* (fan) during the cooling and mixing procedures. Do not refrigerate. The rice will last one day.

Sushi Nori

Toast the nori by passing the shiny side over a high flame. The color of the nori will change from brownish black to dark green. Without toasting, the nori will be gummy and hard to chew. Preheat iron skillet and steam carrot, radish, and jicama strips in vinegar or shoyu, then drain on paper. Add oil and kelp to hot pan. Sauté shiitake, enoke, carrot, and tempeh over medium heat until

Sushi Nori cont.

brown, then remove and drain on paper.

Moisten your hands with vinegar to keep the rice from sticking to your hands as you work. Lay nori on a sushi mat enclosed in a plastic bag, shiny side down. Sprinkle with wine-vinegar mix and firmly pat rice on bottom two thirds of nori closest to you. Alternatively, pat rice on bottom two thirds of the mat and cover with nori. Neatly arrange a few strips of fillings along the closest edge, choosing contrasting colors. Place slices of carrots, radish, jicama, shiitake, enoke, tempeh, avocado, cucumber, and cream cheese as desired, varying ingredients between rolls.

To roll, hold the line of fillings in place with your fingertips and use your thumbs to push up and turn the end of the bamboo mat so that the closest edge of the nori curls away from you over the fillings. While you press firmly along the length of the mat, slowly roll it up, jelly-roll style, so it gradually encloses all the rice in the roll. It helps to slowly pull the mat toward you while maintaining even pressure along its length. Work slowly and tightly — this may take practice. Dampen the exposed edge of the nori with vinegar-water before sealing the roll closed. Squeeze the whole roll tightly before releasing it from the mat, rolling back and forth a few times. Refrigerate at least 30 minutes before cutting the roll with a sharp wet knife into half-inch rounds, trimming ends neatly first. Arrange on wooden tray with dishes of wasabi, shoyu, and pickled ginger.

Difficulty

Recommended Daily Allowances and Suggested Optimal Daily Nutritional Allowances

Nutrient	Men RDA	Men SONA	Women RDA	Women SONA
Fat-soluble Vitamins				
Vitamin A (RE)*	1,000	2,000	800	2,000
Beta-carotene (mg)**	N/A	100	N/A	80
Vitamin D (micro gm)	5	24	5	24
Vitamin E (IU)***	10	800	8	800
Vitamin K (mg)	80	80	65	65
Water-soluble Vitamins				
Vitamin C (mg)	60	800	60	1000
Vitamin B12 (mg)	2	3	2	3
Folic acid (micro gm)	200	2000	180	2000
Niacin (mg)	15	30	15	25
Pyridoxine (B6) (mg)	2	25	1.6	20
Riboflavin (B2) (mg)	1.4	2.5	1.2	2
Thiamin (B1) (mg)	1.2	9.2	1	9
Minerals				
Boron (mg)	N/A	2.5	N/A	3
Calcium (mg)	800	700	800	1200
Chromium (micro gm)	50-200	300	50-200	300
Copper (mg)	1.5-3	1.5-4	1.5-3	1.5-4
Iodine (micro gm)	150	150	150	150
Iron (mg)	10	20	15	20
Magnesium (mg)	350	600	280	550
Manganese (mg)	2-5	10	2-5	10
Phosphorous (mg)	800	800	800	800
Potassium (mg)	99	200-500	99	200-500
Selenium (micro gm)	70	250	55	200
Sodium (mg)	500	400	500	400
Zinc (mg)	15	20	12	17

*I RE = I micro gm = 3.33 IU   ** 1 microgram = 40 IU
***1 IU alpha tocopherol equivalent to I mg alpha tocopherol

Save Your Water

The future of civilization depends on water.
I beg you all to understand this.

— Jacques Yves Cousteau, 1997

We are addicted to petroleum, but that is nothing compared to our dependency on water. A starving animal can live even if it loses nearly all its glycogen and fat, as well as half its body protein, but a loss of 20 percent of the water in the body results in death. A person can live without food for over a month, but without water only a few days. Since the human body is made up of about 65 percent water, we must consider it an important nutrient.

Less than one hundredth of 1 percent of this blue planet's water is fresh, renewed by rainfall. It is this tiny fraction that sustains fields, forests, wetlands, grasslands, and all terrestrial life.

Foolishly, human civilization has been ruining its most vital asset, and the pace of destruction is accelerating. Falling water tables, altered river flows, shrinking lakes, disappearing mangrove swamps, and "dead zones" in our oceans should warn us, but these warnings are mostly being ignored. We are still using rivers for irrigation until they are too dry to reach the sea; still building enormous dam and diversion projects in China, India, Turkey, New Zealand, and elsewhere; still draining fresh-water aquifers at unreplenishable rates; and still dumping our sewage, garbage, and toxic chemicals into our drinking water.

Global warming will soon bring the situation to a head for many nations. Glaciers and mountain snowpacks are retreating in the Alps, Andes, Cascades,

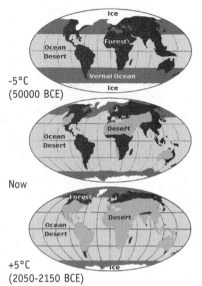

-5°C
(50000 BCE)

Now

+5°C
(2050-2150 BCE)

Climate change with temperature variation (after Lovelock 2006). Our planet was richest in biological activity when it was five degrees cooler. As we warm, habitability declines in the oceans and on land, and biological activity shrinks. We may have already passed the point of no return.

Water Requirements (average individual)	
Intake	
Liquid food	4.7 cup
Solid food	2.1-3.8 cups
Water produced in the body	1.7 cups
Total	8.5-10.2 cups
Output	
Vaporization (lungs & Skin)	3.6-4.2 cups
Feces	0.3-0.4 cups
Urine	4.2-5.5 cups
Total	8.4-10.1 cups

Himalayas, Rockies, and Sierra Nevada at rates never seen in human history. The temporary surge of meltwater creates water abundance for the cities and towns downstream, lulling them into false security. Then it will be gone, and with it, the ability of large populations to live in those places.

Every individual should first, and most importantly, identify and protect a secure supply of water. If we follow the recommendations that each person drink eight glasses of water a day, that's 8 times 8 ounces or 64 ounces per person — two quarts (1.9 liters) of water per person per day for drinking.

Allow an equal amount for cooking, brushing teeth, and minimal cleaning up and you need four quarts or one gallon (3.8 liters) of water per person per day.

For two persons, two gallons. For a family of four, four gallons. For a three-day weekend, the family of four needs 12 gallons. For 30 days, a family of four would need 120 gallons (454 liters)! And this is rationing the amount of water used at all times. No toilet-flushing or clothes-washing is included in calculating minimum water needs.

Assessing Your Water-Readiness

Approaching this problem of water supply from our own situation, we need to ask whether our access to water is both sufficient and assured. Since most people live in or close to cities, they are likely to be dependent on municipal water systems. Municipal systems are almost never solar powered. They run on electricity, and, unless you are in Iceland, the electricity likely comes from oil, gas, coal, nuclear, or hydro. Only the last of those is a renewable resource. The rest will become increasingly scarce.

If your primary supply is rainwater (as it is for river- and reservoir-dependent settlements), you need enough water-storage capacity to make it through dry spells. You might also want some extra storage capacity for times when hurricanes, floods, or other natural catastrophes disrupt or pollute your supply. If your primary source is groundwater, you need enough storage to get through periods when the pump has no power, or when the supply has become contaminated. In exceptionally dry times, during natural disasters, or when there is sudden demand for a limited supply, even the best source may become unreliable.

Saving Water

Bacteria-free water can be kept indefinitely in opaque, airtight containers. The key question is, is it clean? To be safe, both the container and its contents should be disinfected before storage begins. In storage, the

Who Owns Your Water?

One of the more dangerous trends over the past few decades has been the consolidation of the control of freshwater supplies in the hands of commercial interests. The market for water is now a $300 billion global business. Offering water management services are players with names like American Anglican Environmental Technologies, Azurix, Severn Trent Services, and Vivendi Water.

In November 1999, the UK's largest utility, Thames Water, said it would buy the New Jersey utility E'town, owner of Elizabethtown Water and two other providers, to keep pace with bigger rivals Vivendi and Suez Lyonnaise des Eaux. Thames is already managing the taps in Houston and Pittsburgh and is eyeing a move into Latin America. The acquisition of E'town tripled Thames' business in the US. Thames also owns Applied Wastewater Management.

Philadelphia Suburban (PSC), based in Bryn Mawr, PA, is the US's second-largest investor-owned water utility (behind American Water Works) and serves 1.8 million residents in Illinois, Maine, New Jersey, and Pennsylvania. Since 1992, PSC has purchased 27 water systems. Vivendi holds a substantial interest in PSC.

Italy's largest independent energy supplier, Edison SpA, recently agreed to buy 50 percent of International Water Ltd. (IWL), a London-based subsidiary of Bechtel formed in 1996 to manage water-treatment concessions and privatized systems throughout Europe, Asia, and South America. IWL serves a total of about 6 million clients in the three regions. Edison has also purchased 60 percent of the Italian water and gas company Arcadas Sud, which serves about 31,000 people in the Rome area.

International Water, Ltd.

If one "Utility" is owned rent is 4 times amount shown on dice.
If both "Utilities" are owned rent is 10 times amount shown on dice.

Mortgage Value $75.

---

container should be tightly sealed and kept in a dark area, and the water should be taste-tested every six months. Properly stored water can remain fresh for several years.

Disinfecting Water

In an emergency, rivers, lakes, and ponds are possible sources of water, but the water must be disinfected first. Chemical disinfectants are not effective for cloudy water. Run murky or discolored water through ceramic filters or a clean cloth to produce sediment-free water suitable for disinfecting.

Any water to be used for drinking, cooking, brushing teeth, or any other internal use should be properly disinfected. There are several methods for disinfecting water. Boiling it vigorously for three minutes will kill any disease-causing microorganisms. *Giardia* is killed in less than a minute at 176°F, well under the boiling point. Bacteria and viruses last somewhat longer, but most are probably killed in less than five minutes at 190°F. Some viruses may last longer. At 10,000 feet water boils at 194°F, so above this altitude you should boil water an extra minute for each 1,000 feet.

You can improve the flat taste of boiled water by aerating it (pouring it back and forth between two containers), by allowing it to stand for a few hours in a clean container, or by adding a pinch of salt for each quart boiled.

Chlorine Bleach

Common household bleach contains a chlorine compound that will disinfect water. If no disinfection procedure is written on the label of the bleach container, find the percentage of available chlorine and use the table at left as a guide:

If the strength is unknown, add ten drops to each quart. Double this amount if the water is cloudy. The treated water should be mixed thoroughly and allowed to stand for 30 minutes. A simple test of effectiveness is to take a small taste. If the water doesn't taste of chlorine, repeat the dosage and let it stand another 15 minutes.

Once you know the water is free of bacteria (i.e., when it tastes of chlorine), you can reduce the chlorine taste by letting the water sit for a while in an open container or by aerating it (pouring it back and forth between containers). This will allow much of the chlorine to off-gas.

Granular Calcium Hypochlorite

One heaping teaspoon of calcium hypochlorite (approximately ¼ ounce) dissolved in two gallons of water will produce a stock chlorine solution (500 milligrams per liter) since calcium hypochlorite is about 70 percent chlorine.

Disinfected water should have a chlorination of one part chlorine to 100 parts water. That's one pint (16 ounces) of stock chlorine to 12.5 gallons of water. Don't confuse concentrated calcium hypochlorite with stock chlorine! A gallon of drinkable water should have no more than a hundredth of an ounce of calcium hypochlorite.

Chlorine Tablets

Chlorine tablets ready for disinfecting water can be purchased with mixing instructions. When instructions are not available, try one tablet for each quart of water and use the taste test.

Measuring Chlorine	
Available Chlorine	**Drops/Quart**
1%	10
4-6%	2
7-10%	1

Disinfection with chlorine produces hazardous byproducts like trihalomethanes. Chlorine buildup in freshwater ecosystems and the atmosphere is a global concern and one more unsustainable way we are poisoning our planet. Chlorinated drinking water causes at least 6,500 cases of rectal cancer and 4,200 cases of bladder cancer in the US annually. Let's use as little chlorine as possible. We can accomplish this by using the other disinfection techniques first.

Tincture of Iodine

If no chlorine is available, you can use iodine. It is not as helpful as chlorine because it is ineffective against some pathogens, like *Giardia* or *Cryptosporidium*. It is best to use iodine to disinfect well water, rather than surface water, because well water is less likely to have these organisms.

Common household iodine from the medicine chest or first aid kit is 2 percent iodine. Add five drops to each quart of clear water or ten drops to each quart of cloudy water. Let stand for at least 30 minutes.

Iodine Tablets

Iodine water-purification tablets can be found in most drug or sporting goods stores. When instructions are not available, use one tablet for each quart of water.

Ascorbic Acid Powder

Instead of bleach, add ascorbic acid powder to stored water as a preservative. Just half a teaspoon (approximately two grams or 2,000 milligrams) added to a two-quart jar of water may give a very faint lemon flavor, but the water will be fresher. You can obtain soluble, pure, ascorbic acid crystals (Vitamin C) from Bronson Pharmaceuticals, La Canada, California, 91011 USA. It is a good item to be stockpiling.

Containers

Clean water needs clean containers. Once you have disinfected water, you should put it in a container that can block light and that is not too heavy for you to carry to where it will be used. A gallon of water weighs about eight pounds (3.6 kg), so a five-gallon jug (19 liters) is the largest size most people can carry.

When choosing food-grade containers, look for HPDE plastics (high-density polyethylene). They carry the recycling symbol with the number "2" inside the ring. Do not reuse containers that retain strong odors, held toxic materials, or are made from biodegradable plastics, such as milk and distilled-water containers. Biodegradable plastics will break down in about six months.

To prepare jugs for storing water, wash them well, rinse them with a solution of one tablespoon bleach to a gallon of water, and clean the cap. Once you've filled the jugs with water, take a marking pen and label each jug with the date it was filled. Use the oldest water first.

SOUPS

SOUPS

Soups are one way to stretch ingredients farther when times are hard. They are also a good use for dried foods that have been stored a long time. In the first soup recipe I have used potato flakes as an extender, but they could as easily be the main component when whole potatoes are not available.

However, simple soup recipes using stored ingredients do tend to taste a little bland. To fix this we'll start with my cousin Mark's spice herb mixtures and blends. Prepare a jar that you can keep on a kitchen shelf and pull down whenever a soup doesn't quite live up to expectations.

Teotihuacan

Variations in water supply are not a new problem for human societies. Teotihuacan, near Mexico City, was a major center of Mesoamerican civilization around 300 BCE and flourished until 700-800 CE. At its peak it supported a population of 150,000 to 200,000 — the sixth-largest city in the world — in a very dry climate. As the Teotihuacan population outgrew the springs and wells that marked the early settlement period, and as transportation of water from distant sources was impractical, the settlement came to rely on the water that fell generously from the sky in the short rainy season.

Some years ago, excavations in Teotihuacan uncovered the Palace of the Jaguars beneath a later pyramid. Close examination of the palace revealed that it was a cleverly engineered aeration device that even today harvests the rain, adds oxygen by passing the current through the mouths of jaguar-headed flowforms, drops the water onto splash-pans, repeats the process, and then diverts the aerated fresh water into huge reservoirs concealed under the courtyards, ball fields, and boulevards where it stores the water in the dark to prevent the growth of algae.

Aeration discourages anaerobic bacteria and causes some contaminants to oxidize into more benign substances. Bacteria can hitch a ride on suspended solids, so the slow settling process in the reservoirs and cisterns clears the water column. Teotihuacantecos might also have added coagulants like alum to make particles clump together and settle. Time was also on their side. Human pathogens thrive in the human body and similar environments. In a cold, dark, nearly nutrient-free tank, those pathogens gradually die.

Today we have other disinfection techniques that ancient peoples lacked. Ozonation kills pathogens by bubbling chemically unstable ozone through the water column, imparting oxygen much more effectively. Ultraviolet light kills most pathogens with high-energy waves. Chlorination employs a long-lasting environmental toxin that eliminates pathogens, although it has some nasty side effects for healthy ecosystems as well.

Temple of the Jaguars at Teotihuacan

Waterspout flowform at Teotihuacan

You can store full jugs in a basement, in a garage, or outdoors. If you store them outdoors, they should be covered, because sunlight will make plastic brittle over time. If water jugs stored outdoors are likely to freeze, fill them only four-fifths full. This gives the ice room to expand without splitting the sides.

Soft-Drink Bottles

Two- and three-liter soft-drink bottles are useful for water storage, but because they are clear plastic, water quality may deteriorate sooner.

Storage Drums

Although large drums are too heavy to be moved when full, they are good for storage. Local beverage distributors, like Coca-Cola or Pepsi bottling plants, sell used 55-gallon HPDE drums at reasonable prices, often for as little as five dollars. These drums are usually white, so it's a good idea to spray-paint their exteriors a dark color like black, blue, or dark green. Don't store them next to the furnace or fireplace. They melt at 266°F (130°C).

Prior to painting and filling, make sure you have thoroughly cleaned and disinfected the inside. Syrup residue can be a fertile source for bacteria, and it will flavor your water.

Alternative Water Sources

Collecting Rainwater

If you have a house with gutters, begin to collect rainwater. Water storage typically costs 50 cents to $3 per gallon, and rainwater is so superior to most well and spring water that every home should have a supply. It requires no "softener," uses less soap, and is friendlier to work with than even the best water that has come into contact with the ground. Grandmother loved the softness of rainwater for washing her hair, and the country house always had a barrel — topped with some screening to keep out leaves — standing under eaves near the gutter downspout.

You will need the following materials:

- A barrel, cistern, or tank
- Guttering
- A downspout from the gutter into the tank
- Hardware, such as elbows, pipes, and pipe cement, to connect the spout to the tank

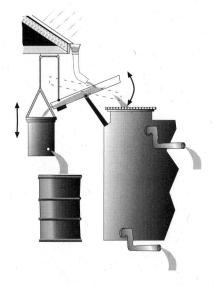

- A "roof washer" to divert the first flow of dirty water away from the tank (see illustration)
- A tank overflow pipe to direct water away from your foundation
- A faucet for the bottom of the tank
- A tight-fitting, childproof, removable cover that will keep out mosquitoes and allow access for cleaning
- Hoses or watering cans to take water from the faucet to the garden or wherever it is needed

Cut a hole in the lid of a large, heavy-duty trash can, then place the can under the drainpipe of your gutter to collect water. Fasten some fine mesh screen under the hole to keep debris out. The illustration shows a simple system for dumping the leaves and dirt that collect on a roof before sending cleaner water to the cistern. You can construct a more elaborate filter by filling a tank or barrel with alternate layers of coarse gravel, charcoal, and sand to cleanse the water before sending it to the house. All filters should be drained and cleaned when not in use.

If you want to use roof-collected water for washing up, brushing your teeth, or drinking, it's a good idea to filter it and then boil it for two minutes first, or use chemical treatment.

If your house doesn't have gutters, maybe it's time to think about adding them. An alternative is to construct a shed roof over a cistern tank at a high point of land and collect water there, then send it by gravity and pipe to your home. Enameled steel makes a good shed roof that stays cleaner.

A really great book about making cisterns and designing ponds is *Water Storage* by Art Ludwig (available from oasisdesign.net). Some home designs are shown in the brochure "Everybody Needs a Rain Barrel" by Kathy Hill (from www.elizabethriver.org/Publications/Publications.asp).

In this design from Bill Mollison, a small bucket is attached to a rope that runs through a pulley and is secured to a hinged section of gutter. As the first raindrops collect on the roof and flow into the hinged gutter, the water in the bucket slowly rises, and the weight causes the bucket to descend, pulling the rope, which raises the gutter section until it no longer empties into the bucket. After an initial period of rain, with the dirty roofwater collected in the bucket, the rainwater flows into the cistern.

Melted Snow or Icicles

If you live in a cold climate, there may be snow or ice outdoors. Have one or more buckets and a shovel handy to collect the snow. Bring it into your warm room and let it melt.

Fill the Bathtub

If you know a storm is coming and utilities may be cut, fill your bathtub with water. This is a great convenience for a bit of washing up. People who have sailboats claim they can wash dishes for the whole crew in a teacup of water, and you may have to do the same. Scoop out a little at a time to wash your face, but put a jar of fresh or boiled water near the bathroom sink for brushing teeth.

Emergency Sources

> There is a time in the life of every problem when it is big
> enough to see, yet small enough to solve.
>
> — Mike Leavitt, 1998

If a disaster catches you without a stored supply of clean water, you can use water from your hot-water tank, plumbing, and ice cubes. As a last resort, you can use water in the reservoir tank of your toilet (not the bowl), but purify it first.

A large picnic cooler may hold 20 to 30 gallons (114 liters), as do large rubberized trash containers. If you keep a bag or two of ice in your freezer, put the bag into a clean, leak-proof container so you can use the water when the ice has melted.

A 50-gallon water heater will have 50 gallons of drinking water even after the water heater has been turned off. Start the water flowing by turning off the water intake valve and turning on a hot-water faucet. If you drain your electric water heater, be sure to refill it before restarting when the power comes back on. If you forget, the heating element could easily be ruined.

Waterbeds hold up to 400 gallons, but some contain toxic chemicals that may not be fully removed by many purifiers. If you designate a waterbed in your home as an emergency resource, drain it yearly and refill it with fresh water containing two ounces of bleach per 120 gallons. Use the water for cleaning and flushing, but don't drink it.

If your water is cut off and you have to use the water in your pipes, let air into the plumbing by turning on the highest-elevation faucet in your house and draining the water from the lowest one.

Do you know the location of your incoming water valve? You'll need to shut it off to prevent contaminated water from entering your home if you hear reports of broken water or sewage lines. Also, in cold climates, frozen pipes may burst if there is no heat. Shut off the water and drain the pipes if there's a strong possibility of this occurring.

Scaling Up

As we become more respectful of the value of our fresh water, we will want to take larger measures to protect it. Communities may reexamine

---

SOUPS

POTATO SOUP
Serves 4 to 6

4 potatoes, scrubbed, peeled, and diced
1 onion, chopped
1 quart water or soup stock
1 tsp sea salt or to taste
¼ cup non-fat dry milk, powdered soymilk, soy cream, blended tofu, or potato flakes
2 Tbsp fresh chopped or dried parsley

Put potatoes, onions, water, and salt in a soup pot. Place over heat. Cover and cook until potatoes are tender. Mix the milk with a little water or stock and stir into the soup. Ladle into bowls, sprinkle parsley on top of each.

Difficulty

SOUPS
SPLIT PEA SOUP

Serves 10

2 cups dried split peas
2 carrots, finely chopped
1 large onion, chopped
10 cups water or soup stock
Salt and pepper to taste
Optional spices: bay leaf, red pepper, garlic powder, thyme, tarragon, marjoram, ground cloves, or allspice

Combine split peas, carrot, onion, and water in large pan. Cover and bring to a boil. Simmer 30 minutes or until all vegetables are tender. Season to taste.

Difficulty

the sources of their water supply and reconsider how they dispose of sewage, runoff, and industrial greywater in ways that threaten those sources. They might come to see expensive mechanical waste-treatment facilities as the capital-intensive engineering nightmares they are, drawing increasingly scarce energy from other needs for only marginal results. Natural and artificial waste-treatment wetlands will be appreciated as low-cost, high-return alternatives in need of expansion and preservation. Laws preventing rooftop rainwater catchment will be repealed. Community-scale seasonal storage tanks will be built. These are all good developments, but they should have been put in place decades ago.

When I was in Israel looking at these large shed dairies, they are like European dairies, but instead of being fed with crops from natural rainfall, the crops in Israel are grown from water which has been pumped with electricity. Vast field crops of corn and wheat are fed to dairy animals. And I said to the people there, "You know, in Australia the glass of milk we drink is about twenty percent oil. In Europe, it's about fifty to sixty percent oil. In Israel, it's about ninety percent oil!"

— David Holmgren, 2004

Manage Your Wastes

*March 15, 1910: The amazing
Lakeview Gusher started spewing crude oil
into the air of the San Joaquin Valley in California.
Oil shot into the air at an estimated 125,000 barrels a
day from a column of oil and sand 20 feet in diameter and 200
feet high (6 meters by 60 meters). Lakeview's roaring and spouting
began to be measured, not in days, but months. It seemed little dis-
couraged by the feeble efforts of humans to control it. Besides the labor
of holding the oil, there was constant anxiety and fear. Adjacent landowners
sued. Workmen cursed the sticky flood and labored in fear that spray from
the well, carried on the wind for up to ten miles, could cause accidental fires.
Preachers and their flocks prayed that oil might not cover the earth and bring
about its flaming destruction. The entire oil industry wilted as this seemingly
inexhaustible fountain brought crude prices down to 30 cents a barrel. Even
Union Oil Company, with endless lawsuits, labor bills and low-priced crude
on its hands, began to despair of having made the "richest" oil discovery
in history. When the bottom of the hole caved in on September 10,
1911, the well died. Although Lakeview No. 1 produced 9.4 million
barrels during the 544 days it flowed, less than half of this oil
was saved — the rest evaporating off or seeping into
the ground.*

— San Joaquin Geological Society

ots of people, when thinking about emergency preparation, think about their supply of food and water. Fewer think about the other

SOUPS

VEGETABLE SOUP PROVENÇAL

Frozen vegetables that have thawed can be added to this soup after the potatoes are cooked tender. Leftover pasta-cooking water can be used as part of the stock.

Serves 6 to 8

4 cups (about ¼ head) cabbage, shredded
2 medium potatoes, scrubbed, peeled, and diced
2 medium carrots, thinly sliced
2 cloves garlic, chopped
1 large onion, chopped
6 cups water or vegetable stock
1 tsp salt or to taste
1¾ cup fresh or 15-ounce can of tomatoes, chopped
1 tsp dried basil
1 tsp dried oregano
Dash of savory, thyme, rosemary, sage, marjoram, and fennel

Combine cabbage, potatoes, carrots, garlic, and onion with water or stock in a large kettle. Add salt. Cover. Place over heat and cook until the vegetables are tender. Add tomatoes and seasonings; heat and serve.

Difficulty

end — their wastes. Disposing of wastes is nearly as important a survival skill as finding food because if it is improperly handled, normal daily wastes can make people too sick to function and can even kill them.

We are so accustomed to having sewage pipes, septic systems, and similar modern conveniences that it is difficult to imagine what it might be like if they stopped working. In industrial societies, most sewage is carried by water from the toilet to treatment, but what would happen if that water became unavailable? What about the power needed to pump the water or to run a large-scale sewage treatment plant? If brownouts and blackouts become more common, what happens to our sewage?

An efficient way to dispose of sewage in an emergency is to dig a trench in the backyard, about one foot deep and six inches wide. Have a pile of sawdust or mulch nearby. Dump the contents of the waste bucket into the trench and cover solids with sawdust or mulch. An apartment dweller could line a dry toilet with garbage bags and use it for solids only, covering each use with newspapers, placing filled bags in a large trashcan designated as a waste receptacle, and planning on trips to a vacant lot to do the burying — while managing liquid waste separately. Obviously this is not something thousands of apartment dwellers could do as a permanent solution.

Over the long term, it is better if organic wastes can decompose aerobically (with air infiltration) rather than by anaerobic processes (in closed containers or underwater). Anaerobic decomposition produces ammonium and other smelly gases, so sawdust or straw piles, turned regularly, are preferable to pit trenches, closed cans, or boxes.

Kitchen scraps, wood ashes, shredded paper, brush, and leaves — anything that decomposes rapidly — should be made into a compost pile and turned regularly to allow aerobic decomposition. Worms can be added to the pile to speed and enliven the process. American red wigglers, African nightcrawlers, and Asian tigerworms are among the best for this kind of work, but any diversity in microfauna is good.

Because of the potential for harm from human pathogens, sewage should never be put into the vegetable garden. However urine, which contains nitrogen and potassium, is an excellent fertilizer, and urinating into a bed of shredded paper, sawdust, or straw before adding the mixture to compost provides two of the elements plants use most: carbon and nitrogen.

Anything that doesn't easily decompose (wood, metal, wire, plastic) should be recycled or stored until it can be collected for recycling.

Dry Toilets

While water-based sewage disposal is considered normal in many Western countries, such systems are extremely expensive, costing about $4,000 for each household to install and using 25 to 60 gallons of water per person per day to operate. In many parts of the world, water is too scarce a resource to be used for sewage, so composting toilets have become the standard. A composting toilet can be safe, sanitary, and efficient if a homeowner is prepared to take the time required to properly manage the system. Many composting toilets are commercially available at prices ranging from $850 to $5,000.

In an emergency, all you may have time to do is build a pit latrine. But if you plan to be prepared for any emergency, or if you find yourself in an emergency that goes on for weeks or months, constructing a composting toilet is worth the effort.

Controlling flies and fly larvae is important to controlling vector-borne disease. Installing a simple flytrap on or near sewage receptacles is a wise precaution. Many flytraps work on the simple principle that flies prefer to fly upward to exit an enclosed space and seldom fly down through a narrow space once trapped. Dead flies can be safely added to compost once they accumulate.

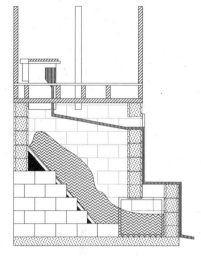

Dry compost toilet.

Joe Jenkins' Design

Joe Jenkins' now famous *Humanure Handbook* describes the simple system his family has used on their farm for 30 years (available from www.jenkinspublishing.com/humanure.html). It consists of a five-gallon bucket that sits under a seat in the bathroom, gathers the solid (not the liquid) wastes, and is emptied daily into a special compost pile. Augmented with sawdust and other compostable materials, and turned weekly, Jenkins' system is odor-free and waste-free. After thermophilic digestion, the finished product goes to the orchard.

Traditional outhouses, which are pit latrines, create health, environmental, and aesthetic problems. Flies and mosquitoes transmit disease over a wide area. Pollutants from the pits leach into the ground and can travel long distances through groundwater. And the pits smell.

Composting toilets recapture the nutrients in humanure but require proper maintenance and treatment to eliminate potential disease vectors and smell. Even urine, which is normally sterile, can transmit disease if it contains blood. Fecal matter carries bacteria, viruses, worm eggs, and larvae, all of which can be harmful to people if they reach the dinner table.

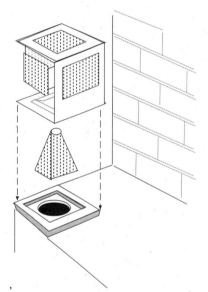

Flytrap.

However, as we change the environmental conditions of the wastes, pathogen die-off rates accelerate. Ninety-nine percent of fecal coliforms (bacteria commonly found in feces) will die in soil after about two weeks in summer and about three weeks in winter. A temperature above 140°F (60°C) will result in near-instant death for most pathogens excreted in feces. Temperatures just ten degrees cooler result in no growth for bacteria and a rapid death, usually within 30 minutes and sometimes less, for most pathogens. You can achieve these temperatures using various methods (such as high-temperature composting). By changing more than one factor at the same time, you can speed the die-off even further. For instance, decreasing moisture and increasing temperature combine to produce a faster die-off than either achieve alone. Good designs for composting toilets take these factors into account.

One reason we humans have not
"fed" our excrement to the appropriate organisms
is because we didn't know they existed. We've only learned
to see and understand microscopic creatures in our recent past. We
also haven't had such a rapidly growing human population in the past,
nor have we been faced with the dire environmental problems that threaten
our species today, like buzzards circling an endangered animal. It all adds up
to the fact that the human species must inevitably evolve. Evolution means
change, or as Rachel Carson stated almost four decades ago, we must realize that
we are now standing at a fork in the road. Change is often resisted, as old habits
die hard, and flush toilets and bulging garbage cans represent well-entrenched
but non-sustainable habits that must be rethought and reinvented.

— Joe Jenkins, 1994

Clivus Multrum

The Clivus Multrum (www.clivusmultrum.com/) is probably the best-known commercial composting toilet. Made of plastic or fiberglass, it is typically installed on the ground floor or in the basement of a house, with the commode pedestal being one or more floors above. Like all composting toilets, the Clivus works best if kept dry, either through a process of continual aeration or through liquid separation at the source and discrete greywater disposal.

Biolytix

The Biolytix® Company of Maleny, Australia (www.biolytix.com), offers a line of wet composting toilets that pass sewer water into a series of

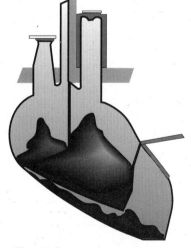

Clivus Multrum.

digestion chambers where specially adapted worms and bacteria break the wastes down into harmless soils. These wet digesters can not only accept shower and sink water, but can also compost kitchen scraps and paper trash. Newer models can be retrofitted between floors of a two-story house. Biolytix also builds neighborhood-scale greywater recycling systems.

Sunny John

Created by John Cruickshank, the Sunny John is a simple set of plans (available from www.sunnyjohn.com) that you can use to build your own composting toilet that dehydrates the pile by evaporation. Air is drawn into the chamber by the thermal siphon effect created when a black-painted stack is exposed to direct sunlight. The Sunny John is low-maintenance and inexpensive.

Village-Scale Systems

In many countries the sprawling steel-and-concrete municipal treatment plant that sits at the edge of some body of water and noisily processes sewage on an enormous scale has become a paradigm of modernity. A huge plume of oily brown sludge at the mouth of the Nile as it enters the Mediterranean is the product of as many as 300 outflows near Cairo. A similar plume flows from the Mississippi into the Gulf of Mexico. There are now 146 "dead zones" covering the planet's oceans, like a pox. Those in the Gulf of Mexico, East China Sea, and Baltic each span more than 7,500 square miles.

Municipal sewage treatment plants are enormously expensive to construct and operate, have to be rebuilt or replaced every few decades, work poorly at returning water to a non-toxic level, and, perhaps most importantly, require a lot of energy.

While they may be necessary for very large cities for the near term, there are alternatives for smaller communities and urban eco-neighborhoods.

Many years ago, Professor James Wolverton, who was designing waste-handling systems for the NASA space program, came to a startling conclusion. Even in the environment of space, none of the mechanical devices for processing human wastes worked as well as natural processes of decomposition. Wolverton stopped fooling around with chemicals and stainless steel pulverizers and started using micorrhyzae and duckweed. In many locations, at varying latitudes, he supervised construction of municipal sewage systems that employed artificial wetlands — lagoons and reed beds — to purify water to a higher standard than that of many freshwater sources, while at the same time producing biomass for fuel

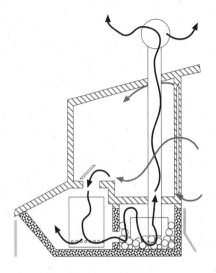

Implicit in the moldering process is a long resting period: the full waste vault must be left undisturbed for a minimum of six months while bacteria and microorganisms break down the waste without any addition of fresh material. This requires that you build a second vault to be used while the first is resting. The Sunny John uses solar energy and wind for heat and ventilation. A thermostatic damper controls the amount of winter venting to prevent deep cooling.

SOUPS

TUSCAN BEAN SOUP

Serves 4 to 6

2 Tbsp oil
3 cloves garlic, chopped
3 cups vegetable broth
2 cups cooked Great Northern or cannellini beans
1 cup cooked whole tomatoes, chopped
1 tsp dehydrated onion flakes
1 tsp rubbed sage

Heat pan; add oil and garlic. Cook 2 minutes. Add broth, beans, tomatoes, onion, and sage and simmer until mixture bubbles. Taste and add a little salt and pepper if desired. You may wish to add a few crushed red pepper flakes.

Difficulty

and providing habitat for wildlife and parkland for recreation. Wolverton demonstrated that we could recapture the intrinsic nutritional value of the solid "wastes" and direct it to ecological restoration. His work illustrated one of the principles of permaculture: everything gardens. Wastes from one organism are always food for another.

Working on a similar track, John Todd and his family enterprise found ways to bring artificial wetlands indoors, reduce their footprint, and increase their efficiencies. Using these indoor wetlands, which they called "living machines," the Todds demonstrated compact sewage treatment in a variety of settings, from college campuses to inner-city neighborhoods. While living machines are more energy-intense than the gravity-flow biological systems built by Wolverton, they consume less energy than standard municipal treatment plants, and the energy they require can be supplied by renewable sources, including their own production of methane. A good example of a living machine is the one at the Findhorn ecovillage on the far north coast of Scotland, where there is a very cold winter climate. Using a large enclosed greenhouse heated by methane and powered by a wind generator, the Findhorn living machine handles the wastes from 300 people.

I think, given the speed with which we are approaching this energy-descent world, and the paucity of any serious consideration of planning or even awareness of it, we have to take as part of the equation that the adaptive strategies will not happen by some big, sensible, long-range-planning approach, but will happen just organically and incrementally by people just doing things in response to immediate conditions. So if you live in an apartment in a multistory building, and you've got to work out how to try and retrofit that in an energy-descent context, there's a lot of complex, technical infrastructure and organization involved. In the suburbs people can actually just start changing houses and doing things — give or take planning regulations — without the whole of society agreeing on some plan. The suburbs are amenable to this organic, incremental, adaptive strategy.

— David Holmgren, 2005

Create Energy

Get up when the light comes on, go to bed when you are tired.
— Adam Turtle, 2004

In most Western countries we have become so accustomed to having cheap energy that we take it for granted much of the time. We use it to heat and light our houses, store and cook our food, wash and dry our clothes and dishes, heat our baths, and provide our home entertainment.

Many Canadians who experienced the ice storm of 1997 will never take electricity for granted again. They were without power for several weeks during a northern winter, in some of the worst weather conditions imaginable. This experience was well-publicized but is not unique. Between 1991 and 2000, North Americans experienced more than 150 power outages greater than 100 megawatts, affecting on average 765,000 homes.

What would you do if electricity or heating fuel disappeared and stayed unavailable for days or weeks? In this chapter I'll suggest how you might keep warm and cook food and have lights without electricity. I'll also describe ways you can make your own low-tech electricity using renewable resources.

Maintaining Efficiency

The first thing to do is look around and see how well you are prepared for living through bad weather, natural disasters, or catastrophic events. Winterize your apartment, house, barn, shed, or any other structure that might provide shelter for your family, neighbors, livestock, or equipment. Install storm shutters, doors, and windows; clear rain gutters;

insulate and repair roof leaks. Check the structural ability of the roof to sustain unusually heavy weight from the accumulation of snow or water, especially if drains should be overwhelmed. Keep plywood, plastic sheeting, lumber, sandbags, and hand tools available and accessible.

If you go outside in inclement weather, dress for the season and for changing conditions. In cold weather, wear several layers of loose-fitting, lightweight, warm clothing rather than one layer of heavy clothing. Outer garments should be tightly woven and water-repellent. Wear a hat. Cover your mouth with a scarf to protect your lungs from extremely cold air. Wear sturdy, waterproof boots in snow or flooding conditions.

Hot-weather clothing should allow air to circulate near your skin so sweat can evaporate. It should also protect you from too much sun. A wide-brimmed hat and sunglasses are necessary even for children. Pay careful attention to the cooling needs of the very young, very old, and infirm when there is no air-conditioning.

Most people living in rural areas know these things and teach them to their children. Those accustomed to short bursts of exposure to the outdoors as they move from house to car, bus to school corridor, or subway to office foyer may not yet appreciate the advice, but times could change.

Solar Heating

It has often been said that our most reliable source of power is 93 million miles away and makes deliveries daily. Most of the world's energy — for growing food, building healthy bodies, and meeting our other basic needs — has always come from the sun.

To make solar power work for you, location is everything. You don't have to live at the equator; you just have to point yourself in that direction.

Heating with sunlight involves capturing the long waves as they arrive from space and either putting them to immediate work or storing them for later use. Probably the simplest capture and storage device for the home is the greenhouse. Stretching glass, Plexiglas, clear fiberglass panels, or clear polyvinyl plastic sheets over a frame of wood, bamboo, metal conduit, or plastic pipe and attaching the resulting structure to the side of your house that faces the equator will provide an enclosure that is warm during most days of the year. If you have straw bales, water drums, or any dark, solid mass (brick, stone, piled firewood) backing this space, the structure will store daytime heat and slowly release it back into the enclosure overnight.

Every house can function much as a greenhouse does, except that direct sunlight only enters through windows on three sides, walls shade

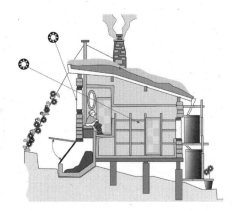

Passive solar heating entails orienting houses toward the equator and allowing the lower winter sun to enter through windows, while screening the higher summer sun with vegetation, overhangs, or window covers. This illustration, based on a demonstration house in Taiwan, also shows good drainage technique, solar-dehydrating compost toilet, the insulating value of a living roof, and rainwater catchment.

out most of the heating effect, and the windows give off heat to the sky at night. It is important to uncover all sun-side windows when the sun is on them, and to cover them again when it is not. The better insulation the cover provides, the more efficient the heat retention.

The sun only shines during the day, so if you want the space to stay warm at night, you have to design and build it to store heat and gradually give it back as needed. There are many ways to accomplish this, but most of them involve solid or liquid storage media, which is called "thermal mass." Thermal mass can be as simple as a jar of water put on a windowsill, or as complicated as a vegetable oil that flows from parabolic collectors into insulated storage containers after reaching a designated temperature. Some greenhouse managers stack available floor space with water-filled drums. Others pump hot air into gravel reservoirs during the day and allow it to slowly radiate back out at night. Some architects specify thick walls to catch the heat wherever sunlight shines. The ancient Anasazi used much the same technique in cliff and canyon villages, capturing direct solar energy in mud bricks of precisely the correct dimensions to insulate houses in the day and give the heat back to the interior in the evening.

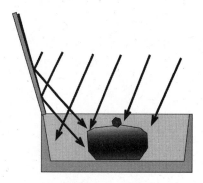

Solar box cooker.

The same principles apply to the basic solar box cooker, window box collector, flat plate and batch water heater, and most other solar-heating devices. They point themselves at the sun, gather light through translucent windows, trap the light when it enters (typically by having black or dark green coatings on walls or tanks), and then minimize heat losses with insulation.

Heating by Burning

Heating more often involves burning a fuel, particularly where solar exposure is poor or you are not able to adequately store daytime heat in your living space. There are wood heaters commercially available for $250 to $12,000. Some of these models can also switch to run on other fuels, like oil, gas, coal, sawdust, pellets, or kerosene.

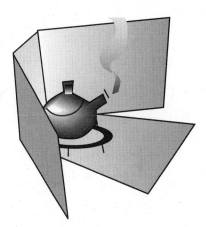

Parabolic box cooker.

If you live near a forested area from which you can obtain firewood, you might consider a woodburning stove. The newest, top-of-the-line wood heaters can be expensive, but they are efficient. Because they are airtight, burn combustion gases in a separate jacket, and have a catalytic converter on the exhaust port, they squeeze every available BTU from each piece of wood, which means it is less work to keep the fire fed. You can find less elaborate models, new or used, for a few hundred dollars, but expect to burn more wood and get up in the night to keep it going.

If You Burn Wood

1. Cure your wood for six months to a year after cutting. If you must burn wet wood, make the best of a bad situation by splitting the wood into small pieces, about three inches in diameter. Small pieces heat up and ignite faster, and burn cleaner. Try to let the wood warm up before burning it. Burn small, bright fires, using no more than five sticks at a time.

2 If you have a battery-operated smoke detector, see that it is working. If you don't have one, try to get one. Get a stovetop thermometer from a local hearth store and keep track of the temperature. Burn creosote out of the chimney every day when you first start the fire. Do this by creating a very hot fire (hotter than 500°F); listen as it roars through the pipe, then cut the draft and bring the temperature down. This will prevent creosote buildup, which can lead to a catastrophic chimney fire. Never leave a wood fire unattended.

3. In a weather emergency or if fuel is scarce, don't try to heat the whole house; concentrate all your activities in the room where the heater is located and let the rest go cold. Drain any pipes in unheated rooms to prevent freezing.

4. Shovel ashes into a metal container, take it outside when it cools, and empty it in the yard away from trees and shrubs. Never put a bucket full of ashes in the basement or on a wooden porch floor, and never put ashes in a wooden or cardboard box. Keep small children away from the stove or fireplace, and fence off the ash pile.

5. Makeshift woodstove installations done by untrained people can be very hazardous. Try to get professional help, even if it is just some advice over the phone. Keep the following points in mind.
   - You need a proper masonry or metal chimney.
   - Check to see that the inside of the chimney flue is clear and smooth.
   - Each joint in the flue pipes between a stove and its chimney must be secured with three sheet metal screws.
   - Don't vent a woodstove out a window using single-wall pipe.
   - Make sure there is plenty of space around the stove and flue pipe.

6. Be careful using decorative fireplaces. If your fireplace doesn't produce much heat, it is a decorative type and continuous use of it might be hazardous. If the unit has glass doors, it may be best to leave them open (with a safety screen) so you receive direct radiation from the fire. Close the damper until the fireplace starts to smoke, then open it until the smoking stops; this will reduce the amount of warm room air drawn up the chimney. Burn small, bright, controlled fires; never overload the unit.

Please burn safely. Don't put your family at risk.

With a good wood furnace and an adequate supply of wood, you can keep a whole house comfortably warm. With less wood available, you may want to go with a smaller woodstove and just heat one or two rooms.

A well-managed woodlot can provide a sustainable supply of wood for a single house year after year. Today we have fast-growing trees, such as hybrid poplar, that can be coppiced, rather than cut down, and which also re-root from cuttings. Selectively bred for their ability to restore damaged soils, these trees convert sunlight into a new form of wealth. You can order cuttings from www.thegreatchange.com.

If you plan to cut your own firewood, be sure you have a large saw or chainsaw and oil for the chain. Laying up a supply of wood is a year-round activity, but the felling is best done when the leaves are off the trees. Properly seasoned firewood yields far more heating value for the labor invested, so a shed, rack, or well-designed drying area is a must. Drying out the sap in firewood also means there will be less creosote buildup in flues, which reduces the risk of chimney fires and protects metal stovepipes from corrosion.

Kerosene Heaters

Kerosene area-heaters are found in most hardware stores. The advantages of kerosene are that it may be easier to buy than other petroleum-based fuels, it is easy to store, and it's easy to pour. It can also be used for lamps, camp stoves, and even some internal combustion engines. The disadvantages are that kerosene is dangerously flammable, and some of us find its odor disagreeable. Mineral Spirits — purified kerosene sold as paint thinner — will work in all kerosene appliances and burn hotter with less odor.

It may not be wise to heat a whole house if fuel is limited. Room heaters, whether wood, kerosene, or gas, may be a better choice than a furnace. But even heating one small room for 15 hours a day will exhaust a five-gallon reusable gas bottle in only five days. In these conditions, preparedness may mean having lots of warm clothes and blankets.

Cooking
Cooking with Wood

Wood cookstoves, which were common 50 years ago, are harder to find now. New, airtight models that use coal, oil, or gas, hold a hot-water reservoir, and have many other wonderful features can cost over $4,000, but you can find more modest models, and good used cookstoves, for less than $1,000. One thing to remember about wood cookstoves is that while they

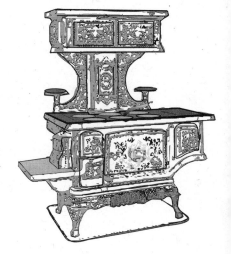

help heat the kitchen in the winter, all that heat is unwanted in the summer months, so you should also consider alternative cooking methods (and summer kitchens).

> Initially governments will try to control
> and limit the effects of depletion. Public money and the medical authorities will be used to help those in need, delivering emergency food supplies and offering vouchers for heat and power for those unable to provide for themselves. Communal food stations and cheap public transport may be made available. Security will be maintained by the state, bringing in new legislation and martial law as need be. Electricity shortages will be managed, with rolling blackouts preventing people suffering for too long and allowing the emergency services to prepare for hardships and looting. Food and fuel queues will be policed so the disaffected public will tend to remain under control. Eventually, and gradually, governments will begin to lose control as we merge into Anarchic Transition. When the blackouts grow too long for comfort and become unpredictable, people will be forced to take things into their own hands. As the state's finances deteriorate, it will be harder to supply those in need with both food and money, and the emergency services will have more to do with less. The poor and hungry will find the power cuts ideal opportunity for finding food from others. The food and fuel queues will turn nasty and constantly occupy the police and army. Protests about the problems and government mishandling will escalate into riots.
> — Paul Thompson, 2004

Cooking with a Fireplace

A working fireplace can give you one warm room for cooking, eating, and even sleeping (bring in mattresses, or sleeping bags if the carpet is comfy), although fireplaces are less efficient for home heating than well-designed heating stoves. Poorly designed fireplaces can send valuable heat out of a house, even when they are not in operation.

The best pots and pans for fireplace cookery are made of black cast iron. You can cook a variety of recipes with a black cast-iron skillet and a Dutch oven that holds several quarts. Try to get a cast-iron lid that will fit both pans. Some lids can hold hot coals. Cooking pans made of Pyrex also work well in fireplaces. Have potholders or mitts handy.

Pots and pans need more watching when you are cooking in a fireplace than they would if you had put them in an oven as they are inclined to tip over and spill as logs burn down and break up. A useful accessory is a folding camp grill that will sit over the logs and coals and

Tamera Solar Village

Jürgen Kleinwächter has designed a modular Solar Village for widespread use in Africa. It is being tested in the Tamera ecovillage in Portugal (tamera.org). A transparent plastic tube carries vegetable oil through reflective solar concentrators and heats it to nearly twice the boiling point of water, then stores it in an insulated tank. As needed, rain or shine, the hot oil is piped to stoves, ovens, water heaters, and even to a greenhouse for growing food in winter and a Stirling engine to make electricity. The prototype system can work a full three days on one sunny day, but a larger storage tank could extend this for a much longer period.

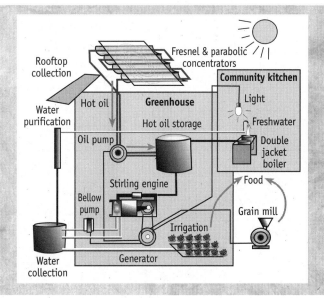

provide a level cooking area. In the Campmor catalog (www.campmor.com, 800-226-7667) these cost from $8 to $14.

If your fireplace is also your source of heat, and your house plan is fairly open, you may want to increase the number of thick tapestries on the walls around the living/cooking area to keep that space toasty warm during winter months. Installing battens and insulated shutters is another easy way to reduce heat loss through windows.

Outdoor Grills

Many people have a backyard barbecue pit or portable outdoor grill. Typically, these are fueled by charcoal or gas, but in a pinch they could be converted to burn firewood. If you have a grill, make sure you have plenty of fuel stored. A large grill can meet the cooking needs of several families. My favorite outdoor stove is the Rocky Mountain Volcano stove (www.rmvolcano.com). It is so efficient that 12 to 20 charcoal briquettes are all you need to feed a large family a full meal of rice, beans, and cornbread. Briquettes are unnecessary — small pieces of wood or biomass pellets work equally well.

In really difficult conditions, you can make a portable outdoor grill by lining a metal wheelbarrow with aluminum foil and filling it with charcoal. Use the shelf from a gas or electric oven as a cooking rack.

Volcano stove.

Camp Stove

An assortment of stoves are available from camping equipment catalogs. For example, a small folding camp stove that uses solid alcohol fuel like Sterno is available for about $8. A more versatile two-burner propane camp stove costs about $50. A small bottle of gas will last 4.5 hours at low heat on one of these camp stoves. At high heat, you will run out of fuel in one hour.

If you want to do some baking, you can get a camp oven that sits on top of a stove and costs about $40. A four-slice, folding, camp toaster, which can be placed over a burner, is available for about $3.

Most camping supply stores have a wide variety of devices you can cook with — using heating sources from solar to Sterno.

Aprovecho Rocket Stove

Over many years, the Approvecho Institute in Oregon refined a series of small, homemade, wood cookstoves that maximize fuel efficiency and are easy and inexpensive to construct. The end result is the Rocket Stove, which can be made from steel cans and insulation. Detailed plans are available at www.efn.com/~apro/AT/atrocketpage.html or www.solar-cooking.org.

Chafing Dish

As the 19th century turned into the 20th century, the chafing dish was the *fin de siècle* epitome of elegant entertaining. Delectable preparations from the chafing dish highlighted intimate candlelit suppers as both gentlemen and ladies prepared fondues, rich buttery sauces, or blazing brandy-lit desserts right in the drawing room.

The chafing dish is heated by small cans of solid ethyl alcohol or similar fuel. To prevent foods from scorching, it's best to use two pans: the bottom pan holds hot water, while the top pan contains the recipe ingredients. Tabletop cooking could not be easier, and one little can of fuel will burn for 45 minutes.

After the dish is served, you can use the hot water in the bottom pan to make tea, instant coffee, or cocoa. Most one-dish meals lend themselves to chafing-dish cookery.

Make a Cob Oven

A basic earthen oven is a simple thing. You build a big mound of cob, scoop out a firebox, and make a door. The door can be a simple piece of wood the same size as the hole, or it can be fashioned from more mud.

Chafing dish.

Cob is a popular poor-man's building material from the British Isles, consisting of approximately equal parts of clay, sand, and gravel, that is wetted and mixed with straw, then pounded or trod until it is stiff.

The oven should be on a fireproof footing, such as stone or brick. My Brazilian friend Marcelo built one on a straw-bale foundation, thinking that the earthen floor would somehow keep the bales from catching fire. He was overly optimistic, and it took him several days to extinguish the slow, smoldering fire.

A chimney is optional. It is enough to build the fire in the chamber. When it gets to 400°F inside, and too hot to touch outside, rake out the fire and put in the bread dough or pizza.

Fire Safety

- If you use candles, place them in a safe place away from any flammable material.
- Be sure all children know the dangers of candles, chafing dishes, potpourri scent pots, the fireplace, and space heaters.
- Never leave children alone near an open flame or with matches.
- Keep clutter away from the stove while cooking. Keep pot handles turned away from you.
- If grease catches fire, cover the pan with a lid. Be careful. Moving the pan can cause the fire to spread. Never pour water on a grease fire or try to beat it out with a towel. Baking soda and salt are effective extinguishers because they exclude air.
- Always keep an A-B-C fire extinguisher close to hand.
- Do not store combustible materials in closed areas or near a heat source.
- Don't leave cooking food unattended for extended periods of time. This is the most common cause of cooking-related fires.
- Only burn wood in the fireplace, and only burn small amounts of paper at a time to avoid a chimney fire.
- Have your chimney cleaned and flue checked before using them.
- Buy a battery-operated smoke detector and carbon monoxide detector. If you already have detectors, clean and test them. A working smoke detector can double your chances of survival.
- Practice home fire drills. Designate two exits from every room, make sure all family members are aware of an outside meeting place, and get out quickly.
- Fire spreads faster than you can possibly imagine — in a matter of seconds. Evacuate immediately. Contact the local fire department *after* you have left the building.
- *Never* go back into a burning building to retrieve belongings or pets.

SOUPS

BORSCHT

Serves 6 to 8

1 Tbsp oil
1 yellow onion, minced
6 beets, peeled and minced, or one 15-ounce can of diced beets, drained
¼ head cabbage, shredded
1 cup carrot, grated
2 potatoes, peeled and diced
1 tsp sugar or equivalent sweetener (stevia, honey, molasses, sorghum, adjusted by sweetness)
1 tsp salt or to taste
3 cups vegetable broth
2 Tbsp lemon juice
¾ tsp ground black pepper or to taste

Garnish

1 cup plain nonfat yogurt
1 Tbsp prepared horseradish
¼ cup chives or parsley, minced

Mix horseradish and yogurt and set aside. Heat a Dutch oven or soup kettle. Add oil; fry onion 3 minutes. Add beets, cabbage, carrot, potato, sweetener, salt, and broth. Cover and simmer until tender. Add lemon juice and pepper and taste for seasonings. Puree and pour into bowls. Add a dollop of horseradish yogurt on each bowl and sprinkle with chives or parsley.

Difficulty

There is a good reason that traditional cob dwellings in Britain have brick ovens, not cob ones. Under the strain of many firings, cob ovens crack and have to be rebuilt. This is a lot of work, so you may find it easier just to use bricks.

Heating Water

Many people are so accustomed to cheap energy that they don't give any thought to having uninsulated 100- or 150-gallon hot-water tanks in their bathrooms or basements keeping all that water at more than 100°F all day, every day, and even for days or weeks when they are away from home. If the house gets too hot from all that hot water, they turn up the air-conditioning. It is not uncommon for these monstrous batch heaters to run on electricity, which is not a terribly efficient way to heat water. This kind of blissful ignorance was recently displayed by US senator Charles Grassley of Iowa in a radio interview:

> You know, what — what makes our economy grow is energy. And, and [US] Americans are used to going to the gas tank [sic], and when they put that hose in their, uh, tank, and when I do it, I wanna get gas out of it. And when I turn the light switch on, I want the lights to go on, and I don't want somebody to tell me I gotta change my way of living to satisfy them. Because this is [the United States of] America, and this is something we've worked our way into, and the [US] American people are entitled to it, and if we're going improve [sic] our standard of living, you have to consume more energy.

Flash Heaters

Electricity is usually the most expensive way to heat water. However, where neither gas nor wood heating sources are available or practical, an electric flash-style heater is better than a tank-style water heater. The tank-style forces you to waste energy keeping many gallons hot at all times unless you turn it off. Even if you turn it off, you have to heat all those gallons before you can get one gallon of hot water.

There are several types of small electric flash heaters that fit under the sink or beside a showerhead and are far more efficient at supplying what you really want, which is hot water on demand.

If you have gas available for heating water, there are gas flash-style water heaters that have been popular in Europe and the Far East for many years. They can save you up to 50 percent of the energy costs associated with tank-type heaters. There are two things you must remember about flash heaters, however. One is that many use a pilot light, which is a constant draw on your gas supply. The second is that they must be installed in a location where they will not freeze. If the heat exchanger freezes, it will split and leak, rendering the flash heater useless.

Solar Water Heating

Solar water heating is the most economical and practical method for obtaining hot water, regardless of your location. City dwellers should be working with their landlords, housing cooperative boards, and municipal authorities to install solar collectors on rooftops and in place of awnings on any buildings that have sky-views toward the equator. For emergencies, it's a good idea to have one portable solar-shower bag for each family member. They can also be used for dishwashing.

Solar showers or handwashing kiosks range from the simple black-plastic-bag variety costing around $20 that is found in sporting goods stores, West Marine, or Campmor, to the more permanent stall design that can be constructed for about $500, with plans from our website, www.thegreatchange.com.

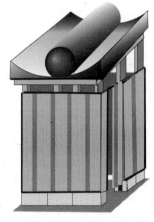

Solar Showers.

Wood Water Heaters

Wood-fired water heaters are commercially available for $250 to $750. Some of these models can also switch to run on either pellets or kerosene. Alternative Energy Engineering, in Redway, California, has a good catalog containing these and other items (www.alt-energy.com, 800-777-6609).

Lighting

Have some or all of the following on hand:

- Kerosene lamps, fuel, and wicks: hurricane-style lamps are the most foolproof. Avoid the kind with thorium mantles (Coleman, Aladdin). They give off brighter light but produce radioactive soot.
- Flashlights and extra batteries: Consider especially the hand-cranked LED flashlights available on the Great Change website. Solar-recharged flashlights are notoriously unreliable, but a solar battery recharger is a good investment. Always buy rechargeable batteries. Greenbatteries.com is an excellent source.

HOT SOUR CABBAGE SOUP

Serves 6

1 Tbsp oil
½ head cabbage, shredded
1 medium onion, chopped
1 large apple, peeled and chopped
5 cups vegetable broth
1 Tbsp shoyu
1 Tbsp lemon juice
1 Tbsp honey
¼ tsp crushed red pepper flakes
¼ tsp allspice

Heat a big pan. Add oil, cabbage, and onion and cook 5 minutes. Add remaining ingredients, cover pan, and cook about 40 minutes until vegetables are tender. Chopped dried mushrooms are a good addition.

Difficulty

- Candles and candleholders: Go for the long-life candles and glass-enclosed candle lanterns.
- Spare 12-volt auto bulbs, wire, and aluminum foil or tin reflectors: You can rig home lighting to run from a car battery and use the car to recharge it. LED bulbs are the best because they deliver the most light for the power and last forever. Now's a good time to start replacing all your incandescent lights with LEDs.

Home Power

Self-reliance is far and away the best solution to the energy problem, but one question confronts anyone planning to make their own power: What technology is the best? The answer is always the same. It depends.

It depends on what natural forms of energy are in greatest abundance at your particular location. It depends on how technically adept you are and whether you have ready access to a "knowledge guild" of skilled people who can assist you and help you learn. It depends on the price of equipment, which changes as technology advances. A few years ago, small wind machines were more expensive than solar cells, but now they are cheaper. New advances in thin-film photovoltaics (PV) promise to give solar cells the cost edge once more.

Generally the cost advantage for home power favors water ("micro-hydro"), then wind, then solar-PV, then biomass and other thermal systems, in that order. If you have enough local waterpower, you can be generating electricity around the clock. The same is true for wind, although it is highly variable in most places.

Wind Turbines

Legal, scenic, and noise issues; terrain features; and variations in local weather all affect whether a particular site will be a good place to set up a wind turbine. While a local airport can give you historical weather data that indicates average wind speed over the course of a year, your site might be subject to wind currents that are considerably different from those at the airport. Valleys that gather heat in the morning and send it up hillsides in the afternoon or channel it into canyons; notches in ridgelines; trees that redirect or scatter wind; and the effects of built structures — all are factors that will not be estimated by airports or the local weather service.

As the operators of many North American wind farms learned to their dismay in the 1990s, the flyways of migratory bird populations must be considered. Some of the largest wind farms in the world now shut down during migration seasons to avoid the unpleasant spectacle of seeing turbine blades act like giant Cuisinarts.

Typically, small turbines in the one-kilowatt range begin making power when the wind reaches 5 to 8 miles per hour and reach their full capacities at 15 to 25 miles per hour. At wind speeds above 80 to 100 miles per hour, they "feather out" — turn away from the wind — so that they are not damaged by turbulence. Visit www.kissenergy.com/PracticalSailor.html to consult a chart comparing the output of many types of turbines at different wind speeds.

There are professional firms that, for a price, will survey wind potential and give you advice on selecting a site, but for less than the cost of that report you can buy an inexpensive turbine and tower and obtain your own data.

Small wind machines come in all sizes and shapes and can cost as little as $1,000 per kilowatt of installed capacity. One of the newer models is the Magnetically-Levitated Axial Flux Alternator Vertical Axis Wind Turbine. It can produce 1,100 kilowatt hours per month where the wind averages 13 miles per hour. It takes up five square feet of roof and is very safe and quiet. If your current electric bill is more than $300 per month, you can recover the cost of putting a Mag-Wind on your roof in three years or less.

Magnetically-levitated axial flux alternator vertical axis wind turbine.

Estimating Hydro Potential

Horsepower (hp) = water current (cubic feet per second) x head (height of drop, in feet) ÷ 8.8.

To obtain one kilowatt (1.3 hp) of power from a ten-foot head, you would need to capture 1.14 cubic feet (8.56 gallons) of water per second. If you had a higher head, such as 100 feet, you would need only 0.11 cubic feet (0.86 gallons) per second to obtain one kilowatt.

You can measure the potential of any nearby stream or waterfall by estimating its width, depth, current speed (toss in a piece of wood and time its passage), and head (measure the drop over distance using a sighting device or topographical map). It is usually not practical — or ecological — to dam small streams when adequate flow can be diverted to a (screened) pipe and then run through a micro-hydro turbine to produce electricity. A long pipe running downhill can provide ample head for most micro-hydro generators.

A one-kilowatt turbine might cost $2,000 installed, but remember that it is able to run 24 hours per day, so it will generate 24 kilowatt-hours every day. The same capacity in solar PV, if exposed to strong sunlight for eight hours, would only generate eight kilowatt-hours.

SOUPS

LENTIL STEW

Serves 4 to 6

1 Tbsp oil
1 onion, chopped small
1 carrot, chopped small
1 stalk celery, optional
1 tsp salt
1 cup dried lentils, rinsed
4 cups water
1 tsp dried tarragon or thyme

Heat Dutch oven. Add oil and onion; cook a few minutes. Add carrot, celery, and salt; cook a few minutes. Add lentils and water; cover and cook about 30 minutes, stirring in the tarragon or thyme. Taste and add a little salt and pepper if desired.

Another great way to improve the experience of soups (as well as pasta, salads, and main dishes) is with a side dish of bread. I like a nice artisanal bread or pita, still warm from the oven, and a small table dish of olive oil, sprinkled with Italian seasoning or zataar, a Middle Eastern blend of sesame seeds, ground sumac, salt, and Syrian hyssop. Here are three variations:

Roasted Black Pepper Olive Oil

¼ cup olive, peanut, or other local cold-pressed oil, with 1 tsp ground black pepper (best if the peppercorns are roasted in a frying pain until lightly brown first).

Hot Pepper Oil

¼ cup olive oil with ½ tsp cayenne or other ground hot chili pepper.

Photovoltaics

Sun power is only available when the sun is shining, which means you will need batteries or some other storage media if you want electricity after dark or on cloudy days. Biomass and other thermal electric systems that might use Stirling or Rankin engines, parabolic dishes, and similar technology also depend on availability of local resources.

While there are differences between the devices you'll use for each of these types of power, some general rules apply. Let's look at a typical photovoltaic system, the kind of power plant that anyone who lives where there is some sunlight at least part of the day might use.

The size of a solar-electric system depends on the amount of power that is required (kilowatts), the length of time it will be used (hours), and the amount of energy available from the sun (hours per day). You have control of the first two; your location controls the third.

Using special crystals, solar-electric cells produce electricity by converting incoming photon energy into an electrical current that moves through a wire. The cost of a solar system is not entirely in the cells, but also in the mounting racks, batteries, inverters, and backup charging devices. Since batteries and chargers are an expensive part of the system, you can sometimes save money by skipping the batteries and wiring to a network. Increasingly, public utilities are encouraging customers to add solar cells to their homes and let the power flow directly into the national grid, essentially running the meter backward. This is a good deal for utilities because it means they can build and operate fewer large power stations. For customers, it means paying off the solar installation in as little as two years and having nearly free electricity after that.

Many people want to learn more about designing and maintaining a solar power system before they make the investment, and I recommend taking a good introductory workshop. Solar Energy International (www.solarenergy.org) and Our Sun Solar (970-948-5304) provide excellent workshops.

Some users will prefer not to be connected to a national grid and the associated risks of brownouts and blackouts. For those people, a standalone system is the way to go. The first thing you need to decide is whether you want to go with a standard high-voltage alternating current (AC) or a low-voltage direct current (DC). In a small home, boat, or RV, low-voltage DC lighting makes sense and keeps system costs down because you don't need an inverter. If you need other appliances, want to have more power, or decide to connect to the national grid, an AC system is the correct choice. That means you may have to buy an inverter to convert battery power into normal house current.

Washing machines, large shop machinery, power tools, and pumps require a large inverter, typically 3,000 watts. A standard washing machine uses between 300 and 500 watt-hours per load. Vacuum cleaners use 600 to 1,000 watts. Electric space heaters use 1,000 to 2,000 watts. Many small appliances like irons, toasters, and hair dryers use even larger amounts, but because they require it for short and infrequent periods of use, they can be managed. Stereos, televisions, VCRs, and computers draw relatively small loads and are also available in 12-volt DC models that don't need an inverter.

Electric cooking (especially baking and microwaving), space heating, and water heating use a prohibitive amount of electricity for all but the most lavish solar-electric systems. Going solar for lighting, radio, and television; refrigeration; and some small appliances makes more sense. If possible, use another means, such as biofuels and passive solar-heating devices, to supply energy for your cooking and heating.

If you are considering going to a solar-electric system, you should also look into other renewable sources of energy like wind power and hydro. It is possible that, depending on your location, you may have a cheaper alternative to solar photovoltaic cells.

A typical Australian or North American home consumes 10,000 to 20,000 kilowatt-hours per year for all purposes, and a European or South African home about a third less than that. You can look at your electric bill to see what your home uses. Most parts of North America and Europe receive from four to six sun-hours per day on average for the year. Armed with a few simple facts, you can calculate what it would cost you to go solar.

Let's say you can get by with 1,200 watt-hours per day (for lights, refrigerator, fans, TV, radio) and you live in an area with four sun-hours per day.

Multiply the number of sun-hours by the rating on your photovoltaic module (we'll use 150 watts in this example) to see how many watts per day (W/d) each solar panel produces.

$$4 \times 150 = 600 \text{ W/d}$$

Divide that number into your electric load to see how many panels you will need.

$$1,200/600 = 2 \text{ panels}$$

Multiply each panel's price by the number of panels.

$$2 \times \$1,000 = \$2,000 \text{ total cost of panels}$$

Multiply the daily load by number of cloudy days to have in battery storage.

$$1,200 \times 7 = 8,400 \text{ watt-hours}$$

Divide this by 12 to get amp-hours (ah). Add 20 percent to prevent deep discharge (discharging below 50 percent of the batteries' capacity), which would damage the batteries and shorten their lives.

$$8,400/12 = 700 + 20\% = 784 \text{ ah}$$

Industrial chloride batteries start at about $1,350 for 525 ah. Deep-cycle lead-acid batteries (L16s) cost $225 for 370 ah. We'll need two of the chlorides or four of the L16s (because they are six-volt and need to be wired in series), so let's estimate $1,000 for batteries.

The Non-Renewables in Renewables

Oil and gas are not the only resources that are becoming scarcer. Raw materials like copper and rare earths are also being mined out, and even where they are still plentiful, it takes a lot of fossil energy to bring them to market. Steel, cement, and aluminum are the end products of enormous energy inputs.

Because large wind turbines require a lot of steel, many are now being installed on concrete masts, but the day may come when wooden masts are again standard. In solar thermal absorbers, scarce and expensive copper is giving way to laser-welded aluminum, but coated ceramics may some day replace them both.

We don't think of silicon as a scarce material since it makes up a large fraction of the Earth's crust, but we've recently seen that the highly refined silicon used to make photovoltaic cells can be in short supply, and that can affect prices. Between 2003 and 2004, demand for PV silicon went up 120 percent as parts of Europe and North America suddenly doubled and tripled the amount of photovoltaic electricity being installed. The chemicals industry had warned that it couldn't keep up with higher demand for both computer-grade silicon and solar-grade silicon, and when the crunch came, deliveries slowed and prices doubled. In 2005 the manufacturers streamlined their processes, making wafers thinner and more efficient, and improved the design of the production lines. This stabilized costs, but supply remained tight. The bottleneck may have consequences that will accelerate over the coming years as demand for solar-grade silicon jumps from 5,000 tons to 50,000 tons (or more) per year by 2010.

System cost: $2,000 (panels) + $500 (mounting brackets) + $2,000 (inverter & controls) + $1,000 (batteries for one week storage, 25-year life) + $1,000 (installation) = $6,500

Unless you have very deep pockets, it should be evident from this quick exercise that with solar-electric systems, a little conservation goes a long way. Using energy-efficient appliances and non-electric alternatives whenever possible can bring your expenses down dramatically.

If you want to learn more about electric-generating options, I recommend *Home Power* magazine. A complete archive of past articles is free for downloading or available on CD-ROM at a very reasonable price from www.homepower.com.

For the past 30 years we have been expecting photovoltaic systems to become cheaper as they become more common and as technology improves. The price has come down a bit, but not nearly as much as had been predicted. Anyone who is still waiting for solar cells or batteries to get a little cheaper before buying them should stop waiting and make the purchase now. For at least the next ten years, demand will not drive prices lower, and costs may well rise instead. Design, install, and use your solar-electric system now. Get to know how it works, how to optimize it, and how to repair it when something goes wrong. Even if you have wind and hydro at your location, adding a little solar PV power into your energy mix is a good investment.

Yes, solar electricity is expensive. You may find it is worth every cent you spend.

> *I'd put my money on the sun and solar energy.*
> *What a source of power! I hope we don't have to wait until oil*
> *and coal run out before we tackle that.*
>
> — Thomas Edison, 1910

Biomass

The word "biomass" describes any organic, non-fossil material, typically living or dead biological tissues. Cellulose fibers used for biodegradable plastics and paper, timber-frame houses, and Antarctic krill are all biomass. The entire Earth contains about 75 billion tons of biomass, including the 0.33 percent that is presently in human form.

As we move from a hydrocarbon-based economy (fossil fuels) to a carbohydrate-based economy (solar energy), we will be exploring many new ways to use biomass to provide our energy. One such use is "biofuels," such as ethanol, methane, and biodiesel made from biomass.

Sweden accelerated its biofuel conversion by introducing a Renewable Energy Certificate System in 2003. Every certified power generator, large or small, selling wind, solar, hydro, or biomass heat or electricity now gets a subsidy payment of 20 to 30 euros per million watt-hours sold. This may not seem like very much — about $100 per year for a home-sized small producer — but it works out to substantial incentive for a power company producing thousands of megawatts. It was enough to push one-quarter of Sweden's electricity into bioenergy sources — the equivalent of three nuclear power plants — since 2003.

Lovelock's Folly

I find it hard to believe that large-scale solar energy plants in desert regions, where the intensity and constancy of sunlight could be relied on, would compare in cost and reliability with fission or fusion energy, especially when the cost of transmitting the energy was taken into account .... The nuclear waste buried in pits at the production sites is no great threat to Gaia and dangerous only to those foolish enough to expose themselves to its radiation.
— James Lovelock, 2006

In the natural environment, our species has always been enveloped in radiation: from our sun and moon; from distant stars and cosmic winds; and from elements distributed in the soil, rocks, and oceans of the Earth. All human populations pass through life exposed to some part of this radioactive environment. It is now estimated that up to half of all new cancers are caused by this "background" radiation, which had previously been thought harmless or even beneficial. The small dose that we receive from natural background radiation, typically in combination with free radicals of oxygen, is a significant factor in the normal aging process — the process that takes place in the bodies of living organisms by which abnormal cells gradually replace normal cells until a vital function is sufficiently impaired to result in death.

Before life could begin upon the Earth, it took millions of years for our planet to quench the radiation at its surface and to erect atmospheric barriers to radioactive bombardment from space. Yet background

Also since 2003, the share of Finland's energy mix provided by bioenergy has passed petroleum's. As well as having giant power stations providing electricity, heat, and steam, Finland has become a leader in small home generators using woodchips and pellets. Some are sold in Sweden, where the city of Kristianstad is calling itself the "Bioenergy City." Kristianstad provides free energy consultations, a biogas carpool for city employees, biogas public buses, free parking for biofueled cars, and a district heat and power station that replaced oil and gas for 75,000 residents. Solid organic material from domestic waste is mixed

radiation has continued to play a vital role in our billion-year process of evolution. By continual death and replacement, and by continual minor mutations over many eons, the human species, as well as all other life forms, have developed into what they are today.

Very early in this evolutionary process, primary emphasis was placed on the protection of our genetic code through the development of extremely efficient and sophisticated chemical repair mechanisms. Only in this way could the advances of evolution be protected against the deteriorating effect of oxygen and natural radiation, and the stability of the human species over periods of millions of years be assured. For evolution to proceed, however, it was also necessary that a balance be struck between the ability of the human organism to repair itself and the need for continual death and replacement to evolve the species. This fine balance between the evolving human organism and the relatively constant natural background level of radiation was achieved over the course of millions of years, and it is an extremely delicate one.

When a marauding high-energy particle rips a nucleoprotein out of a DNA sequence, the entire code is thrown askew unless and until fortuitous breaks occur elsewhere that restore the correct sequence. Radioactive bombardment endows biological molecules with such unstable properties that they can produce all kinds of energetic chemical reactions that would never have been possible before the exposure, multiplying the genetic damage in many invisible and enduring ways.

When a mutated gene is responsible for regulating normal cell growth, an uncontrolled proliferation of damaged cells, or cancer, can develop. When mutation occurs in the procreative cells or in the developing embryo, birth defects can result. When mutation occurs in the blood-forming tissue, the immune response system can be impaired, which may increase susceptibility to an entire spectrum of human disease and lower resistance to environmental toxins.

Early studies of genetic mutation demonstrated that only 1 percent of the latent damage of exposure to radiation may appear in each generation. We will have to wait through 100 generations of human population to see the full genetic effects of the late 20th century's nuclear dalliance, including Hiroshima, Nagasaki, the atmospheric tests, Chelyabinsk, Windscale, Three Mile Island, Chernobyl, and whatever comes next.

SOUPS

MEDITERRANEAN VEGETABLE STEW

Serves 6

2 Tbsp oil
1 large onion, chopped
4 cloves garlic, sliced thinly
2 cups cabbage, shredded
1 tsp salt
2 carrots, thinly sliced
2 potatoes, diced
2½ cup fresh or 30-ounce can of tomatoes, chopped
2 tsp orange rind, finely minced
2 tsp fennel seed, ground
1 quart stock
1 cup cooked red kidney beans or chickpeas

Heat a Dutch oven or big pan. Add oil and onion; cook a few minutes. Add garlic, cabbage, and salt; cook 5 minutes more, stirring. Add remaining ingredients except for the beans. Cover pan and let simmer until potatoes are tender. Stir in the beans. Heat.

Difficulty

with liquid manure from surrounding Swedish farms to make fertilizer and electricity.

While these measures are all signs of government foresight, they can also be replicated on a small scale (at the household, neighborhood, and village level) wherever governments are still behind the learning curve or simply too timid to act. Individuals can install pellet stoves and Finnish generators to make use of local energy sources. Neighbors can create energy consultation and installation guilds and biofuel co-ops, collecting organic wastes and farm products to make fuels for heating, lighting, and transportation in the neighborhood or region.

The women of Chapaldi in Andhra Pradesh, India, make fuel from pongamia seeds and use it to provide electricity for their village. Every family has to pay for the electricity, but not in rupees. They pay in pongamia seeds. They have to grow about 15 pounds per family per week to run their lights, radios, and refrigerators — and they need a little extra if they run an irrigation pump.

In 2003, the cooperative went a step farther. It sold 900 tons of petroleum-equivalent emissions reductions to Germany for $4,164 as part of the Kyoto CO_2 trading system. The payment from Germany was equal to a year's income for the entire village. By 2006, biofuel electrification on the Chapaldi model had spread to 100 other villages in India.

Even at today's prices, a dime buys enough electricity to lift a pickup truck 500 feet in the air. A gallon of gasoline contains as much energy as that expended riding a bicycle across the United States or hiking 300 miles across Arizona. Because energy was affordable and abundant, we learned to consume enormous quantities. In recent decades our "burn rate" has been the equivalent of 100 pounds of coal per person-day. [US] Americans now consume their body weight in petroleum products each week. Energy may be a sliver of gross domestic product — but try running the rest of the economy without it. Energy, not money, is the original currency, the source of all wealth.

— Matthew R. Simmons and Stewart Udall, 2005

Grow Your Food

*Our recent focus upon productivity, genetic
and technological uniformity, and global trade — all
supported by supposedly limitless supplies of fuel, water and soil —
has obscured the necessity for local adaptation. But our circumstances are
changing rapidly now, and this requirement will be forced upon us again by
terrorism and other kinds of political violence, by chemical pollution, by increasing energy costs, by depleted soils, aquifers, and streams, and by the spread
of exotic weeds, pests and diseases. We are going to have to resume the
breeding of plants and animals to fit the region and the farm.*

— Wendell Berry, 2005

*The pleasures of gardening are
many — getting outdoors, exercising, putting
your hands in the soil, growing things, and the special
pride of accomplishment that comes with the harvest. Many
gardeners want to experience the feeling of being self-sufficient or at
least partly so, and to have some control over what they eat, particularly
to have fresh, wholesome food without any additives or preservatives. All of
these are good reasons for gardening.*

— Mel Bartholomew, 1981

Consider the oil we eat. In 1945 the average farm produced 2,500 calories of food for every calorie of energy employed by the farm. By 1975 that ratio had become 1:1. Today, thanks to fertilizers, pesticides, herbicides, farm machinery, refrigeration, and trucking, we use 2,000 calo-

SOUPS

SWEET POTATO SOUP

If cooking fuel is dear, or if you are trying to keep your home cool without air conditioning, consider baking many things at one time, as cooks in many countries have done for centuries.

Serves 12

2½ pounds medium orange-fleshed sweet potatoes or sliced yams, skinned and cut into 1- to 2-inch chunks
1 large white onion, coarsely chopped
1¼ tsp sea salt
3 Tbsp nutritional yeast
¼ cup olive or other local cold-pressed oil
4 stalks celery, finely sliced
Dash of caraway seed
2 Tbsp fresh lemon juice
½ tsp dry mustard
½ tsp freshly ground black pepper, and more to taste
¼ cup chopped fresh mint, cilantro, and/or parsley

Preheat oven to 400°F. Toss the potatoes, onions, salt, and nutritional yeast with oil in a large bowl and spread on a rimmed cookie sheet. Top with any leftover oil. Bake, turning occasionally, until the chunks are tender when pierced with the tip of a knife, about 20 to 30 minutes. Transfer the potatoes and onions to a large pot; add celery and caraway and bring to a boil over high heat.

ries of energy to produce each calorie of the food consumed by 6 or 7 billion people. In the past 25 years, the number of family farms in the United States has dropped precipitously, by more than 300,000, replaced by well-oiled agribusinesses. In an era of energy scarcity, these businesses will pass fuel cost increases on to consumers in the form of higher grocery prices.

Today many of us are accustomed to eating food grown out of the local season and out of the local region. We go to a grocery store or a restaurant and seldom think twice about consuming fruit from Mexico, Indonesia, or Spain; lettuce grown in California or Argentina; cheese from Denmark or Greece; or a host of other foods that have traveled halfway around the world to reach our plate. The diversity and styles of modern cuisines, most available in virtually any city of more than 100,000 people, have all been made possible by the Age of Oil.

When oil becomes more expensive and in short supply, who gets to use it will be determined by social needs (in countries where social needs matter to those holding the reins of power) or by money (in countries where they don't). In either scenario, the biggest price increases are likely to hit the transportation sector. That will affect the price of food. The farther food travels, the more it will cost.

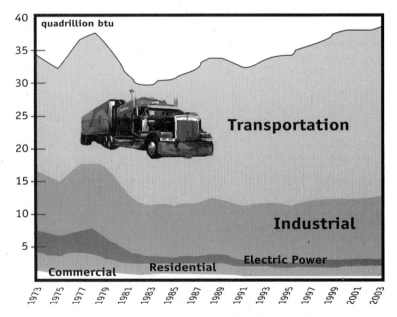

United States petroleum consumption by sector, 1973–2003 (after SAIC/MISI, 2005).

Urban Agriculture

Some smart farmers have been anticipating this change and have demonstrated how practical it is to grow food inside or close to cities where it is consumed. Michael Ableman farms 12 acres of land in suburban Goleta, California. In a neighborhood where the average income is $65,000 per year, his farm produces 100 different organic fruits and vegetables. The land was saved from real estate developers by a conservation easement, and Michael has been farming it for the past 25 years. A couple of years ago he loaded his tractors and rototiller on a truck and went to Los Angeles, where, with the help of local community volunteers, he removed ten tons of asphalt, old wiring, trash, rubble, and tires from three acres of urban blight on the corner of 103rd and Grape. A few months later, Michael and his Los Angeleno friends were harvesting tomatoes, melons, and squash. Says Wendell Berry, in *Fatal Harvest: The Tragedy of Industrial Agriculture*, "Michael Ableman's farm is a landmark, a source of comfort to all of us who love good farming and good food. A lot of people are grateful to him, and I am one of them."

David Blume had two acres of land — one on a 35-degree slope that he terraced; the other in a flat field — in suburban California. From those two acres he produced enough vegetables to feed 450 people. Each year his soil became more fertile, darker, richer, deeper, and easier to work. His losses to pests dropped so much that, by his fourth year, he stopped worrying about them.

Blume explained that "the keys to the success of that long-term experiment were some of the basic tenets of permaculture. Work with nature, not against it. Everything is a yield, it's up to me to realize its value and find what to use it for. Be allergic to any extra work (put things in the right place in relation to other things). Never fight gravity (it wins). The problem is the solution. Every design component has to have at least three purposes and depend on three other systems. And any energy flow crossing into my farm was mine to use, not a force to battle (rain coming from uphill into my property for instance)."

Does "permaculture" work in the real world or is it just some hippie hunter-gatherer gardening system? Blume's operation ranked in the top 15 percent of the more than 2,000 California organic farms in terms of income, even though his acreage was a small fraction of the size of most of those farms.

The United Nations Development Program estimates that 800 million people are engaged in urban agriculture worldwide. In many countries, up to a third of total agricultural production is from urban lands. In

Sweet Potato Soup cont.

Reduce the heat to medium; add lemon juice, mustard, and pepper; and stir occasionally until the potatoes blend well and the soup thickens. Garnish with mint, cilantro, or parsley and serve hot.

Difficulty

SALADS

CLEOPATRA SALAD
Serves 6

Croutons

3 to 4 slices hard artisanal bread, trimmed and cubed (about 1½ cups)
2 Tbsp cold-pressed oil
½ tsp dried rosemary
½ tsp dried marjoram
1 tsp garlic powder
Dash of black pepper

Dressing

2 Tbsp flaked almonds or local nuts, sliced
3 cloves garlic, minced
Pinch dry mustard powder
3 Tbsp nutritional yeast flakes
1 tsp shoyu
3 Tbsp Worcestershire sauce (optional)
3 Tbsp fresh lemon or similar citrus juice
¼ cup water

Salad

2 large heads romaine lettuce, torn into bite-size pieces
¼ pound firm tofu, cubed and pickled in vinegar for 1 day

Croutons

Preheat oven to 325°F. Lightly coat bread cubes with oil (a spray bottle works well here). In small bowl, mix remaining crouton ingredients and toss again to coat. Spread in a single layer on baking sheet. Bake until lightly toasted, 10 to 15 minutes. Remove from oven and cool. A variation would be to coat and toast the cubed tofu at the same time.

Cairo, over a quarter of households raise small livestock, which provides more than 60 percent of household income. In Dar es Salaam, urban agriculture is the second-largest employer. In Accra and Havana, 80 percent of the vegetables consumed, and a fair number of the chickens, ducks, and guinea fowl, are grown right in the city or, in the case of Shanghai, on junks in the harbor. Throughout Europe, you can see tens of thousands of small plots for home gardeners in cities like Berlin, St. Petersburg, and Copenhagen. Two-thirds of households in England now maintain compost piles. In Vancouver, 44 percent of households grow some of their own food. There are an estimated 12,000 vacant lots in New York City, which is enough land to provide food for thousands of people, even before we get to the rooftops and window boxes.

In Russian cities, when the economy suddenly changed in the early 1990s, people started gardening cooperatives in apartment buildings. Three residents in each building, farming the rooftops with soils made in worm-bins under the stairwells, could make a living for themselves by supplying the hundred or more other residents with the fresh fruits and vegetables they grew in containers, sometimes using heating vents and chimneys from the buildings to warm greenhouses through the long winter.

In *Fatal Harvest: The Tragedy of Industrial Agriculture*, Michael Ableman says, "Urban agriculture does not require the construction of expensive facilities, the destruction of existing buildings, or new transportation networks. The land, the people, and the cultural knowledge already exist to make it happen. All that stands in the way is the lack of political support and of a shared vision of how we can transform our cities into biologically and culturally alive gardens."

Organic Food

When people think of organically grown food, they primarily think of the absence of harmful chemical additives, pesticide residues, and other poisons that have become all too common in industrial agriculture and are doubtless contributing to the huge increase in cancer rates in the developed world. Organic food is much more than this. The roots of the movement can be traced back to agronomist F.H. King, who traveled through China in the early 1900s and wrote a book, *The Farmers of Forty Centuries* (1911), which inspired Paul Keene, J.I. Rodale, Bill Mollison, and countless other readers who have kept *Farmers* in print for nearly a century.

The premise in *Farmers of Forty Centuries* has little to do with chemicals and a lot to do with soil. Chinese farmers, King observed, were constantly improving the soils that grew their food. They did this by recapturing scrap wastes from the kitchen, "night soil" (humanure), and animal byproducts (manures, water from fish farms, slaughterhouse wastes) as compost. Microflora do the rest, digesting the wastes and enzymatically enriching humus with nutrients ready to be absorbed by the roots of plants. In contrast to the chemical processes of agriculture, which leach valuable elements and trace minerals from soils and bleach out important fungi, helpful microorganisms, and companion plants, the ancient methods of responsible farming created a legacy of constantly improving soil health. From healthy soils came healthy vegetables, grains, and fruit and nut crops.

> In 200 years, when they are
> brushing seeds into baskets with their
> fingers, and a stranger appears with a new
> threshing machine that will do the same thing with less
> time and effort, they will need to say something smarter than
> "the Gods forbid it" or "that is not our Way." They will need the
> knowledge to say something like: "Your machine requires the seed to be
> planted alone and not interspersed with perennials that maintain nitro-
> gen and mineral balance in the soil. And from where will the metal come,
> and how many trees must be cut down and burned to melt and shape it? And
> since we cannot build the machine, shall we be dependent on the machine-
> builders, and give them a portion of our food, which we now keep all for
> ourselves? Do you not know, clever stranger, that when any biomass is removed
> from the land, and not recycled back into it, the soil is weakened? And what
> could we do with our "saved" time, that would be more valuable and
> pleasurable than gathering the seed by hand, touching and knowing every
> stalk and every inch of the land that feeds us? Shall we become allies of cold
> metal that cuts without feeling, turning our hands and eyes to the study of
> machines and numbers until, severed from the Earth, we nearly destroy it as
> our ancestors did, making depleted uranium and polychlorinated biphenyls
> and cadmium batteries that even now make the old cities unfit for living?
> Go back to your people, and tell them, if they come to conquer us
> with their machines, we will fight them in ways the Arawaks and
> Seminoles and Lakota and Hopi and Nez Perce never imagined,
> because we understand your world better than you do
> yourself. Tell your people to come to learn."

> — Ran Prieur, 2006

Cleopatra Salad cont.

Dressing

Process almonds, garlic, mustard, yeast flakes, shoyu, and lemon juice. Add ¼ cup water. Blend until smooth.

Salad

Toss together lettuce, tofu, and dressing. Add croutons and toss again. Serve promptly. This faux Caesar has fewer calories than a regular Caesar and can be vegan if you eliminate the Worcestershire sauce.

Difficulty

SALADS

MARINATED CANNELLINI BEANS
Serves 4

1¾ cup cooked or 15-ounce can of cannellini beans or small limas, drained
1 clove garlic, minced
¼ cup cold-pressed oil
2 Tbsp red wine vinegar
1 tsp dried parsley
½ tsp crushed oregano
½ tsp crushed basil
¼ tsp dried tarragon
Salt and pepper to taste

Mix all together, cover, and let stand several hours to develop flavors.

Difficulty

If organic farmers and gardeners have learned anything in the past half-century, it is how to make soil. If you can make soil — and anyone, almost anywhere, can — you can feed yourself. It doesn't matter if you live in the city, in a suburb, in the country, or on a remote mountain. If you can make soil, you can eat.

Some cities, like Lismore in New South Wales, have turned their municipal garbage dumps into soil-making factories. Compostables are separated at curbside and hauled to the composting facility, where they are pulverized, mixed with shredded cardboard and paper wastes from offices, inoculated with worms, and bedded into carts that move on rails under light misting sprays of water as the worms gradually do their work. At the end of the line, the rich black soil is bagged and sent off to be sold in garden stores, from where it makes its way back to produce the food consumed by Lismore residents and begins the process all over again.

Organic vegetable farming is now the most prosperous segment of the Chinese food industry, having grown by 30 percent annually for most of the past decade — twice the growth rate of the Chinese economy as a whole. While organic fruit is mostly still at the conversion-to-organic stage, organic vegetable farming is a mature segment, with about 80 percent of production for export, mostly to Japan. This is earning China about a billion dollars per year, but it is just the beginning. The Chinese government is encouraging the development of the organic industry, and local governments are implementing different incentive policies, such as offering free land, to support organic production. More than 4,000 different organic fruits and vegetables are now being produced.

Organic farming is first and foremost stewardship of the land and the wildlife that inhabits it. It is also environmentally and socially responsible methods of production, processing, and shipping. It is the humane treatment of animals. It is preservation of heirloom seed and gene lines. Organic integrity relies on openness, honesty, and direct public communication. Organic standards embrace fair trade, food security, fair pricing, and farmworker rights. As Michael Sligh, director of sustainable agriculture at the Rural Advancement Foundation International says in *Fatal Harvest*, "it's not about 'just' having lunch but about having a 'just' lunch."

Extending Your Season

You can construct a simple straw-bale greenhouse using 36 bales of straw that are covered by one 20-by-20-foot sheet of clear poly draped over struts made from five 12-foot sections of bamboo, saplings, conduit pipe, or steel rebar. To attach the clear poly, create "clothespins" by cutting plastic pipe (one size larger than the struts) into three-inch lengths and splitting them up the middle. Snap the pins onto the struts over the poly cover.

One advantage of this design is that it allows solar gain through one side while insulating against heat losses on the other sides. Plastering the straw bales will extend their life, but if you allow them to get wet and gradually decompose, it will add to the heat of the interior.

In subfreezing temperatures it takes 6,000 BTUs/hr to heat a 200 square foot room (20 by 10 feet). There are 92,000 BTUs per gallon of propane and 1,000 BTUs per cubic foot of natural gas. Therefore, you will need one gallon of propane or 90 cubic feet of natural gas every 15 hours to heat a small greenhouse with gas. As gas prices rise, this will quickly become unaffordable, so you'll need to consider alternatives. A wood, pellet, or sawdust stove will serve equally well. If you have animals, keeping them inside the greenhouse at night and piling their manure outside, in front of the clear poly side, will create a thermal curtain that helps retain heat.

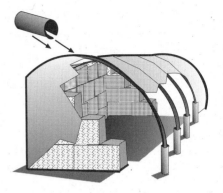

Straw-bale greenhouse.

Making Soil

Soil is the product of decay, which is part of the normal cycle of life. All living things die, and their elemental parts are recycled by microscopic workhorses we call "primary decomposers." Compost is material that is no longer alive but is not yet soil. If it is actively composting, a compost pile is alive with activity.

There are two techniques for making compost happen — hot and cold. Building a hot compost pile takes more effort, but it composts faster than a cold pile, taking six weeks rather than six months. A hot pile is built with optimum mass, moisture, air, and materials in a 30:1 carbon-to-nitrogen ratio and reaches over 140°F at its center. When it is really cooking, you can bake potatoes in it.

Turning the pile allows all the material to be exposed to the hot center and increases aeration. The pile's heat should peak every time you turn it, although the peak temperature will be lower and lower with each turn.

The compost is done when it looks like dark rich soil and smells sweet and earthy, crumbling through your fingers.

If you build your compost bins under a group of rabbit hutches, the rabbits add manure (nitrogen) without prompting. Chickens turn the pile by scratching for worms and centipedes and make their own nitrogen contributions.

What Non-Vegetarians Need To Know about Soyfoods

Food is going to become more expensive as a result of sharper competition for food crops from biofuels, higher farm and fertilizer costs, transportation constraints, the world's dwindling freshwater resource, and climate change. With 6.4 billion people to feed — a number likely to grow before it shrinks — we might expect horrible famines in the 21st century were it not for a simple legume that at present occupies a fringe position in most of the world's cuisines.

I'm talking about the soybean. George Washington Carver made cars out of it; Brazil, the United States, and China export enormous quantities of it for animal feed and cooking oil; and vegetarians actually eat the thing as veggieburgers and tofurky. Because soy is a complete protein, grows on six continents, is inexpensive to produce, and fixes nitrogen in the soil, it has the potential to keep those billions of people alive if they will only stop feeding it to their pets and eat it themselves. Those who prefer to make derisive jokes about tofu can start basing their diet on it after they've eaten their pets.

An acre of soybeans produces more than 300 times the edible protein of range-fed cattle, with a fraction of the water requirement. To turn those soybeans into delectable food for humans entails a little processing, but it is not complicated and can be done at home. Soy contains a digestive inhibitor that needs to be cooked or fermented before the bean becomes safe for human consumption. In the process of deactivating this enzyme, our ancestors, principally in Asia, came up with some wonderful foods. The recipes in this book employ these foods in many different ways, but primarily as meat substitutes because they are likely to be available long after meat has become much scarcer and more expensive. These are some of those foods:

Tempeh is a fermented bean cake made from soybeans, okara, grains, or nuts that have been injected with *Rhizopus oligosporus* and allowed to ferment. It is high in nutritional and dietetic value and fiber, and has a chewy texture with a mushroom-like, nutty flavor.

Textured soy protein (TSP) is a healthy meat substitute (contained in foods like Hamburger Helper) made from defatted soy flour. It comes as dried and seasoned flakes, granules, or chunks, and it has a chewy, meaty texture when cooked.

Soymilk is the creamy white liquid that is left when dried soybeans are soaked and boiled and the skins are skimmed off. A little salt, oil, honey, and vanilla will take away the "beany" flavor.

Tofu is a curded soymilk that is pressed into blocks. It is cheap, high in protein, low in fat, and very versatile. You can eat it raw or cooked, but its bland flavor is improved if allowed to absorb other flavors.

Those who prefer to make derisive jokes about tofu can switch over to it after they've eaten their pets.

Silken and soft tofu are relatively moist, well suited for making shakes, dips, and dressings. Regular tofu is good for scrambling or using in place of cheese. Firm and extra-firm tofus hold their shape in fried dishes and on the grill. When frozen or dried, tofu takes on different textures, and its absorptive qualities improve. Tofu is also available smoked, pickled, flavored, baked, and deep-fried.

Soy yogurt is made from soymilk that has been cultured.

Soy ice cream is made from soymilk that has been chilled and whipped.

Soy frogurt is made from soymilk that has been cultured and then chilled and whipped.

Soy mayonnaise, a substitute for egg-based mayonnaise, is a blend of tofu, vinegar, and lemon juice.

Making Soy Mayonnaise

½ cup finely ground cashews (use coffee grinder)   1¼ tsp sea salt or kosher salt
1 medium clove garlic   1¼ tsp lemon juice
1 pound silken tofu   1 Tbsp oil

Combine all ingredients and blend until smooth. Makes 1½ cups.

Fermented bean curd is cubed tofu immersed in a broth. It has a pungent aroma and strong flavor. If fermented in wine, it is called "sufu."

Okara, the pulp that's left over after soymilk is squeezed from soybeans, is full of protein and fiber and is good for burgers and granola.

Yuba, made from the skin that forms on the surface of heated soymilk, is also known as "Buddhist duck" because it takes on the texture of a roasted duck skin when fried or baked.

Miso is a thick paste made from soybeans and grains that have been fermented and then aged. It is used to flavor soups, dipping sauces, and stir-frys. *Hatcho miso* is a strong, salty, reddish brown, fermented soy paste aged for up to three years. *Shiro miso* is a pale yellow miso that is sweeter and milder than other miso. It is best for light soups, salad dressings, desserts, and marinades.

Natto, a fermented soybean that is pungent, mucilaginous, and highly nutritious, is an acquired taste.

Nama nori san are colorful sheets of soy paper used to wrap sushi.

Soya powder is made from soy flour that has been cooked. The texture is lighter and finer than soy flour and leaves no aftertaste.

Tofu sour cream is a low-fat, more nutritious substitute for sour cream.

Making Tofu Sour Cream

1 pound silken tofu   ½ tsp rice vinegar
4 tsp lemon juice   ¼ tsp sea salt

Combine all ingredients and blend until smooth. Makes 1½ cups.

Soynuts are roasted soybeans that you eat like peanuts. To make your own: Soak dried whole soybeans overnight, then rinse and drain. Season the beans if you like, then bake them in a 350°F oven, stirring occasionally, for about an hour, until they're light brown. Alternatively, fry them in oil until they're light brown, about ten minutes.

Soynut butter, made from roasted soynuts, has less fat than peanut butter.

Soy coffee is made from ground, dark-roasted soynuts.

Cold Process

If you don't want to spend a lot of time with compost, just get the pile started and leave it alone. It will take longer but will still give you soil in the end.

Look for nearby sources of good organic wastes that can supplement your kitchen and garden wastes. Sawdust, horse manure, flourmill wastes, and oilseed meal may be local waste products that you can help get rid of.

Some people add a shovelful of soil per layer to introduce microorganisms to the pile. You might need to do this if your pile is located on pavement, but otherwise it's probably not necessary, though you may want to introduce some worms.

Worm Compost

Worms produce a high-quality compost in a short amount of time and don't require you to turn the pile as often. Worm composting, or vermiculture, is also a way to sterilize compost (even humanure) because the bacteria in the worms' intestines completely digest harmful pathogens and expel sterile castings. To make a worm pile, you need to be able to contain the worms, so you will need to buy or construct a bin.

Observe these three rules:

- Worms like a dark, moist environment.
- Worms need to breathe.
- Worms need to be protected from pests and pets.

Compostables

Good to include:
- Chicken and duck manure
- Coffee grounds
- Corncobs
- Dried grass clippings
- Eggshells
- Flours and meals
- Ground bones
- Hedge trimmings
- Horse and cow manure
- Kitchen scraps
- Old sod
- Pine needles
- Rabbit and guinea pig droppings
- Reject fruits and vegetables
- Sawdust
- Seaweed
- Shredded leaves and twigs
- Straw
- Tea bags

Best to avoid:
- Bones (whole)
- Cheese
- Dog and cat manure
- Dried weeds (contain seeds)
- Eggs
- Fruit pits
- Grease
- Hay (contains seeds)
- Meat and fish
- Thick or long material
- Unshredded paper and cardboard

Compost Tea

When I am weeding my garden, I don't throw away the weeds. Instead I toss them into an open garbage can where they accumulate and begin to decompose. I leave the lid off the can during the first few rainfalls so that the rainwater soaks and immerses the weeds. Eventually I will put a lid on the can and let the material steep for some weeks or months. At that point I'll begin filling another can with fresh weeds. When I am starting new plants, I'll go to my can of "compost tea" and take some cupfuls of the brew to apply as fertilizer.

Compost tea recognizes that anything we call "weeds" are actually just plants we haven't found a better use for. All of these plants are dynamic accumulators of valuable minerals that can and should be returned to the soil to nourish the plants we want to grow. Plants don't live on carbon and nitrogen alone, any more than humans can live on a diet of Big Macs and Pepsi. So we make compost tea, and the plants slowly sip and enjoy the sunlight.

Of all the thousands of books, magazines, pamphlets, and other advice on growing food, I have only two books I recommend above all others: *Gaia's Garden* by Toby Hemingway and *Square Foot Gardening* by Mel Bartholomew. Anyone seriously interested in growing his or her own food successfully, and not burning out after a single season of disappointment, should invest the money and time to buy and read these two books. You can save yourself a whole lot of back-break, heartbreak, and half-bake.

Mulch

All bare soil should have a cover of mulch to protect it, including ground underneath shrubbery and trees. Never leave bare soil exposed, even in indoor greenhouses. Mulch can be pine needles, various types of wood bark, sawdust or chips, nutshells, shredded leaves or cardboard, hay or straw, or even crushed rock. It's best to use organic materials that won't mat easily or blow away.

The real purpose of mulch is to protect the health of the soil. It lessens the effect of extreme temperatures, increases moisture retention, prevents topsoil from washing or blowing away, and reduces soil compaction. With a mulch covering, weeds do not receive enough light to grow, and the few that do survive are so weak they can easily be removed.

Food Animals

Before the petroleum era, meat occupied a much different place in the world's diet. Recipes from cookbooks in the 1800s focused on stretching

Sheet Mulch

Water the area to be mulched. Before you lay down mulch, first cover the ground with sheets of wet newspaper or cardboard. You can put fresh or partially digested compost under the paper if you like, because the wet paper will attract worms. Make small openings where your seeds and plants will be growing. Spread mulch thickly over the wet paper and wet it down.

Be careful not to lay mulch so that it is touching plants. Keep it two to three inches away from plant stems. Try not to lay it so thick that plant leaves are resting on it.

You can "sheet compost" by adding raw, undigested compostables right on top of the mulch and then adding more mulch to cover. While this is slower and more prone to pests than a hot compost pile, it is also less effort. The process of composting will steal nitrogen from soil, so by not tilling the raw materials into the ground, you protect the nitrogen in your mulched garden and force the compost to draw its nitrogen from the air or from the surface of the garden, not from the root zone.

a small amount of meat over many meals, usually to enhance the flavor of other foods.

Since the mid-20th century, meat production has paced oil consumption, with a worldwide growth rate of 2 percent per year. In the industrial world, a pattern of bacon and eggs for breakfast, chicken or hamburger for lunch, and fish or steak for dinner is often considered normal. The developing world now aspires to the same profligate standard, with a current growth rate in meat consumption closer to 6 percent annually. The International Food Policy Research Institute projects that by 2020 the average Chinese adult will consume 161 pounds of meat per year, up 55 percent from current levels and just 15 pounds less than the average in the West.

The high cost of energy will bring about a major restructuring of the global meat industry. At the end of the 20th century, the factory-farm method of raising animals had almost completely taken over Europe and North America and was well on its way to conquest of Asia and South America. Global cattle and pig populations were up 38 percent from 1961. Livestock had moved to occupy two-thirds of the world's agricultural land and consumed two-thirds of mined freshwater resources. Producing just eight ounces of meat requires 6,600 gallons of water (equal to the capacity of a 10 foot by 18 foot swimming pool, five feet deep), compared to the 145 gallons (three bathtubs full) that goes into a loaf of bread. And it takes energy to lift and move the water needed to produce meat.

*The first big test of
the international community's capacity to manage scarcity may come with oil or it
could come with grain. If the latter is the case, this could
occur when China — whose grain harvest fell by 34 million
tons, or nine percent, between 1998 and 2005 — turns to the world
market for massive imports of 30 million, 50 million, or possibly even
100 million tons of grain per year. Demand on this scale could quickly
overwhelm world grain markets. When this happens, China will have to look
to the United States, which controls the world's grain exports of over 40 percent of some 200 million tons. This will pose a fascinating geopolitical
situation. More than 1.3 billion Chinese consumers, who had an estimated
$160 billion trade surplus with the United States in 2004 — enough to buy
the entire U.S. grain harvest twice — will be competing with [US]
Americans for U.S. grain, driving up U.S. food prices. In such a situation 30 years ago, the United States simply restricted exports. But
China is now banker to the United States, underwriting much
of the massive U.S. fiscal deficit with monthly purchases of U.S. Treasury bonds.*

— Lester Brown, 2005

Another major boost to meat production was the availability of cheaper grain, primarily corn and soybeans, with yields greatly enhanced by fossil fuel inputs. Beef calves can grow from 79 pounds to 1,200 pounds in just 14 months on a diet of corn, soybeans, antibiotics, and growth hormones. In North America 70 percent of the corn harvest is now fed to livestock. Worldwide, 80 percent of soy production and a third of the world's fish catch goes to animal feed. The result is the destruction of global fisheries through unsustainable harvesting and the steady deforestation of Earth to make room for grain plantations and cattle ranches. The forests being removed were the atmospheric scrub brushes that kept global warming in check. Cheap oil fueled the chainsaws and bulldozers that cleared the forest; made the fertilizers and pesticides for the corn and soybeans; powered the tractors, combines, and fishing fleets; and hauled the harvest to distant markets.

Because of cheap fossil fuel inputs, the world price of beef has fallen 25 percent over the past 30 years, and the amount of saturated fats in the global diet has increased proportionately. More than 300 million adults are now obese, and 115 million adults in the developing world suffer

SALADS

BASIC HERB DRESSING
Serves 4

5 Tbsp oil
2 Tbsp balsamic or red wine vinegar, cider vinegar, or lemon juice
1 tsp honey
¼ tsp salt
½ tsp dried basil or oregano, or both

Mix ingredients in a small jar and shake. For variation, add a pinch of powdered hot pepper or crushed and minced garlic.

Difficulty

from obesity-related health problems. Avian flu, mad cow disease, foot-and-mouth disease, nipah virus, campylobacter, listeria, salmonella, *E. coli*, super-resistant bacteria, and hazardous hormones are all public health threats deriving from the meat industry.

Reversing these health and environmental disasters should become less politically difficult when we are confronted with the undeniable reality of shrinking supplies of natural gas and petroleum. Fewer animals will make their way to market, and, because of higher transportation costs, those markets will become more local. As a result, the price of meat will rise, perhaps even faster than the price of gasoline.

In the future, farmers and homeowners will have more small fish or shrimp ponds as part of their home and neighborhood gardens. They will use chickens, goats, and rabbits to control weeds and pests, or perhaps they will have fast-reproducing guinea pigs as household pets. Adopting a delicious vegan diet or producing animal protein on a small, local scale are ways to stay happily well-fed.

*As you realize that the breakdown really is
going to happen and it is not just another scare story,
you may have thoughts of retreating to a couple of hectares in the
wilderness where you can endure the end of the world on your own little
piece of independent paradise. This should be treated with caution. A self-
sufficient community needs a certain minimum size to survive. Growing food
and maintaining a farm is labor intensive — the smaller the group, the
harder it is to deal with the inevitable illnesses and injuries. During the
harvest, you will need every hand you can find.*

— Paul Thompson, 2005

Sprouts

Sprouts will provide you with fresh, nutritious food. You will need the following items:

- A wide-mouth jar with a mesh top (made from window screening or cheesecloth)
- Shade and warmth (a closet, cupboard, or cloth cover)

The process is:

1. Cover seeds with water; rinse several times.
2. Cover with water; soak overnight. Keep in darkness until sprouts appear, then place in partial shade.

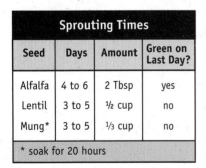

Sprouting Times			
Seed	Days	Amount	Green on Last Day?
Alfalfa	4 to 6	2 Tbsp	yes
Lentil	3 to 5	½ cup	no
Mung*	3 to 5	⅓ cup	no
* soak for 20 hours			

3. Drain, rinse, keep jar inverted at an angle. Rinse at least twice a day until sprouts are of the desired size. Spread on a towel to dry before using as salad or in stir-fry or sandwiches. Seed hulls may be floated off and composted.

Remember, the larger the seed, the longer the soak. You can use the soaking and rinsing water for cooking. It's rich in nitrogen, and houseplants love it.

Mushrooms

Some years ago I was introduced to shiitake mushrooms by Bob Harris, who recommended them as an alternative therapy for high blood pressure. I was immediately wowed.

Besides being one of the most delicious foods known, and a balanced whole protein, shiitake is antibacterial; anti-candida, anti-staphylococcus, anti-listeria, anti-streptococcus, anti-pseudomonas, anti-tuberculosis, anti-tumor, and anti-viral (herpes; HIV and influenza); a blood sugar moderator; a cholesterol reducer; an immune-system enhancer; a liver and kidney tonic; a sexual potentiator; a stress reducer; and specifically effective against cancers of the breast, liver, skin, and prostate.

Instead of paying for expensive vitamin supplements, I now grow shiitake, maitake, nameko, and oyster mushrooms that are rich in thiamine, riboflavin, niacin, pantothenic acid, vitamin D, iron, potassium, and selenium.

Bob taught me how easy it was to grow shiitake in green hardwood logs, using techniques developed in Japan after World War II to assist rural farmers whose wartime employment had depended on making charcoal for gunpowder. In the latter half of the 20th century, the shiitake industry saved much of Japan's mountain oak from being cut down because it provided greater financial returns from standing forest than did conversion to timber farm or cattle ranch — a lesson that could be learned today by Brazil and Indonesia.

You will find a stand of a dozen or more shiitake logs in the shade a short distance from my kitchen. Like many people in my community, I have a steady supply of fresh mushrooms from spring to fall. When they occasionally overproduce, which might happen after a strong rain, I dry them for winter.

I don't recommend shiitake alone. I believe everyone should have logs, sawdust buckets, and stumps inoculated with oysters *(Pleurotis var.)*, reishis *(Ganoderma var.)*, maitake *(Grifola frondosa)*, pom pom *(Hericium*

*The chanterelle (*Cantharellus cibarius*) is a fruity, flavorful, wild delicacy that contains all eight essential amino acids in good proportion. The sporophore also contains vitamin A. In China it is used to improve eyesight, moisturize dry skin, and relieve certain infectious respiratory illnesses. The ethanol extract of the sporophore of this fungus has an inhibitory effect on certain cancers in white mice.*

Inoculating logs with mushrooms. Shiitake and oyster mushrooms are produced by drilling holes in freshly cut hardwood logs and inserting young mycelium spawn. The logs then incubate for six months to two years before yielding their first harvest. Over a few years they will produce the weight of the green log in mushrooms.

erinaceus), and sulfur shelf *(Polysporus sulfurus).* In *Mycelium Running,* Paul Stamets lists 184 varieties of wood that can be inoculated to grow mushrooms. They grow everywhere, even indoors at the McMurdo Research Station at the South Pole.

Complete starter kits, including instructions for growing your own supply of mushrooms year-round, are available from Mushroompeople (PO Box 220, Summertown TN 38483 USA; www.mushroompeople.com). Mushroompeople is the world's oldest mail-order supplier of spawn and tools for home and industry and provides high-quality products at reasonable prices.

> *In this new world, the price of oil begins to set*
> *the price of food, not so much because of rising fuel costs for*
> *farmers and food processors but more because almost everything we eat*
> *can be converted into fuel for cars. In this new world of high oil prices,*
> *supermarkets and service stations will compete in commodity markets for basic*
> *food commodities such as wheat, corn, soybeans, and sugarcane.*
>
> — Lester Brown, 2006

Begin Storing Food

We recognize four main stages of the pulsing cycle:
1. growth on abundant available resources, *with sharp increases in a system's population, structure, and assets, based on low-efficiency and high-competition (capitalism and monopolistic overgrowth);*
2. climax and transition, *when the system reaches the maximum size allowed by the available resources, increases efficiency, develops collaborative competition patterns, and prepares for descent by storing information;*
3. descent, *with adaptations to less resources available, a decrease in population and assets, an increase in recycling patterns, and a transmission of information in a way that minimizes losses; [and]*
4. low-energy restoration, *with no-growth, consumption smaller than accumulation, and storage of resources for a new cycle ahead.*
The pulsing paradigm has always been in front of our eyes. Forest ecosystems never did anything different.
— Howard and Elizabeth Odum, 2000

If in 1936 we had told the [Latter Day] Saints, "You would better prepare, because the time is coming when" — remember, in 1936 the problem was money; there was always enough to buy, but the problem today is something to buy, not money — if we had told you then that the time would come when you could not buy all the meat you wanted, and perhaps not any at times; that you could not get butter, and that you could not get sugar, and that you could not get clothing, and that the farmers could get no machinery, and so on down the whole list of things that you can not get now and that therefore you should prepare for a stormy day, we would have

SALADS

THREE BEAN SALAD

Serves 6

1¾ cup cooked or 15-ounce can of French-cut green beans
1¾ cup cooked or 15-ounce can of red kidney beans
1¾ cup cooked or 15-ounce can of yellow wax beans, cut
½ cup onion, chopped small
½ cup oil
¼ cup red wine vinegar
2 Tbsp sugar or equivalent sweetener
Salt and pepper to taste

Drain the beans (liquids can be added to soup pot), rinse, and combine with onion in a large bowl. Whisk together the oil, vinegar, and sweetener and pour over beans. Let stand several hours. Stir occasionally. Add salt and pepper to taste. This is traditionally very sweet.

Difficulty

been laughed to scorn. But I say to you again, the advice then given is good today, and you would better prepare for the times ahead, that you may not be like the five foolish virgins with no oil in your lamps.

— J. Reuben Clark, Jr., 1946

If we want to be able to eat food out of season, like fruit and vegetables in winter, we need to learn how to properly store food. Storing food without refrigeration is something humans learned to do more than 10,000 years ago, and most of our families have only lost this knowledge in the past century.

Canning Food

Canning homegrown food can save you half the cost of buying commercially canned food, even including your labor. Canning your favorite foods, to be enjoyed later by family and friends, is a fulfilling experience and a source of pride for many people.

Some people think that canning and drying food will be impractical on a small scale in an era of energy scarcity, but canning and drying was common in most homes in the days before petroleum was discovered, and the decline of home processing of food exactly parallels the expansion of the oil economy. Today we have grown accustomed to fast foods and convenience foods and have lost touch with the old-fashioned ways of putting up food in season so that it will be fast and convenient later. We need to relearn.

If vegetables are handled properly and canned promptly after harvest, they can be more nutritious than fresh produce sold in local stores. The advantages of home canning are lost when you start with poor-quality fresh foods; when jars fail to seal properly; when food spoils; and when flavors, texture, color, and nutrients deteriorate during prolonged storage.

Label and date your jars of canned food and store them in a relatively cool, clean, dark, dry place, preferably between 50°F and 70°F. Do not store them near hot pipes, a range, a furnace, in an uninsulated attic, or in direct sunlight. Under these conditions, food will lose quality in a few weeks or months and may spoil. Dampness may corrode metal lids, break seals, and allow contamination and spoilage.

Can no more food than you will use within a year.

Hot-packing

Hot-packing is the practice of heating freshly prepared food to boiling, simmering it two to five minutes, and promptly filling jars loosely with the boiled food. Whether food has been hot-packed or raw-packed, the juice, syrup, or water to be added to the foods should also be heated to boiling before it is poured into the jars. This practice helps to remove air from food tissues, shrinks food, helps keep the food from floating in the jars, increases vacuum in sealed jars, and improves shelf life. Preshrinking food gets more food into each jar.

Hot-packing is the best way to remove air and is the preferred pack style for foods processed in a boiling-water canner. At first the color of hot-packed foods may appear no better than that of raw-packed foods, but within a short storage period both color and flavor of hot-packed foods will be superior.

Tips for Canning

If you're canning tomatoes, you should scald them, peel them, and pack them into quart jars, then put the jars into a big kettle of boiling water for 45 minutes. They don't have to be pressure-canned; a water bath is enough. Alternatively, you can make a tomato sauce with onions, peppers, garlic, oregano, basil, and other seasonings. Cook it for 15 minutes. Tomato juice can also be water bathed for 15 minutes.

To make fruit juices, put cherries, blackberries, grapes, blueberries, raspberries, or pears in jars with eight parts water to one part honey and water-bathe them for 20 minutes. Jams and jellies get the same process, but with pectin added to firm up the mixture. You can turn apples into applesauce and bathe for 20 minutes or press them into cider in half-gallon jars and hot-bathe them for 30 minutes.

Make pickles by scalding cucumbers, beets, sliced eggplant, baby onions, or banana peppers and then packing them into jars with pickling spices, dill, garlic, a grape leaf, and a half-and-half mixture of good white or cider vinegar and water. Add one tablespoon of salt to each cup of liquid. Water-bathe the jars for 15 minutes.

Leave a half-inch of space at the top of the jar when you fill it, wipe the rim with a clean towel, and tighten the band by hand. Once the jars have cooked, let them set for a day to cool and dry. You might remove the bands so they don't rust and stick.

Sauerkraut

Two hundred years before Vitamin C was ever heard of, sauerkraut was used for curing scurvy and rickets. Sauerkraut is a favorite winter food in both Europe and Asia because of its health-giving properties and long shelf life. It is also one of the easiest fermented foods to make.

SALADS

BLACK BEAN SALAD

Serves 4 to 5

1 Tbsp oil
2 tsp cider vinegar
½ tsp salt
½ tsp dried basil
⅛ tsp black pepper
1⅔ cup cooked or 14-ounce can of black beans, drained
2 Tbsp onion, minced
1 carrot, grated

Mix oil, vinegar, and spices. Stir in beans, onions, and carrots.

Difficulty

Using a Pressure Canner

Follow these steps for successful pressure-canning:

1. Put two to three inches of hot water in the canner. Place filled jars on the rack, using a jar lifter. Fasten canner lid securely.

2. Leave weight off the vent port or open the petcock. Heat at the highest setting until steam flows from the petcock or vent port.

3. Maintain high heat setting, exhaust steam ten minutes, and then place weight on the vent port or close the petcock. The canner will pressurize during the next three to five minutes.

4. Start timing the process when the pressure reading on the dial gauge indicates that the recommended pressure has been reached, or when the weighted gauge begins to jiggle or rock (you might have to tap it lightly).

5. Regulate heat under the canner to maintain a steady pressure at or slightly above the correct gauge pressure. Quick and large pressure variations during processing may cause unnecessary liquid losses from jars. Weighted gauges on Mirro canners should jiggle about two or three times per minute. On Presto canners, they should rock slowly throughout the process.

6. Cook at ten pounds pressure: peas for 40 minutes; corn for 95 minutes; green beans for 25 minutes; beets for 30 minutes.

7. When the timed process is completed, turn off the heat, remove the canner from the heat if possible, and let the canner depressurize. Do not force-cool the canner. Forced cooling may result in food spoilage. Cooling the canner with cold running water or opening the vent port before the canner is fully depressurized will cause loss of liquid from jars and seal failures. Forced cooling may also warp the lid of older model canners, causing steam leaks. It's best to time the depressurization of older models. Standard-size heavy-walled canners require about 30 minutes to depressurize when loaded with pints and 45 minutes with quarts. Newer, thin-walled canners cool more rapidly and are equipped with vent locks. These canners are depressurized when their vent-lock piston drops to a normal position.

8. After the canner is depressurized, remove the weight from the vent port or open the petcock. Wait two minutes, unfasten the lid, and remove it carefully. Lift the lid away from you so that the steam does not burn your face.

9. Remove jars with a lifter and place them on a towel or cooling rack.

To make one gallon of sauerkraut you will need five pounds of cabbage and three tablespoons to a quarter cup (more in summer, less in winter) of sea salt (not iodized salt — it can inhibit the bacterial action). Approximately 45 pounds of cabbage will fill a five-gallon crock, but let's start small until we get the hang of it.

Shred the cabbage to about the thickness of a pocketknife blade. Mixing green and red cabbage will give you a bright pink kraut. Sprinkle the salt into the cabbage as you chop it. The salt makes the cabbage sweat, and this creates the brine.

For variation you can add other vegetables, like onions, garlic, brussels sprouts, and other greens.

Mix the cabbage and salt thoroughly and let stand five minutes. Then pack the mixture hard into a clean container (a cylindrical crock is best) by hand and press to draw the juice, continuing for as many batches as it takes to fill the container.

Cover the cabbage with several layers of clean cloth and tuck the cloth down the sides. Close the container with a lid that fits snugly inside, and cover it with a weight of such size that the juice comes to the bottom of the lid but not over it. A water jug works great. You may have to vary the weight over the first few days of fermentation to keep the cabbage submerged in brine. Cover the whole crock to keep dust and flies out and store it at 68°F to 85°F for two to six weeks. The warmer the temperature, the faster the fermentation.

Visit the crock every day or two and press down on the weight until the brine comes to just below the lid. Promptly remove any white scum that forms at the brine surface or it will use up the acid and spoil the kraut. Lift the cloth carefully so that the scum adheres, rinse the cloth and lid, and replace. If the brine becomes too low, you can create more brine by adding salt water — two tablespoons salt to one quart water.

The cabbage should taste tangy after a short time, and the taste gets stronger the more it ages. In cool weather it can keep aging for months, but eventually it will hit a peak and begin to decline. When it gets soft, the flavor becomes less pleasant.

Once the sauerkraut has matured (light color, no rotting smell) you can sterilize and preserve it by the hot-pack canning method. My friend Sandor Katz (author of *Wild Fermentation*) has been making kraut for many years and never hot-packs his. So much of the power of sauerkraut is its aliveness, he says, so why kill that? He scoops out a bowlful at a

SALADS

CHICKPEAS WITH ROASTED PEPPERS

Serves 4

1²/₃ cup cooked or 15-ounce can of garbanzo beans or chickpeas, drained
3 fresh red peppers or 12-ounce jar of roasted red peppers with liquid
2 Tbsp minced onion
1 Tbsp oil
2 tsp lemon juice or rice vinegar
Salt and pepper

To roast fresh peppers, heat a dry griddle or heavy skillet. Roast the peppers in the skillet, turning frequently until blistered and blackened. This can also be done on a cooking grate over an open fire. Cool peppers, then place them in a paper bag and rub the bag from the outside, removing blackened skins in the process. Dice the roasted peppers. If chickpeas are uncooked, you need to soak them for 24 hours, then cook them for 25 minutes. Combine all ingredients in a glass bowl, adding salt and pepper to taste.

Difficulty

SPICY CABBAGE SALAD

Serves 6 to 8

1 Tbsp oil
1 medium onion, thinly sliced
½ head red cabbage (about 5 cups), shredded
1 tsp salt
½ tsp powdered ginger
1 tsp turmeric
¼ tsp crushed red pepper flakes, or to taste
2 Tbsp peanut butter
2 Tbsp water
1 tsp sugar or equivalent sweetener
1 large carrot, grated

Heat a big skillet, add oil and onion, and fry 2 minutes. Add cabbage and salt and fry about 10 minutes, until it softens. Mix spices, peanut butter, water, and sweetener. Pour over vegetables and cook 2 minutes. Stir in carrot. Mix well.

Difficulty

time and keeps it refrigerated. Every time he opens the crock, he carefully repacks it tightly with a level surface and clean cover.

Butters, Jams, Jellies, and Marmalades

Sweet spreads are a class of foods with many textures, flavors, and colors. Fruit jelly is a semisolid mixture of fruit juice and sugar that is clear and firm enough to hold its shape. Other spreads are made from crushed or ground fruit.

Jam will also hold its shape, but it is less firm than jelly. Jam is made from crushed or chopped fruits and sugar. Jams made from a mixture of fruits are usually called conserves, especially when they include citrus fruits, nuts, raisins, or coconut.

Preserves are made with small, whole fruits or uniform-size pieces of fruit in a clear, thick, slightly jellied syrup. Marmalades are soft fruit jellies with small pieces of fruit or citrus peel evenly suspended in the transparent jelly. Fruit butters are made with fruit pulp that is cooked with sugar until it thickens to a spreadable consistency. The best way to learn how to preserve fruits by canning is to read the free instruction booklets provided by makers of canning jars and supplies. You can also visit the Great Change website for recipes and advice.

Drying Food

The oldest method of food preservation is drying. The practice of sun-drying fruits and vegetables was developed before biblical times by the Chinese, Hindus, Persians, Greeks, and Egyptians. The advantages of dried foods are that they take up very little space, they do not require refrigeration, and they provide variety to the diet. They are good for backpacking, lunches, camping, and snacks in general.

Drying is a comparatively simple process, requiring little outlay of equipment, time, or money. Even though drying is not difficult, it does take some time and requires constant attention, skill, and understanding of the principles of food-drying methods.

To preserve food you must control enzymes and microorganisms. Drying controls the microorganisms that grow rapidly on raw or fresh food products because the lack of water limits their growth; however, drying does not kill the microorganisms. Enzymes, which can catalyze undesirable flavor and color changes, are usually controlled by a pretreatment.

Because drying removes moisture, dried food shrinks, decreasing in size and weight, thus requiring less space for storage. When water is added to the dried product, it returns to its original size. Yields of dried products are directly related to the amount of water in the original product. Twenty-five pounds of apples will yield about four pounds of dried apples. Twenty-five pounds of onions will yield about three pounds of dried onions.

Fruits and vegetables selected for drying should be sound, fresh, and in peak condition; that is ripe but still firm, and at the right state of maturity. Wilted material will not make a satisfactory product — it has already begun to deteriorate. One moldy bean may give a bad flavor to an entire lot. Immature fruits will be weak in color and flavor. Over-mature vegetables are usually tough and woody. Over-mature or bruised fruits are likely to spoil before the drying process can be completed. Fruit and vegetables that are inferior before drying will be inferior after drying.

Heat for drying is supplied by the sun or electrical heat. If the drying temperature is too low, the product will sour. Drying should be done as quickly as possible, at a temperature that does not seriously affect the texture, color, and flavor of the fruit or vegetable. If the temperature is too high or the humidity too low, there is a danger that moisture will be removed too fast. This can cause case hardening, which means the outer cells of the product harden, preventing water vapor from diffusing from the inner cells. Drying is best accomplished when the process is continuous. When heat is applied intermittently, temperatures conducive to bacterial growth can develop.

Each piece of food should have good exposure to air. The food being dried should be only one layer deep with space around it. There does not

SALADS

EASY COLESLAW
Serves 6

½ head green cabbage (about 5 cups), shredded
½ cup cider vinegar
⅓ cup sugar or equivalent sweetener
½ tsp salt
½ cup evaporated milk, reconstituted dry milk, blended tofu, or soymilk

Pour vinegar over cabbage. Sprinkle on sweetener and salt. Pour milk over all and let stand 20 to 30 minutes. Be sure to follow this order so dressing doesn't curdle. Mix well and chill 2 hours. Optional ingredients include carrots, celery, onions, raisins, and pineapple.

Difficulty

Nutritional Value of Dried Fruits and Vegetables

- Calories: No change. However, the calorie content of the dried food will be higher per unit of weight because nutrients become more concentrated as water is removed.

- Fiber: No change.

- Minerals: Some may be lost in soaking, but no data are available. None is lost in the drying process.

- Vitamins: Those most often found in fruit and vegetables are A, C, and the B vitamins. If vegetables are blanched, vitamin A activity is maintained to a high degree. Vitamin C losses vary widely depending on treatment. It's best to dry the product quickly, keep it out of the sunlight, and decrease the air temperature as it nears complete dryness in order to maintain ascorbic acid (Vitamin C) levels. Only moderate amounts of B vitamins are lost during drying.

SALADS

PINEAPPLE-BEET WOK HAY COLE SLAW

Owning a wok opens your kitchen to a universe of delights. The semi-spherical curve of the wok provides maximum cooking surface while using minimal fuel, which is one reason it comes from regions where fuel is scarce and foods must be cooked quickly. Because the curve of the wok allows flame or heated air to rise rapidly, smoothly, and evenly, liquids evaporate quickly, so woks are perfect for curries and stir-fries. Woks made of pottery are still used in Southeast Asia for slow stewing, just as they were in the Han Dynasty, but most woks today are hand beaten from steel, with a round bottom and two handles. The first choice of wok chefs is a wok of cast iron.

Serves 6

2 Tbsp vegetable oil
1½ Tbsp minced fresh ginger
2 large cloves garlic, minced
1 medium red onion, thinly sliced
2 bunches watercress, stemmed, washed, and drained
¼ cup fresh basil, coarsely chopped
Pinch sea salt and freshly ground black pepper
½ head green cabbage (about 5 cups), shredded
1 cup cooked beets, diced and cooled, or 15-ounce can of diced beets, drained
1 cup or 15-ounce can of pineapple tidbits
2 Tbsp vinegar (or to taste)

need to be a lot of space since the product will shrink during the drying process. A good flow of air is also necessary. The air will absorb all the moisture it can hold; therefore, it's a good idea to force the fresh air to circulate so it removes water vapor and carries moisture away from the food being dried. The force of the circulating air should not be so strong that it blows the dried food off the rack.

There are three methods commonly used for home drying: sun drying, oven drying, and dehydrating (using a cabinet-type dryer with controlled heat and air circulation). Whatever the method used, the prepared food should be placed carefully on trays so that air can circulate around the product and between the trays.

Preparing Food for Drying

Any food that is to be dried will go through the following sequence:

- Sort — Carefully discard any bruised or undesirable product.
- Wash — Clean the product carefully and thoroughly.
- Peel — Slice product according to the recipe.
- Blanch — Prepare all vegetables, with the exception of onions, garlic, horseradish, and herbs, by blanching: drop pieces of vegetables into boiling, salted water; boil for one to two minutes; drain and put in cold water to stop the cooking process. Blanching preserves flavor and color.
- Dry — Spread the product one layer thick on racks and allow it to dry.

If possible, gather the vegetables early in the morning and start the drying process as soon as possible.

ASCORBIC ACID

Pure crystalline ascorbic acid is a good antioxidant, which makes it a great flavor preservative, but it is sometimes difficult to find. It is a good item to store. Look for it in drugstores or from chemical companies.

For apples, dissolve 2½ teaspoons of crystalline ascorbic acid in each cup of cold water. For peaches, apricots, and pears, dissolve one teaspoon of ascorbic acid in each cup of cold water. One cup of solution will treat about five quarts of cut fruit.

As the fruit is prepared (peeled, diced, sliced, etc.), place it in a large (one gallon) plastic bag. Add the ascorbic acid solution. Shake thoroughly so that all parts of the fruit are coated with the solution. Drain well.

Ascorbic acid powders contain ascorbic acid and are found in grocery stores for use on "fresh fruit." They do not work as effectively as pure ascorbic acid. Follow the directions on the package.

Fruit Juice Dips

Soaking fruits in a fruit juice that naturally contains ascorbic acid will help keep the natural color and prevent further darkening. The juice will also add its flavor to the product. Soak the fruit pieces three to five minutes, remove, and drain well. Only use the juice twice before replacing. (You can safely consume the used juice.) Use orange, grapefruit, lemon, lime, or pineapple juice.

Vitamin C Tablets

Crush 500 mg vitamin C tablets to a powder and mix one teaspoon of the powder with one quart of water. Vitamin C tablets contain carriers that do not dissolve as well as pure crystalline ascorbic acid, so there may be harmless white particles floating on the solution. Soak the fruit in the solution for three to five minutes.

Other Treatments

Saline: Soak sliced fresh produce in a saltwater solution (four to six tablespoons salt to one gallon water) for ten minutes.

Honey dip: Dissolve ½ cup sugar in 1½ cups boiling water. Add ½ cup honey. Dip fruit in small batches. Allow fruit to soak three to five minutes. Remove with a slotted spoon and drain.

Honey lemon dip: Slightly heat and dissolve 1½ cup of honey with the juice of one lemon in ½ cup of water. Dip the fruit, then spread on drying trays.

Hot syrup: Combine one cup each of corn syrup, sugar, and water. Bring to a boil. Add fruit. Simmer 10 to 15 minutes. Drain well. Lift fruit gently from the pan and place it on trays that have been sprayed with oil to prevent the fruit from sticking. Syrup dip will increase the drying time. The final product is like a candied fruit.

Sun Drying

There are many excellent designs for solar dryers — we have a number of them pictured on the Great Change website. They all share some common

Pineapple-Beet cont.

A carbon-steel or Chinese-made cast-iron wok must be heated on high heat until a faint wisp of smoke rises. You can test the "Wok Hay" (breath of wok) by flicking a bead of water into the pan; if it vaporizes within a second or two, the wok is hot enough. Quickly turn off the heat, swirl in the oil, and then return the heat to high. This prevents the oil from smoking. Swirl in ginger and garlic and quickly add onion, watercress, basil, salt, and pepper. Stir-fry until watercress wilts. Turn into a bowl and toss with the cabbage, beets, pineapple, and vinegar. Serve at room temperature. Wash the wok with hot water and a soft sponge. Dry over low heat for 1 to 2 minutes. This keeps the wok cured, unlikely to rust, and ready to use.

Difficulty

Crazing

Some fruits (such as prunes, plums, cranberries, blueberries, and grapes) have a natural protective wax coating. If they are to be dried whole, it is best to pretreat these fruits by dipping them in boiling water for 15 to 60 seconds (according to the size and toughness of the skin) and then immediately dipping them in cold water. This process crazes the wax coating on the skin and allows the moisture to escape, thus speeding the drying time. Unlike blanching, it is not desirable to have the heat penetrate to the center of the product.

features: a large, flat, transparent or translucent surface aimed toward the sun; a chamber where air is heated; and a place where the food sits on racks as the hot air flows past. Good designs have good heating, good airflow, insulation to keep heat from being lost from the drying chamber, and easy access to put the food in and take it out. The ability to move the dryer easily may also be a design advantage because it needs to be oriented to the sun, and you may need to take it out of the weather when it is not in use.

Sun drying requires temperatures of 98°F or above. You should have a good thermometer to ensure your product is at the proper temperature.

To sun-dry fruit: After fruit has been treated, place it, one layer deep, on trays. You can speed up the drying time by ensuring there is air circulation below as well as above the fruit.

Place the trays in direct sun and turn the fruit occasionally. A light covering of cheesecloth or a screen suspended above the food will protect it from insects. If the trays are on a table, place the table legs in cans of water to prevent insects from crawling up into the food.

Several days in direct sun are sufficient to make fruit about two-thirds dry. At this stage, stack the trays in the shade where there is good air circulation and continue drying until the fruit is leathery.

To sun-dry vegetables: Spread vegetables in a thin layer on trays. Place the trays in direct sun and turn the pieces occasionally. Too much direct sun on vegetables can cause sunburn or scorching. Drying can be completed in the shade.

Beans and peas that are allowed to dry on the vine need to undergo a pasteurization process for insect control. Freeze the dried product for 48 hours or spread it one layer thick on a tray and heat in a 150°F oven for 30 minutes.

To sun-dry meat: It's difficult to sun-dry meat as rapidly as necessary to avoid food poisoning, so I'd recommend using a dehydrator or oven instead. Only sun-dry meats that have been treated with curing salts containing nitrates and/or nitrites. Cover meat with suspended cheesecloth or mesh to keep the flies off.

Air Drying

Air drying is an alternative to sun drying for such products as herbs and chili peppers. The material is tied into bunches or strung on a string and suspended out of the sun until dry. This can be in a shady porch, shed, or corner of the kitchen. Enclosing herbs in a paper bag protects them from dust and other pollutants. Some herbs can be dried simply by spreading them on a dishtowel or tray and leaving them on the counter for two or three days.

Using a Dehydrator

Dehydrators with thermostatic-controlled heat and forced air circulation are available from a number of commercial sources. They can also be constructed from a variety of materials available to the home carpenter. Dehydrators require an enclosed cabinet, a controlled source of heat, forced air to carry away the moisture, and venting.

Place a thermometer on one of the shelves inside your working dehydrator. Desirable dryer temperatures are 140°F to 160°F, and the dryer's

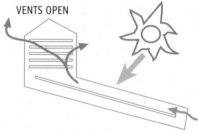

VENTS CLOSED

VENTS OPEN

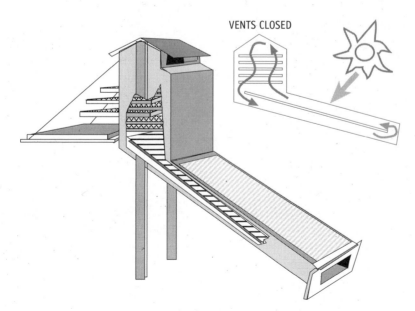

Solar food dehydrater. You can control airflow through a simple solar dryer to speed or slow drying depending on the climate and the type of food being cured. Warm air rises as it is heated under a clear fiberglass or glass panel, passing through drying racks and exiting through upper vents.

DISHES

SPICED SEITAN WITH BUTTERED LEEKS

Serves 4

Seitan
2 cups gluten flour
1 tsp garlic powder
1 tsp ground ginger
Pinch chili powder
Pinch caraway seed
1 tsp liquid smoke
1¼ cups water or vegetable stock
3 Tbsp light tamari or shoyu
1 to 3 tsp toasted sesame oil (optional)

Broth
4 cups water
¼ cup tamari or soy sauce
3-inch piece of kombu
3 to 4 slices ginger (optional)
½ cup nutritional yeast

Leeks
1 large or 2 small leeks (2 cups sliced), thinly sliced lengthwise, white and light green parts only
4 Tbsp unsalted butter
2 tsp fresh lemon juice
2 Tbsp coarsely chopped tarragon
Pinch chervil
Pinch dill
Pinch marjoram

Seitan
Mix dry ingredients. Mix liquids and whisk into dry mixture. When it forms a dough, knead it until very stiff. Let the dough rest 2 to 5 minutes, then knead it a few more times. Let it rest another 15 minutes before proceeding. Cut dough into 6 to 8 pieces and stretch into half-inch-thick cutlets.

controls to adjust temperature should be accurate. It is vital that the temperature inside the dehydrator be uniform if you wish to avoid having to rotate shelves during the drying procedure. You can check temperature uniformity by measuring the temperature at the front and back, top and bottom of the dehydrator.

The airflow through the dehydrator is also important. Dehydrator designs vary, but all will have an air intake and exhaust. The air intake is frequently on the bottom or back and the exhaust on the top or front of the dehydrator. With the dehydrator turned on, light a match or a candle, hold it in the outflow of air, and slowly move it toward the dehydrator. The airflow should blow it out at two to four feet from the exit port.

Oven Drying

Oven drying is harder to control than drying with a dehydrator; however, some products can be successfully dried in the oven. It typically takes two to three times longer than using a dehydrator. Thus, the oven is not as efficient and uses more energy.

Set the oven at the lowest setting, preferably around 150°F, and leave the door open two to three inches (block open if necessary). Position a small fan to the side of the oven door, blowing inward, to help remove moist air. *Caution: This can be hazardous in a home with small children.* many convection ovens already have a built-in fan system.

Fruit Leathers

Fruit leathers provide nourishing snacks and are easy to prepare. This product can be made by pureeing fruit, either fresh or a canned product that has been drained.

Follow these steps to make leathers:

1. Wash fresh fruit and peel if desired. Remove pits and seeds. Slice or cube if the fruit is large.

2. Make a puree from the desired fruit. You can use a blender or food processor for fresh or precooked fruit. If you are using a blender for fresh fruit, puree the fruit first and then bring the puree to a boil while stirring continuously. If you are using a food mill or potato masher, it is best to cook the fresh fruit with a small amount of water in a covered pan until it is tender and then puree it. The heat process will deactivate enzymes that can cause the leather to discolor.
   Canned fruit does not need to be heated, but it should be well drained.

The pureed product can be lightly sweetened if desired. Heavily sweetened fruits will remain sticky and will not dry well.

3. Spread the puree in a thin layer on a plastic film. The plastic film can be on a cookie sheet, a pizza pan, an oven-safe dinner plate, or some dehydrator racks. Make sure that the plastic sheet edges do not fold over and cover any of the puree. The puree should be about ¼ inch deep.

4. Dry the leather in a dehydrator or oven. The leather is adequately dried when you can peel it from the plastic. The dried product should have a bright translucent appearance, chewy texture, and a good fruit flavor.

5. Store leathers by rolling them up while they are still on the film and placing them in a glass jar with a tight lid or in a plastic bag. They will retain their color and flavor for several months at room temperature, but you can extend storage life by refrigerating or freezing them.

How to Vacuum-Pack Dried Produce

Fill canning jars with dried fruit or leathers. With the lid lightly screwed down, place the jars in a 325°F oven for 15 minutes. Remove the jars from the oven and tighten the lids. Test the lids on the dried fruit after the jars have cooled to ensure that you do have a vacuum seal. Never vacuum-pack your dried vegetables unless you know they are truly dry, either by drying to a brittle stage or by calculation (vegetables should be dried to 90 percent solids level).

Conditioning or Curing Dried Foods

Pieces of food taken from the drying trays are not always uniformly dry. To condition them, place cooled dried fruit loosely in large plastic or glass containers until they are about two-thirds full. Cover with a cloth and store in a warm, dry, well-ventilated place. Stir and feel the food every day for a week. If there is evidence of moisture, return the food to the dryer. The food can be left this way for one to two weeks. It assures an even distribution of moisture and reduces the chance of the product's spoiling.

If you dried the product to a calculated final solids content, you can package without the conditioning step. Variations in moisture content will equalize between the pieces in the package.

Foods exposed to insects before or during the drying process should be pasteurized to destroy insect eggs. Preheat oven to 175°F. Spread the food loosely, not more than one inch deep, on trays. Do not put more than two trays in the oven at once. Heat brittle, dried vegetables for 10

Spiced Seitan cont.

Broth

Combine broth ingredients except nutritional yeast in a large saucepan or wok and bring to a low boil. Rub both sides of the cutlets with nutritional yeast and add cutlets to broth. Reserve remaining nutritional yeast rub. Reduce heat to barely simmer, covered, for 30 minutes.

Leeks

Fresh leeks may have a surprising amount of dirt in their tightly rolled leaves. After trimming, slice each leek end to end and rinse, gently separating leaves to dislodge dirt. If you chill them for a few days after they are picked, they will soften and gain flavor. Add leeks and half of the butter to the broth with the cutlets and simmer over medium heat until leeks are tender, about 8 minutes. Remove the cutlets and reserve them on a warm platter. Increase the heat under the leeks to high and stir in lemon juice, remaining butter, nutritional yeast, and spices. Do not boil. Remove any large pieces of kombu or ginger. Pour the leeks and broth over the cutlets and serve.

Difficulty

DISHES

BROCCOLI ALMONDINE
Serves 8

4 tsp olive oil, divided
¼ tsp crushed red pepper
3 cloves garlic, minced
1 cup diced onions or
½ cup scallions or ¼ cup ramps
2 cups (1 pound) sliced baby
carrots
8 cups broccoli florets
1 cup stock
1½ tsp shoyu
2½ Tbsp chopped fresh dill or 1
tsp dried dill
½ cup nutritional yeast
1 Tbsp cornstarch or flour of
any kind
½ cup soymilk
½ cup slivered almonds
3 Tbsp lemon juice
½ tsp cider vinegar

Add 2 tsp oil and crushed red
pepper to a heated iron skillet and
simmer for 1 minute. Add garlic,
onions, and carrots. Sauté for 3
minutes; add broccoli and cook for
4 minutes more, stirring
occasionally. Add stock, reduce
heat to low, and add shoyu and
dill. Stir in half of the nutritional
yeast. Make a paste of remaining
yeast, cornstarch, and soymilk, and
add to pan with almonds. Cook for
3 minutes, stirring in 2 tsp olive
oil, lemon juice, and cider vinegar,
and season with shoyu to taste.
Remove from heat and keep warm
until ready to serve.

Difficulty
🐓🐓🐓🐓

minutes; heat fruits 15 minutes. Oven pasteurizing results in additional loss of vitamins and may scorch food.

Freezer method: Seal dried food in heavy freezer containers (bags or boxes). Freeze for 48 hours to kill insects and insect eggs. Remove and let the product reach room temperature before packaging for permanent storage.

> *From the point of view of*
> *Buddhist economics, production*
> *from local resources for local needs is the*
> *most rational way of economic life, while depend-*
> *ence on imports from afar and the consequent need to*
> *produce for export to unknown and distant peoples is*
> *highly uneconomic and justifiable only in exceptional cases*
> *and on a small scale.*
>
> — E.F. Schumacher, 1973

Staples and Other Foods

Many staples and canned goods have a long shelf life. Always buy the newest product or batch on the store shelf. Buy fresh-looking packages and avoid dusty, rusty, or old-looking packages. Never purchase dented or bulging cans.

Cereals and Pasta

Edible grains have been found in ancient tombs, but you may have encountered small insects in grains that were purchased fairly recently. One way to insure a longer shelf life is to freeze the grain as soon as it is purchased. Leaving it in the freezer for just one day will kill the tiny, invisible eggs of insects so they cannot hatch when the grain remains on the pantry shelf for a year or more. This also works for organic nuts, legumes, and other pest-prone foodstuffs.

In addition to rice, cornmeal, and oatmeal, consider having other grains on hand. Couscous, bulgur, kasha, millet, and buckwheat groats will add variety to your menus and require little time or water to cook. Just pour a hot liquid (water, bouillon, fruit juice) over the tiny grains and let stand for 15 minutes. Bulgur wheat needs to stand for about one hour after hot water is added. For kasha or buckwheat groats, cook in twice as much water for 15 minutes.

A can or jar of popcorn in its original container will keep for three years in a dry basement; in a box or package, it keeps three months.

Whole-wheat flour has a short shelf life ranging from a few weeks to a few months. Enriched white flour in a rigid container will keep for one year in a dry basement. To restore food value to white flour, add one tablespoon nutritional yeast, one tablespoon bran, and one tablespoon dried milk to each cup of flour when preparing breads or gravies.

Store dry goods in their original paper or plastic containers, packed into rigid mouse-proof containers. Store in a dry pantry, basement, or closet away from heat and light.

Rice

Rice is a versatile, economical food for family meals. It is a good source of energy and can supply necessary vitamins and minerals for the diet. There are 7,000 varieties of rice produced in the world, but one need only be aware that there are generally three different lengths of rice grain and five different types.

Long grain rice is distinguished because its length is four to five times its width. The grains are clear and translucent, and they remain distinct and separate after cooking. Medium grain rice is about three times as long as it is wide. This type is less expensive than long grain rice due to the fact that it requires a shorter growing season and produces a higher yield per acre. It is also easier to mill than the long-grained variety. Short grain rice is only one and a half to two times as long as it is wide. It is generally the least expensive of the three lengths.

Because B vitamins are added to rice in the form of powder, much of the valuable nutrients are lost if the product is not handled properly.

- Except where a recipe calls for it, or when the rice is imported in loose bulk, do not wash rice before cooking or rinse it after cooking. Rice is one of the most sanitary foods. Nutrients on the surface of the rice are washed away if it is washed or rinsed before cooking.

- Do not use too much water when cooking rice. Any water drained off means wasted food value. Too much water makes soggy rice. Too little water results in a dry product.

- Do not peek when cooking rice. Lifting the lid lets out steam and lowers the temperature.

- Do not stir rice after it comes to a boil. This breaks up the grains, which makes rice gummy.

Cooking Times of Rice			
Rice	Water*	Salt	Cooking Time
Brown	4 to 6	2½ tsp	45 min
White	2	1 tsp	14 min
Parboil	2¼ tsp	1 tsp	20 min
Instant	1	½ tsp	soak in hot water
* cups of water per 1 cup of rice			

DISHES

CHILLED HACHIWARI

Serves 4

12 ounces dry hachiwari soba noodles (80 percent buckwheat)
Dash of sea salt
1 cup instant dashi (kelp and bonito broth), prepared according to package instructions. Substituting a kelp broth makes this recipe vegan.
3 ounces enoki mushrooms
½ cup shoyu
1 Tbsp rice vinegar
¼ cup mirin
1 sheet nori, toasted lightly and flaked
¼ cup finely sliced scallions, for garnish
¼ cup finely grated daikon, for garnish
Wasabi paste

Noodles

Bring a large pot of water to a boil, add salt and noodles, and reduce heat to medium. When the water returns to a boil, stir the noodles with chopsticks or fork and add about ¾ cup cold water. When the water returns to a boil, add more cold water and repeat this process one more time. Cook until noodles are al dente, 6 to 8 minutes. Drain and rinse under cold running water, running your fingers through the noodles to untangle them. Drain noodles on a paper towel or cut brown paper bag and refrigerate, covered, until they are cool. If the noodles clump together, rinse and dry again.

- Do not leave rice in the pan in which it is cooked for more than five to ten minutes or the cooked rice will pack.

Beans

Canned beans are easy to use. You only have to heat them, or you can take them right from the can for salads. Dried beans need to be sorted, with shriveled and spotted beans removed, then the good beans washed and soaked. They can be slow-cooked in a Dutch oven over a fireplace or woodstove or in a pressure cooker.

A pressure cooker will save time and energy in cooking beans. Never fill the cooker more than about one-third of its capacity to allow room

Cooking Times of Beans				
Bean	Soaked, open-kettle	No soak & pressure cook	Soak & pressure cook	Yields per 2 cups dry beans
adzuki	30 min	15 min	5-10 min	6⅔
anasazi	60 min	25 min	15 min	5
black	90 min	30-35 min	20 min	5
black-eyed peas	25 min	10 min	5-8 min	4¾
garbanzo	4 hr 25 min	35 min	25 min	5
Great Northern	90 min	25 min	20 min	5
kidney	35-40 min	30 min	15-20 min	4½
lentil, brown*	20-25 min	**	**	5
lentil, orange*	15-20 min	**	**	3⅓
lima, baby	30 min	10-15 min	8 min	4
navy	35-40 min	22 min	15 min	5
pinto	90 min	35-40 min	20-25 min	5
soybeans	**	60 min	45 min	4
split peas*	75-90 min	7 min	**	4

* It is not necessary to presoak lentils and split peas
** Do not use this method for this variety of beans

This table courtesy of Barb Bloomfield, author of Fabulous Beans *(Summertown, TN: The Book Publishing Company, 1994).*

for expansion and foaming. You can minimize foaming by adding one tablespoon of oil. Approximate cooking time is 20 minutes at 10 pounds of pressure or 10 minutes at 15 pounds of pressure. Never pressure-cook split peas or lentils.

Textured Vegetable Protein

Textured vegetable protein or TVP is made from soybeans after the oil is extracted. It's available in granules or chunks in many different flavors from the Mail Order Catalog for Healthy Eating (www.healthy-eating.com, 800-695-2241). Pour 7-8 cups of hot water over one cup of granules to reconstitute, then use in recipes as you'd use ground meat. It has a long shelf life.

Eggs

Water glass is a liquid sodium silicate. One gallon bucket of pure water glass (about $20 worth) will preserve 50 dozen eggs, keeping them fresh for months. These directions are from *The Boston Cooking School Cook Book* by Fannie Farmer, 1886:

Mix one part water glass with ten parts cooled, boiled water and pour into a large stone crock. Wipe fresh eggs with a flannel cloth and place them in the solution (eggs should be covered by at least two inches of the mixture). Cover the crock and store it in a cool, dry place.

When eggs come from the chicken, they are coated with a light layer of a natural sealing agent called "bloom." A good wash may make a batch of eggs look more attractive, but it removes this natural protective coating, leaving the eggs more vulnerable to aging and attack by the air and bacteria. If eggs with a natural bloom are kept at 35°F to 40°F, they smell good, taste good, have a good texture, and seem almost fresh, even after many months.

Dried Milk

Regular and instant nonfat dry milk are made from skim milk. The milk is dried by spraying it into hot air. Instant milk is regular milk that has been further processed so it clumps together. This results in a product that is easier to reconstitute with water than is regular nonfat dry milk. They both have the same nutrient composition. Regular nonfat dry milk is more compact and will require less storage space. The most common type of dried milk to be found in grocery stores is instant nonfat dry milk. Dried whole milk will not store as well as nonfat dry milk.

Chilled Hachiwari cont.

Dipping Sauce
In a small saucepan, combine the dashi, enoki, shoyu, rice vinegar, and mirin and bring to a simmer. Remove from the heat and let stand 5 minutes, then strain the sauce into a serving bowl, cool, and chill. Enoki can be reserved or offered as a garnish. Serve soba in bowls, sprinkling each with toasted nori. Serve garnishes and individual small bowls of the dipping sauce on the side.

Difficulty

In any recipe calling for milk, simply add the dry milk to other dry ingredients. Sift to blend, then substitute water for the amount of milk called for in the recipe.

Other Vegetables and Fruits

Dig potatoes when the vines die and quickly set them out in a single layer in a dark storage area. Any light will turn them green, and solanine, a potentially toxic alkaloid, develops in the same conditions as the green chlorophyll. The bitter taste associated with greened potatoes is caused by solanine, not chlorophyll. The amount of greening is not a direct measure of its solanine, but bitterness is, so pay attention to taste. Rotten potatoes must be culled as soon as decay appears or they will spoil their neighbors.

Turnips and beets can go directly to the root cellar with their tops removed and roots left on.

Pull and dry onions and garlic, hanging them in an airy place until late fall and then moving them to a cool, dry place indoors. A root cellar may be too damp for onions.

Winter squash and pumpkins should also be moved indoors when outdoor temperatures approach freezing. Jerusalem artichokes keep well in the root cellar.

Take apples to the root cellar in the fall, but check them regularly for rot, which can spread quickly to a whole batch. Don't store apples with onions; the gases given off by the onions can spoil the apples.

To keep vegetables fresh in higher latitudes, you can try the method used by Jan and Judy Speyers on their farm near Prince George, BC (Zone 2). After the first killing frost, they dig up their carrots, beets, parsnips, turnips, and potatoes and pack the most perfect, unblemished ones into mesh onion bags. They wrap cabbages and brussels sprouts in newspaper. Then they dig trenches in the garden, drop the packed and wrapped veggies into the trenches, cover them with soil and two feet of leaves, and mark the spot with sticks that are longer than the depth of coming snows. Throughout the winter, whenever they need more for the kitchen, they dig up a cache and bring in a sack.

I saw one lady that put storage under almost anything. She even had food in her walls. She took the sheetrock off and used the 2 x 4s for shelves.

— C.L. Rose, 2004

Containers

Food should only be stored in food-grade containers. A food-grade container is one that will not transfer non-food chemicals into the food and that contains no chemicals hazardous to human health.

Some good examples of containers *not* approved for food use are trash or garbage bags, industrial plastics, and fiber barrels that have been used for non-food purposes. Do not risk contaminating your stored food with non-food chemicals that could be hazardous to your health.

Plastic films and containers of food-grade quality are made from polycarbonate, polyethylene, and polyester. They differ in their density, strength, and barrier properties. To increase their barrier properties, which keep moisture and oxygen away from the food, some films have been laminated. Laminated plastics may include a metallic layer that will further increase their barrier properties. Military food packaged in metalized polyester or metallized polyethylene wrap has a long shelf life (five years) if it is kept cool.

Glass jars, especially if they have tight-fitting lids and no open crevices or seams, are the storage containers of choice. Tin cans can rust or leak toxic solders into their contents. Besides being made from fossil fuels, plastics can, over extended time, leach estrogen-altering chemicals into food. Glass jars are long-lasting, sterile, and have an advantage over tin because you can see what's in them.

When you have identified safe packaging materials, there are a few other things to keep in mind in terms of size and durability. Containers for storing dry foods such as wheat, beans, rice, oatmeal, and cornmeal should have a maximum of 20- to 25-pound capacity. These are sizes that can be moved easily by one adult. More importantly, these smaller amounts of food will be used up in a relatively short period of time, thus reducing the chance for contamination or infestation by insects. Smaller containers allow you to use the food without exposing large quantities to the environment. Containers should be filled as full as possible without crushing the food.

Metal cans used in the canning industry are designed to last a few years. Loss of canned foods usually occurs due to can breakdown rather than extensive deterioration of the food under normal storage conditions. For example, older tinned tomato products can wear down the enamel that coats the inside of the tin, producing hydrogen. This will cause the can to swell, and there will be a hissing noise, or a release of gas, when it is opened. Do not use the contents of any suspicious can. If the

DISHES

SUN-DRIED TOMATO QUICHE

This is a recipe that depends greatly on the quality of the tofu. Fresh or water-packed silken tofu creates a light creamy quiche, while packaged firm tofu gives a harder quiche.

Serves 8

Pastry dough
The pastry dough is better if made a day in advance and kept in the refrigerator. Warm the dough to room temperature before filling.

2 cups pastry flour
⅓ cup rolled oats
¼ tsp sea salt
⅓ cup tofu
1 Tbsp oil
1 Tbsp brown rice syrup or similar syrup
⅓ cup cold water

Filling
One 3-ounce package dry-packed sun-dried tomatoes
1 cup hot water
½ cup soymilk
2 Tbsp lemon juice
2 tsp oil
¼ tsp crushed red peppers
4 cloves garlic, minced
1 large shallot or ½ cup of chives, minced
½ cup sliced black olives
2 Tbsp chopped fresh basil leaves
1 pound silken tofu
3 Tbsp mild white miso
¼ cup dry sherry or apple cider
⅓ cup potato flakes
⅓ cup nutritional yeast
¼ tsp turmeric
1 tsp dried basil

product spurts out when the can is opened, it indicates that the contents are under pressure due to a buildup of gas, which could mean fermentation is taking place.

Sealed number 10 cans are popular containers for dehydrated foods, mainly due to their size, convenience, and the fact that they allow minimal exposure of the foods to the environment.

Glass jars, which are popular among home canners, are inert compared to metal cans (in other words, there is less chance of a reaction occurring between the metal and the food), but they are less shock-resistant. Cardboard boxes, such as the original containers for glass jars, make excellent storage containers for jars of fruit since they exclude light and effectively separate individual jars to prevent breakage.

Flexible plastic containers last longer and are more durable if placed inside a rigid container. There is limited information on flexible plastic containers' ability to protect food from insect infestations. If the food is insect-free to begin with, and if the packages are properly sealed, they should prove satisfactory.

One trick you can use to increase the shelf life of dry foods in packages is to freeze them when you have prepared them or brought them home from the grocery store. Make space in your freezer to store rice, flours, dried milk, cereals, beans, and other dry goods temporarily. One to two days of freezing will kill any insect eggs that were left in the product when it was packaged by the manufacturer. Keep rotating new purchases into the freezer space reserved for packaged foods.

It's usually not a good idea to freeze canned products. When the food expands during freezing, it may rupture metal, break glass, or break the seal and allow the food to be contaminated. This could pose a serious safety risk when the food thaws. Once canned goods have thawed, do not continue storing them. It is unsafe to consume canned goods that have thawed and been refrozen several times.

Do not store non-food household chemicals like bleach and cleaning solutions in the same area with food. Volatile chemical compounds can be transferred to the food and affect the flavor and odor. These chemicals should be stored in a separate area where children do not have access to them.

Good housekeeping helps prevent insect infestations. To prevent or at least minimize insect infestations in stored food products, it is ideal to store them in a location with a temperature between 35°F and 45°F. Anything below 65°F will be helpful.

Bay leaves will also deter insects. Buy an ounce of dried bay leaves at a health food store, and as soon as you open a package of flour or grain, place one or two bay leaves in the package. Scatter extra leaves on pantry shelves. Freshen leaves monthly.

Fumigation with Dry Ice

At approximately 75 cents per pound, dry ice is a reasonably priced and efficient method of fumigating. However, it does require careful handling. Take an insulated cooler lined with newspaper when you pick up the dry ice, and wear heavy gloves when handling it.

To fumigate home-stored wheat or similar products, spread about two ounces of crushed dry ice on three or four inches of grain in the bottom of a five-gallon container, then add the remaining grain to the container until it is at the desired depth. (If fumigating large quantities, use 14 ounces of dry ice for 100 pounds of grain or one pound of dry ice for each 30 gallons of stored grain.) Replace the lid on the container but leave it slightly ajar.

Since the fumes from vaporizing dry ice are heavier than air, they should readily replace the existing air in the container. Allow sufficient time (about 30 minutes, depending on container size) for the dry ice to evaporate (vaporize) before closing the lid, but don't close it tightly until the dry ice has pretty well vaporized and has replaced the regular air. Then it can be placed firmly on the container and sealed. Should pressure cause the container to bulge after the lid has been put in place, cautiously remove the lid, keep it off for a few minutes, and then replace it. Carbon dioxide will stay in the container for some time provided the container lid is tight. When practical, follow the above procedure in a dry atmosphere to reduce the condensation of moisture in the bottom of the can.

Dry ice tends to control most adult and larval insects present, but probably will not destroy all the eggs or pupae. If a tight-fitting lid is placed firmly on the container after the dry ice has vaporized, it may keep enough carbon dioxide inside to destroy some of the eggs and pupae. After two to three weeks, you may want to fumigate again with dry ice to destroy adult insects that have matured from the surviving eggs and pupae. If properly done, these two treatments should suffice. Yearly treatments are not necessary unless it's obvious you have an infestation.

Quiche cont.

Pastry dough

Lightly coat deep-dish pie plate with oil. Process flour, oats, and salt until well mixed. Add tofu, oil, and rice syrup and blend. Slowly add cold water and process until mixture comes together in a ball. Turn onto lightly floured surface. Sprinkle dough with flour and roll out to ⅛- to ¼-inch thickness. Press into pan and trim edges, leaving a 1-inch overlap. Using thumb and forefinger, press decorative edge. Refrigerate.

Filling

Preheat oven to 375°F. Combine tomatoes and hot water in a small bowl and set aside. Combine soymilk and lemon juice in separate bowl and set aside. Add oil and crushed red peppers to a large hot iron skillet and simmer over medium-high heat for about 1 minute. Add garlic and shallot and sauté 3 minutes until transparent or beginning to brown. Reserving soaking liquid, add tomatoes, olives, and basil to pan. Reduce heat to medium-low and simmer 5 minutes, stirring occasionally. Blend tofu until smooth. While processing tofu, add miso, sherry, soymilk-lemon juice mixture, potato flakes, yeast, and turmeric. Spoon mixture into pie shell and sprinkle with dried basil. Bake 35 minutes or until lightly browned. Remove from oven and let stand 15 minutes. Serve lukewarm.

Difficulty

DISHES

MUSHROOM LATKES
Serves 8

4 cups peeled and quartered baking potatoes (about 4 medium)
1 medium-sized onion
2 medium shiitake mushrooms, fresh or rehydrated
½ pound tofu
¼ cup nutritional yeast
2½ Tbsp flour
2 Tbsp cornmeal
1 Tbsp flaxseed meal
1 tsp aluminum-free baking powder
1 tsp sea salt or kosher salt
½ cup soymilk
½ cup mashed potato flakes
3 Tbsp olive oil plus additional oil for sautéing
1 tsp Italian seasoning
Dash of shoyu

Garnish
Applesauce
Cinnamon
Sour cream

Preheat oven to 200°F. Grate potatoes using coarse holes of hand grater and press out excess moisture. Dice onion; mix with potatoes in large bowl. Set aside. If mushrooms need to be rehydrated, immerse them completely in warm water and let stand 60 minutes. Reserve the liquid for latke filling, gravies, or soups. Stem and cut shiitake mushrooms into narrow slices across cap. Halve the slices and set aside. Blend tofu with yeast, flour, cornmeal, flaxseed meal, baking powder, and salt. Gradually add soymilk and pureé. Add tofu

Creating Good Storage

Storing food properly requires that you pay attention to several factors:

- Temperature
- Moisture
- Air circulation
- Light
- Insect and pathogen paths

Temperature is very important. Generally speaking, the warmer your storage location, the shorter the shelf life of the food being stored. A recording thermometer will not only show you the current temperature, but will also track the highest and lowest temperature recorded in that location until you reset it. Place one of these thermometers in a potential storage area, record the temperature range after 24 hours, and then try another place.

Potential storage areas in your home include the basement, attic, garage, closet shelves, or under beds and tables. Space under a deck or porch might work with some additional protection such as bales of straw or fencing to keep animals away.

Refrigeration

Most refrigerators are electric. Gas-powered models do exist, but they tend to be quite a bit more expensive. The Danby Gas Refrigerator and Freezer, made in Brazil, costs 1,800 reais (US$840). The Norcold AC/LP, made in Sweden, costs 8,800 kroner (US$1,120) but runs on either gas or electricity. A large gas refrigerator uses about 1,550 BTU/hr, or one gallon of propane every three days.

Under average pre-crisis conditions, it costs about $75 per year to power a standard electric refrigerator. Running a gas refrigerator costs about $150 per year. There is no telling how high the price of propane and liquid natural gas may rise in the future, but alternative fuels, such as homemade biogas, will work in these refrigerators. Still, many people are finding that it makes economic sense to switch to solar-electric refrigerators like the SunFrost, which runs on either 12 or 24 volts. A SunFrost running without problems is cheaper than a comparable electric fridge over 16 years, or a comparable gas refrigerator over 8 years, at pre-crisis prices.

Keeping a long-term supply of food in storage is a wise policy from both economic and environmental standpoints. It is a religious duty for

If the electricity goes off ...

FIRST, use perishable food and foods from the refrigerator.

THEN use the foods from the freezer. To minimize the number of times you open the freezer, post a list of contents on the freezer door. In a well-filled, well-insulated freezer, foods will usually still have ice crystals in their centers (meaning foods are safe to eat) for at least three days.

FINALLY, begin to use nonperishable foods and staples.

some people. If food is to be stored longer than two years, it makes economic sense to buy from suppliers of long-term storable food (dehydrated and vacuum and gas packed). Start paying attention now to the shelf life of foods you normally purchase and eat: date packages, boxes, or tins; rotate supplies to maintain freshness; and keep a record. How long does a five-pound bag of flour last in your house? Sugar? A carton of oatmeal? A pint of olive oil? Make shopping lists, save them for a month, and add up the quantities.

Planning What Foods to Store

1. Write a list of frequently eaten dishes or a list of favorite meals.
2. Go back over the list and add foods needed to balance meals.
3. Inventory food you have on hand.
4. Be a good shopper as you replace and add to inventory.
5. Store foods your family likes.

Food Planning for 6 Weeks of Storage				
Product	Number of times served	Serving size	One person	Four persons
Fruit, tomatoes	7/wk	1 cup	10 qt.	40 qt.
Broccoli, squash, spinach, carrots	4/wk	½ cup	3 qt.	12 qt.
Asparagus, peas, cabbage, green beans, corn	7/wk	½ cup	5 qt.	20 qt.

Mushroom Latkes cont.

mixture, potato flakes, and oil to the bowl containing grated potatoes and onion. Mix well. Heat cooking oil in large iron skillet over strong heat and add Italian seasoning and shiitake. Sauté until brown, adding a dash of shoyu at the end. Stir browned shiitake into tofu pureé and return batter to lightly oiled skillet in spoonfuls. Fry latkes 3 minutes on each side, or until they are golden brown with crisp edges. Transfer to baking sheet, cover with foil, and keep warm in oven. Serve hot with cinnamon-sprinkled applesauce and sour cream.

Difficulty

Shelf Life	
Storage Time	**Product**
3 to 5 years:	dried pasta (in a rigid container) Textured Vegetable Protein (TVP) dehydrated potatoes in sealed cans
24 months:	canned vegetables and fruits, white rice, dehydrated potatoes (place boxes or bags in rigid containers), coffee in cans, loose or instant tea (in a jar), sugar, artificial sweeteners vinegar, baking soda, bouillon cubes or granules
18 months:	baking power, confectioner's sugar, jams and jellies, mustard, ketchup, condiments, molasses, hot roll mix, instant coffee, cocoa, tea bags
12 months:	dried beans, peas, lentils, white flour, dried fruits (air & moisture proof packages), honey, nuts in airtight packages, syrups (unopened), dried soup and instant pudding mixes, grits, cornmeal, condensed or evaporated milk (inverted at 2-month intervals), cold breakfast cereals (unopened)
6 to 12 months:	fresh food in ventilated boxes in a moderately dry basement at 35 to 60°F, gravy and sauce mixes, dried vegetables, instant potatoes, pancake mix, crackers, oatmeal, biscuit, brownie and cake mixes, rice mixes, brown rice, canned fruit juices,

6. Store absolute emergency items, too.

7. Consider the food value of items you store.

Shelf Life

Dried products will keep for a year or more if sealed in moisture-proof containers and stored in a cool, dark, dry place. Heat and light have an adverse effect on the quality of dried foods. As mentioned above, the lower the temperature, the longer the shelf life. If you store foods in a garage at an average temperature of 90°F, you should expect a shelf life less than half of what could be obtained at room temperature (60°F to 70°F), which in turn is less than half the shelf life in cold storage (40°F).

Keep a felt-tip marker with your food supplies. As you put groceries away, write the expiration date on the top of the package or can. Also note the date you bought the product, but remember that shelf life is based on the date of manufacture, not the date of purchase. Sometimes you can decode the manufacture date from the packing code on the label. To learn more about packing codes and what they mean, visit the Walton Feed website (www.waltonfeed.com/grain/faqs/vb.html).

Remember: first in, first out (FIFO). Even if a product is not at the end of its shelf life, use it when the need arises and then replace it with a fresher one.

You can extend shelf life up to five times longer by using a vacuum-packing machine such as the Tilia Food Saver (www.foodsaver.jardendirect.com). You can reuse the special plastic bags several times.

Building the Home Storage Area

Find a cool, dark place to store food. This might be the basement, the garage, or a shed out back. Our grandparents always had a root cellar, and it made good sense. Warm and humid climates shorten the shelf life of many items.

You should store food in a place where you can keep the average temperature above 32°F and below 68°F. Remember that the cooler the storage area, the longer your food will retain its quality and nutrients. Avoid spaces that regularly reach temperatures above 68°F, such as the area near an appliance that produces heat or a shelf that is high up in a room or in a building.

The storage area should be dry (less than 15 percent humidity) and adequately ventilated to prevent condensation of moisture on packaging material. It should be large enough that shelves can accommodate all the stored food, with adequate space to keep the area clean. A 9-by-12-foot room with 10-foot ceilings will provide enough space for a family of six to store an 18-month supply of food.

Food should not be stored on the floor. Your lowest shelf should be two to three feet off the floor, especially if you live in a flood-prone area. Design shelves so that you can put in place a simple rotation system that will allow you to use the oldest food first and ensure the newest food is used within its shelf-life period.

When designing and building a food storage area, minimize areas where insects and rodents can hide. Seal all cracks and crevices with steel wool. Eliminate any openings that insects or rodents may use to gain entrance to the storage area. Heat-producing electrical equipment such as a freezer, furnace, or water heater should not be housed in the storage area.

Root Cellars

The main reason for having a root cellar is to keep vegetables from freezing in the winter. The temperature of the Earth ten feet below the surface stays at a constant 55°F. Air movement usually keeps root cellar temperatures between 50°F and 70°F, which is optimal for storing many types of vegetable. Because they are constructed underground, most root cellars will be damp with condensation, especially in tropical or temperate climates with predictable rainfall. For this reason, root cellars may not store some crops — like grains, onions, garlic, and fruit — as well as they store potatoes, squash, cabbages, and carrots.

Do what you can to prevent your cellar from heating up.

- Make sure you locate your root cellar in a place where it will be in the shade throughout the day.
- Use insulation wisely.
- Include an access hatch that opens to the top (hot air rises, cold air falls).
- Build on the side of a hill facing away from the equator.
- Build in the basement of your home.

In high latitudes, it's a good idea to have a second door on a snow-proof side so you don't end up having to search for the hatch door when it is under three feet of snow.

You can borrow coolness from the air. Often the temperature of the night air will be cooler than the air in your cellar. During these times of

Shelf Life continued	
Storage Time	Product
6 to 12 months:	salad oils, salad dressings, nonfat dried milk, brown sugar, hot oat and wheat breakfast cereals
2 months:	cookies (packaged), mayonnaise, pretzels, potato chips and most snacks, dry cheeses (in containers), potatoes (in a ventilated box), carrots, cabbage, beets, sweet potatoes, winter squash, onions (in a net bag or individually wrapped), apples (wrapped individually), oranges, grapefruit, tangerines, lemons, limes

Calculations assume containers are unopened, stored in a dry basement, below 70°F

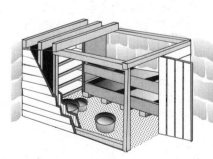

A root cellar.

DISHES

SHIITAKE JOES

This is a very simple and timeless recipe that lends itself to a world of substitution for seasonal and local ingredients. When trying this out recently, I found an old jar of dried peppers marked "2004" that didn't look especially hot. Wrong. The one tiny dried pepper I selected was more than enough heat for a double recipe of these, shared with a dozen friends.

Serves 6

1 cup TVP, can be granulated, chunk, strip, and/or flavored
1 tsp dehydrated onion flakes or ½ medium onion, finely diced
6 rehydrated or fresh shiitake mushrooms, stemmed and diced
1 Tbsp oil
1 Tbsp shoyu
2 tsp chili powder or 1 small chili pepper, finely diced, and 1 tsp cumin
1 6-ounce can of tomato paste and 2 equal portions of water
1¾ cup cooked or 15-ounce can of tomatoes, diced
Salt to taste
2 Tbsp fresh cilantro, chopped finely

Immerse TVP and onion in hot water and let stand 20 to 60 minutes. Bigger, chunk-style TVP should be reconstituted longer or pre-cooked until soft. If mushrooms need to be rehydrated, immerse in warm water and let stand 60 minutes. Reserve the liquid to mix with tomato paste.

the year, open your vents (and perhaps the door, taking precautions to keep pests out) at night when the temperature is dropping below the temperature of the air in your cellar. Close them early in the morning before the outside air warms up. (Don't do this if the temperature is expected to drop below freezing.)

Another important consideration is humidity. In a dry environment, your vegetables will soften and shrivel up. Underground root cellars will generally maintain humidity if they have a dirt floor.

The best root cellars have vents. This is because the vegetables in your cellar give off gases that are conducive to either spoilage or sprouting. For example, apples naturally give off ethylene gas, which makes potatoes sprout prematurely.

The following points are good venting fundamentals:

- Have an inlet vent and an outlet vent.
- The outlet must always be at the highest level in the cellar, and the outlet tube should be flush with the inner wall.
- The inlet should come into the cellar at the bottom. This is easily done if your cellar is built into a hill, and nearly as easily if it is buried in flat ground. Although your inlet vent opens on top of the ground near your outlet vent, the inlet vent pipe must go all the way to the floor before opening into your cellar.
- Keep shelves a couple of inches away from the walls of the cellar. This will promote circulation around the vegetables stored on these shelves. Use rot-resistant or pressure-treated wood.
- To prevent your potatoes from sprouting prematurely, keep your apples above them so the circulating air moves away from the potatoes.
- Have a system in place to close your vents in freezing weather. Something as simple as a big sponge can work for this. If you have very cold winters, you may wish to block off both ends of each vent pipe.

Food Storage Calculator

It's important to remember that most of the recommendations you receive are just that ... recommendations. In the end you need to decide how you will incorporate the recommended foods into your storage plan. The difficult experiences of the early Mormon settlers in Utah endowed church members with good practices for food storage that continue 150 years later. The Mormons provide an online calculator that will help you determine the minimum amount of food you need to store (not including water). It is at www.lds.about.com/library/bl/faq/blcalculator.htm.

Because energy content is the most critical consideration in an emergency food supply, it should be considered first. Dried beans, flour, wheat, rice, sugar, dried fruits or vegetables, pastas, and dried skim milk all provide about 1,600 calories per pound. While 1,600 calories will not adequately meet the energy needs of a hard-working large person, it will quiet hunger pangs for individual members of a family. One pound of dry matter per person per day is a good target volume for food in storage.

Personal actions will clearly depend on your own circumstances. If you are a single person with ample funds and no ties, your choices are different from somebody with a spouse, 2.2 children, a mortgage and a bank account in permanent overdraft. The most important thing to bear in mind is that our present society will not continue for much longer. Ideas of finding a job at 18, marrying, acquiring a house and a family, then retiring at 60 or 70, belong to history and the sooner you accept this, the sooner you can consider what needs to be done.

— Paul Thompson, 2005

Since our emergence as a species, human populations have continually run up against local environmental limits: the inability to find sufficient game, grow enough food, or harvest enough wood has led to sudden collapses in human numbers and in some cases to the disappearance of entire civilizations. Although it may seem that advancing technology and the emergence of an integrated world economy have ended this age-old pattern, they may have simply transferred the problem to the global level.

— Lester R. Brown and Christopher Flavin, 1999

Shiitake Joes cont.

Preheat iron skillet. Add oil and mushrooms and lightly brown. Stir in TVP mix, shoyu, chili powder, tomato paste, and tomatoes. Salt to taste and sprinkle on cilantro. Heat and serve on open-faced biscuits or buns. Substitutions: cooked beans for TVP; potatoes, rice, corn chips, or pasta for buns.

Difficulty

Fallout Shelters

A nice thing about having a root cellar is that it can double as a tornado or fallout shelter. To prepare for this contingency, a few modifications are needed. Nuclear refugees should plan to remain sheltered for at least two weeks and then, depending on ambient radiation readings, work outside for gradually increasing amounts of time (Perhaps four hours a day at three weeks, and so on). The normal work is to sweep or wash fallout into shallow trenches to decontaminate the area. Refugees may have to sleep in the shelter for several months.

**FALLOUT SHELTER
IN THIS CORRIDOR**

Ventilation

Radiation can enter through air passages, so you will need airtight seals around the door and any vents. Put HEPA screens over air intake and exhaust ports to trap particulates. HEPA screens become clogged and ineffectual after extended use, so you may want to wait and slide the filter in when you actually need it. You should store at least one handheld Geiger meter in every shelter.

Sanitation

You can create a basic latrine using a plastic toilet seat that fits on top of a steel, plastic, or fiber drum. You will need plastic bag liners and disinfectant. Don't forget toilet paper. Keep it in plastic or metal storage containers.

Blast and fallout

A one-foot cover of dirt will provide protection from most blast and fallout, but you may need thicker shielding if you live closer to ground zero. Three feet of dirt reduces gamma rays by a factor of 1,024. Radioactive rain may continue for weeks. Remove nearby trees to reduce the fallout that settles on branches and leaves (tall distant trees can provide shade for the shelter when it is used as a root cellar). It won't be possible to cover the door with dirt so you may want to design a sheltered entrance that diverts rain and does not collect windborne fallout.

Other Storage Items

- Potassium iodide (130 mg/day per adult; 65 mg/day per child)
- Food and water (at least a three-week supply)
- Water filters
- Cots and bedding
- Disinfectant
- Medical kit
- Self-protection and survival gear
- Reading material, board games, musical instruments, writing pads
- Communications devices (CB or ham radio, shortwave, cell phone with power sources or chargers)
- Extra clothing, especially foul-weather gear
- Oxygen in tanks
- Alternative energy sources, batteries

There is more information about purchasing meters and designing a fallout shelter at www.thegreatchange.com

Be Prepared

When will we see $6-7 dollar gasoline?
In the unlikely situation nothing untoward happens,
than it could be around the end of the decade. However,
given the likelihood something really bad will happen — an assas-
sination, coup, a civil war, hurricane, major cold snap — then the
real troubles could start at any time.

— Tom Whipple, 2006

ry this experiment: Go to the main electrical breaker box for your home. Turn it off. Do the same for your gas inlet.

Take a few days, maybe longer, and begin the experience of living off the grid.

If it is still light outside, you better get busy, because it is easier to prepare your home for low-energy living when it is not dark. You will need to have candles, oil lamps, or some battery-powered flashlights for evening use.

The first thing you may think to do is visit the refrigerator, but it is not a good idea to stand there with the door open, gaping at the contents. If you do that, you are allowing the interior of the fridge, and its contents, to equalize with the temperature of the room. You might take a quick glance, especially in the freezer, to see what you should plan to eat over the next day or two.

If it is a cold time of year, this will be less of a concern. You can box up the contents and put them outdoors, out of direct sunlight, and they will stay fresh a little longer. But if it is a cold season, you might start

Candle lantern.

wondering how you are going to stay warm overnight. Do you have a sleeping bag? A space heater that doesn't need electricity or gas?

If you draw water from a well with an electric pump, you might want to turn off the water to any flush toilets, find a shovel and dig a pit privy, or get a bucket for indoor use. Save and ration whatever water is still available. That tank behind each toilet probably holds a couple of gallons.

You will need to have a place to prepare and cook food, and some kind of fuel to use for cooking. If you have a camping stove, great, but do you have fuel for it? Do you have a charcoal grill and briquettes? A barbeque?

If you want a hot shower or bath and don't have any fuel with which to boil water, rig a solar collector using a black hose or black container that can hold water. You need to orient it toward strong sunlight early enough in the day to give it time to get good and hot, then move it somewhere it will retain as much of that heat as possible until you use it. An insulated box (like, for instance, an unused refrigerator) would work.

Without central heating, fans, or air-conditioning, you may find the bedroom is not the best place to sleep. Move your bed where the temperature and ventilation are best for you.

I'll stop the description here, but you can see it could suddenly become difficult just to eat, sleep, and be sanitary. This exercise might have been easy for some people, especially rugged outdoorsy types who like to camp, but for those at higher latitudes or altitudes, in cities where you can't bury human wastes in the backyard, or with large families and maybe some special needs, it is not as easy.

Still, you get better with practice. You can go a few days, then a week, then indefinitely if you need to. Your comfort level in this self-imposed state of deprivation rises as your knowledge, skills, and toolkit improve.

Survival really boils down to attitude. It's all mental. People die needlessly because of panic. Panic is the over-magnification of fear. A little fear can be just good old common sense — awareness and caution in a hostile environment. People who have learned to control their fear, maybe though exercises like this one, will control their own destiny.

If you were to go to a wilderness-survival training school, the instruction might vary, but essentially it would begin by teaching you how to react to life-threatening situations by staying calm and keeping your wits about you. It would teach you to assess your needs and your available resources and to devise a strategy to get yourself through in as good a shape as possible. You would learn that you have to set priorities based on a hierarchy of needs. You can't go long without oxygen. You can also die quickly if you are exposed to extreme cold. You need clothes and shelter, then water, then food, usually in that order.

Coping with the end of the oil era is not so very different. It's unlikely that civilized society will collapse abruptly, and the process of change may unfold so gradually that most people hardly notice it. A child born during the transition will quickly develop improvisational skills to use tools and appliances that no longer work the way they did in a era when oil was cheap and abundant. But for many of us, especially the elderly, the change could be disorienting. And when big things don't work well — electric power grids, airlines, governments, currencies — the situation becomes dangerous for the unprepared.

Crashproofing

Energy has always been the basis of cultural complexity and it always will be. The past clarifies potential paths to the future. One often-discussed path is cultural and economic simplicity and lower energy costs. This could come about through the "crash" that many fear — a genuine collapse over a period of one or two generations, with much violence, starvation, and loss of population. The alternative is the "soft landing" that many people hope for — a voluntary change to solar energy and green fuels, energy-conserving technologies, and less overall consumption. This is a utopian alternative that, as suggested above, will come about only if severe, prolonged hardship in industrial nations makes it attractive, and if economic growth and consumerism can be removed from the realm of ideology.

— Joseph A. Tainter, 1996

The first step to becoming a survivor is finding out how vulnerable you are. Take a pad of paper and a pen or pencil. Physically go to every room in your house or apartment. Write down for each room:

- Every appliance and fixture (medical devices, sink, tub, mirror, light, window, heater, fan, vent, etc.) connected to, operated by, or dependent upon fossil fuels
- Everything else in the room (clothes, furniture, towels, medications, toothpaste, toilet brush) supplied by fossil fuels
- Everything in all the drawers, boxes, and storage containers supplied by fossil fuels

DISHES

PEANUT RICE NOODLES
Serves 6

4 cups water
8 ounces dry rice noodles (angel hair pasta can be substituted)
1 Tbsp oil
3 cloves garlic, minced
½ cup shredded cabbage
1 carrot, peeled and grated
1 small onion, shredded
½ cup or 7-ounce can of sliced water chestnuts
12 ounces tofu, diced small
¼ cup shoyu
3 Tbsp rice vinegar
2 Tbsp sugar or equivalent sweetener
2 Tbsp peanut butter
1 cup fresh bean sprouts (optional)
1 Tbsp finely chopped peanuts

Pour 3 cups of warm water over the rice noodles and soak for 20 minutes. Drain the noodles and set them aside, saving liquid for soup. Bring 1 cup of water to a boil and pour over the vegetables. Let stand 1 minute, drain, and reserve liquid. Heat a wok or large skillet and add oil, vegetables, and drained noodles. Stir-fry 1 minute; add tofu. Combine shoyu, vinegar, sweetener, peanut butter, and reserved liquid and stir into vegetable mixture. Add sprouts. Cook 3 minutes. Serve garnished with chopped peanuts.

Difficulty

DISHES

PORTOBELLO FILET

Serves 4

Gravy

2 Tbsp olive or other local
cold-pressed oil
1 small onion, diced
1 chile de arbol or similar hot
pepper, finely minced
1 tsp Italian seasoning or basil,
thyme, and oregano
1 tsp nutritional yeast
¼ tsp garlic powder
Pinch caraway seed
1 tsp shoyu
1 large portobello mushroom
A few chanterelle, shiitake, or local
wild mushrooms
¼ cup flour

Filets

2 large cloves garlic
½ tsp dried oregano
¼ tsp crushed dried hot pepper
(jalapeño, ancho, cayenne, or
peperoncini) or crushed red pepper
½ cup oil
2 large portobello mushrooms
Sea salt and freshly ground black
pepper
4 slices fresh artisanal bread
4 small sprigs of parsley as garnish

Gravy

Heat a skillet. Add oil, onion,
spices, shoyu, and finely sliced
mushrooms, including sliced stems
of all 3 portobellos. When brown,
add flour and begin whisking in
lukewarm water until a gravy forms.
Simmer on low heat for 5 minutes
or until thickened. Reduce heat to
warm until serving.

• Every utility and service in the room (natural gas, electricity, water, batteries)

Walk around the exterior of your dwelling and note where all the utilities enter and where the shutoff valves are. Note outside lights, security systems, sprinklers, and propane or oil tanks. Go through the garage, into the storage shed, under the porch, and into the attic and crawl space and write down everything you find, even the smallest items.

List the services you purchase regularly: newspaper delivery, garbage and recycling, grocery, laundry, transportation. How many of those are dependent on fossil fuels?

Sit down with your lists and indicate which items are:

• Not essential (they are merely a convenience)

• Essential but not critical (you could get by without them for a while)

• Critical (health and safety would be jeopardized without them)

Mark which items could not possibly work or be available if there was a loss of fuel, electricity, telecommunications, water, or sanitation services or if currency collapsed and your money was worthless. For all those items designated to be at risk, you now need to find alternatives.

The greatest antidote to worry,
whether you're getting ready for a space flight or
facing a problem of daily life, is preparation. The more you
prepare, the more you study, the more you think, the more you
try to envision what might happen and what your best response and
options are, the more you are able to allay your fears about the future ....
Obviously, there's a limit to how well you can prepare for everything, because
our lives are continually made up of unforeseen events. That's why I stressed
so much to my own children the value of education — this encapsulated expe-
rience of everyone who has lived before us. It enabled them to have as much
preparation as possible for the unknowns that are in the future for all of us.
— John Glenn, 1998

If you think that such detailed preparation is silly, think again. The people left behind in New Orleans as Hurricane Katrina approached in the summer of 2005 thought that their government would be there with emergency relief; that the shelters would have food, water, and sanitary facilities; that the levies would be properly constructed and closed; even that ambulances would come for the dead. They were wrong.

The petroleum crisis is only one of several civilization-threatening changes now in progress. We have a population bomb exploding, especially in Asia; global warming and its associated storms, droughts, pestilences, and fires; pandemics of super-viruses and super-bacteria; leaking nuclear power plants; weapons of mass destruction in the hands of religious fanatics; and _____ (your crisis goes here).

Preparing for ... Whatever

During any sort of emergency, information becomes extremely important. Make sure you have a portable battery-operated AM/FM radio with good reception, rechargeable batteries, and an inexpensive solar charger. You can time how long the radio will operate and charge batteries accordingly.

A hand-cranked radio needs no batteries and gives 10 minutes of sound for 30 seconds of effort. Useful features include an LED light, solar battery charger, and shortwave antenna.

If a family member will be away for more than a couple of hours, they should have a means to communicate with you (i.e., cell phone, walkie-talkie, CB).

Televisions, stereos, DVD players, and VCRs usually don't run on batteries, so make sure you have a few simple (non-electronic) instruments — guitars, flutes, and drums — books, and games around for entertainment.

If you find yourself cut off from telephones, electricity, rapid transit, or other comforts and conveniences that we have come to expect, it is still possible to enjoy yourself. And if you find yourself out of work for days or weeks, recognize it as the blessing that it is. This might be that time you have been waiting for to write a great novel, catch up on your pleasure reading, or do some outdoor walking.

As you implement your alternatives, make sure you keep all manuals and warranties, learn how to use each tool properly and how to fix what you install, and keep spare parts and repair tools on hand.

From 38 to 68 percent of the US population experienced one of the following ailments in the past 12 months: common cold, headache, tiredness, muscle aches and pains, minor cuts and grazes, bruises, upset stomach, indigestion/heartburn, joint stiffness, and back problems. Survey the contents of your medicine cabinet and check basic supplies. You should stock the appropriate remedy whenever possible.

Portobello Filet cont.

Filets

Puree the garlic, spices, and oil and let sit at room temperature. Clean the mushrooms with a damp cloth and trim away any bad areas. With a sharp wet knife, slice each cap once laterally to create 4 filets. Arrange the caps on a platter and marinate with the spiced oil at room temperature for at least 15 minutes or up to a couple of hours. Prepare a grill or heat a grillpan and brown the filets on both sides. Move the mushrooms away from the hottest coals, or reduce the heat to medium-low, and cover with a pot lid for 2 minutes to steam tender. Season with salt and pepper. Lightly coat or mist sliced bread with oil on one side and toast. To serve, divide toast on 4 plates, cover with a mushroom filet, cover with hot gravy, and garnish.

Difficulty

Talk to your doctor about any prescription drugs a family member takes regularly. Try to have a three-month supply on hand. Think about alternatives, especially herbal ones you might be able to grow yourself or obtain locally. Be sure to have on hand a book of home remedies, such as *Prescription for Nutritional Healing.* You should also try to acquire a recent edition of *Emergency Care and Transportation of the Sick and Injured,* a standard text for training paramedics.

For everyone in your home, gather any information that may be needed in an emergency. Include the following:

- Information on all medications, over the counter and prescription, that all family members use. Don't forget emergency items such as medication for allergic reactions to bee stings.

- Any supplies used with the medications, such as needles, alcohol swabs, lancets, etc.

- Information on all medical conditions, allergies, predispositions, surgeries, etc.

- All devices used at home or at a medical facility (e.g., dialysis machine, pacemaker, glucose testing equipment, inhalers, respirators, etc.).

Discuss with your doctor:

- How to order enough medication and supplies in advance and store them safely.

- How to handle medical conditions in an emergency. Do you need to purchase additional equipment or get training?

Get hard copies of your medical file, x-rays, etc., to keep at home.

Make sure you have spare parts for all the medical equipment you use, have practiced making simple repairs, and have the proper tools on hand. Practice your emergency plans and training.

Take an advanced first-aid class and learn CPR. Learn especially how to tell the difference between life-threatening and non-life-threatening conditions. When in doubt, however, always err on the side of caution. Learning how to deal with such situations yourself will reduce the likelihood that you will panic and increase the chances that an ill or injured person will survive.

If you can't contact an ambulance, you'll need to transport the person yourself, properly and safely. Make sure you know the location of the nearest emergency facilities, and try to contact them before you set off.

Tip: Most people with public or private medical care plans don't reorder their prescriptions as often as they can but wait until they run out. When they inadvertently skip a dose, it's even longer before the time comes to reorder. If you have a prescription that lasts 30 days, reorder it every 30 days whether you are out or not. Eventually you will accumulate an advance supply of the prescription that can see you through an emergency loss of service.

Remember, if there is a general emergency in your community, don't expect the same quality of care you are used to. Try to help out, and don't demand immediate treatment unless you really need it.

Get Fit

> *So, you had better be on
> your way to physical fitness or you will
> be swallowed up by the bear of peak oil. The
> more physically fit you are, the less sick you will be.
> Further, in a culture that will be more and more dependent
> upon physical labor, you will be prepared to take on that chal-
> lenge. This means you start eating right and getting some exercise.
> If you smoke, quit. You don't have to join a gym. You don't have to
> buy anything. All it takes is a little discipline to set aside some time
> each day. Exercising a mere three times a week and practicing some disci-
> pline at the dinner table will put you ahead of millions of others. Do some
> pushups and sit-ups three times a week, and run, walk or bike three times a
> week and you will be okay — cut the desserts and fried foods.*
>
> — Chris Lisle, 2005

One of the benefits of the past century of abundant fossil fuels has been the greater availability of food. This has resulted in an enormous increase in human population in the world and the reduction of malnutrition, at least in the industrialized world, but it also is having some less healthy side effects. Worldwide, people are getting fat. It isn't just the *volume* of food we consume — although portion size in restaurants has been steadily increasing — it is also *what* we consume that is making us wider. It is difficult to avoid ubiquitous additives like refined sugar, sodium, trans-fatty acids, and bovine growth hormone in processed foods. Cultures that traditionally had lean cuisines are becoming more Westernized, putting dairy, meat, and potatoes in the place of rice and beans. Obesity is rising most dramatically in Japan and China.

At the same time, automation, especially computerized workplaces, has created a far more sedentary lifestyle than most people knew two or three generations ago. Now, we even spend many of our leisure hours in a cyberworld, with plasma televisions, TiVo, and videogames. The muscle sets getting the most exercise are in our fingers and thumbs.

In response to this crisis of fat, dieting to control weight has never been more popular. In North America and Europe, diet books consistently

SEA SALT AND KOSHER SALT

Salt is a crystalline compound that comes from the oceans. It is either harvested from seawater through evaporation or mined from inland deposits left by ancient oceans. The human body needs salt to regulate the electrolyte balance inside and outside its cells.

Sodium chloride, the main ingredient in refined salt may make up only 35 percent of sea salt. Other ingredients include potassium, calcium, magnesium, copper, zinc, manganese, iron, iodine, fluoride, boron, barium, beryllium, cobalt, gallium, gold, nickel, palladium, sulfur, selenium, silver, and thallium — over 80 minerals in all. Kosher salt is refined to just sodium chloride but usually contains no additives, and it has big crystals with large surface areas. The size and shape allow it to absorb more moisture than other forms of salt. The salt itself is not kosher, meaning it doesn't conform to Jewish food laws, but the flavor is distinct from ordinary table salt, and some cooks prefer to use it in all their cooking.

I recommend sea salt, such as Le Paludier or Celtic, as the most healthful form and least dependent on fossil fuels.

DISHES

HOT TOFU WITH PEANUT SAUCE
Serves 4

Peanut Sauce
4 Tbsp peanut butter
3 Tbsp shoyu
3 Tbsp white or cider vinegar
3 cloves garlic, chopped
1 tsp sugar or equivalent sweetener
½ to 1 tsp cayenne pepper
½ cup water

Tofu
1 red bell pepper
1 pound firm tofu
¼ pound thin asparagus
½ tsp Szechuan peppercorns
4 Tbsp shoyu
2 Tbsp light brown sugar
3 garlic cloves, minced or pressed
5 tsp roasted peanut oil
5 scallions, including greens, sliced into ½-inch pieces
2 tsp oil
¼ cup roasted cashews, minced
¼ cup roasted walnuts, minced

Garnish
3 medium jalapeños, chopped
1 bunch fresh cilantro
1 bunch fresh basil
1 bunch fresh mint
⅓ cup chives

Peanut Sauce
Mix peanut butter, shoyu, vinegar, garlic, sweetener, cayenne, and water. If you'd prefer your garlic less assertive, blanch it with steam or pour hot water over it and let stand 1 minute.

Tofu
Roast the bell pepper in a dry skillet, turning frequently until

rank at the top of bestseller lists. Celebrities churn out videos and workout books. Subscription gyms are popping up even in small towns. We know we need to lose weight to be more healthy, yet most of us just can't seem to accomplish it in the current cultural environment.

In spite of the plethora of diets, exercise tapes, and fitness fads, losing weight and getting fit actually involve a very simple equation. If you consume more calories then you use, you will put on weight. If you use more than you consume, you will lose weight. A hundred or more years ago, a 180-pound male would normally consume, and burn, 2,640 calories per day.

A crash diet or any other fast weight-loss plan usually won't help restore the balance. The body adjusts its metabolism in response to sudden shortages, so instead of losing weight, a dieter simply loses energy. A host of other problems, including loss of immunity to colds and infection, menstrual irregularities, and reduced libido, can also occur.

Increasing exercise while limiting calories through a moderate diet is the best course (visit www.calorierestriction.com for more information). Intelligent choices in diet, exercise, relaxation, recreation, and relationships all matter.

Gather a Group

The best security is a prepared neighbor. Instead of trying to prepare for post-petroleum challenges all by yourself, get together with your neighbors to discuss preparation. Organize a meeting for your floor in the apartment building or a block party on your street. Show the video *Escape from Suburbia*. Suggest that your neighbors take advantage of the low prices of buying food in bulk as members of a group.

Talk to your neighbors. You don't have to persuade them Peak Oil is a problem. Merely explain that it's something you're concerned about. Let them know that you are preparing and they're welcome to talk to you any time about what you have learned.

If several neighbors become interested, start holding regular meetings. Discuss some of the neighborhood problems that worry you and brainstorm ways you can pull together to handle them, or propose how you might share resources to help those of the group who are physically or financially disadvantaged. You may want to elect a committee to come up with a plan.

Providing Support

People who experience a serious loss, such as a death or major injury, go through a grieving process. It is important to be available during this period and also to provide support after the crisis is over. When the crisis has passed and other people have returned to their routines, feelings of sadness and aloneness are often greatest.

To pause your present reality, become still inside and frame the moment. Then look to your heart to gain the objectivity and clarity you need.

As we near any crisis moment, many people will feel overstressed or on the edge of personal chaos. It is vital that you keep a thread of coherent communication going in an increasingly noisy world.

The post-petroleum transition challenges our society to become even more adaptable and resilient at a time when a "bunker mentality" could seem quite reasonable. We must recognize that there will be life after the change. If we do, we can grow in experience and friendships through this important time.

In any planning sessions for your personal or organizational response to Peak Oil, keep the emotional volume to a minimum. As the media starts to catch on to this topic as the next stimulating story, and the typical frenzied coverage begins, we could be in for a wild ride.

Children

Well before disaster strikes, consider how your children might react to sudden changes in their environment, not to mention what your own reactions might be. How might a crisis affect each person's emotional and physical wellbeing?

The best way to build confidence is to make a plan. Discuss the plan with your family members. You can treat emergency situations as an unplanned camp-out, but tell children simply and matter-of-factly about the problem and how it is to be handled.

Remember that children mirror their parents' anxieties. To reduce your children's fears, be calm yourself. In a bad situation a child may exhibit unusually childish behavior. Most children are not capable of understanding the magnitude and severity of a crisis. Be understanding and patient. Use a familiar toy or book to provide comfort.

If your child's behavior appears unusual, he or she may have lost something — maybe a pet or favorite toy. Ask the child, regardless of age, what he or she misses and try to replace the lost belonging.

Hot Tofu cont.

blistered and blackened. This can also be done on a cooking grate over an open fire. Cool, then place in a paper bag and rub the bag from the outside, removing blackened skins in the process. Cut the pepper in half lengthwise, remove the veins and seeds, then cut each half into 3 long strips. Cut tofu into cubes about ½ inch wide. Cut asparagus into 2-inch lengths. Toast the Szechuan peppercorns in dry skillet until aromatic, then grind to a powder and set aside. Combine shoyu, brown sugar, garlic, peanut oil, and scallions in a bowl and stir to dissolve the sugar. Heat 1 tsp oil in an iron skillet and sauté the tofu until slightly browned, then add another tsp of oil and the asparagus, bell pepper, and peppercorns. Tofu is sometimes difficult to brown, depending on how firm it is, so additional oil or a splash of shoyu might help when the tofu is all alone. Cook 5 minutes over medium-high heat. Pour in the shoyu-sugar mixture and cook over medium heat, moving the pan back and forth rapidly to coat the tofu and peppers. Serve over rice, noodles, or mashed potatoes, topped with peanut sauce, cashews, and walnuts.

Garnish

Chop fresh jalapeños, cilantro, basil, mint, and chives and serve separately in small dishes. People love to tear things into their meals.

Difficulty

DISHES

BARBECUED TOFU WITH SESAME NOODLES

Serves 6

2¾ pounds firm tofu, sliced in ½-inch wedges
2 Tbsp oil
4 Tbsp shoyu
3 Tbsp hoisin sauce
½ cup beer
2 tsp brown sugar
2 cloves garlic, crushed
½ tsp five-spice seasoning
8 ounces thin noodles
1 Tbsp sesame oil

Heat an iron skillet and brown tofu on both sides using a small amount of oil and 1 Tbsp shoyu. Remove and cool. Combine remaining shoyu, hoisin sauce, beer, brown sugar, garlic, and five-spice seasoning in a bowl and mix well. Add tofu to bowl and marinate for 30 minutes or up to 2 hours. Drain and reserve marinade. Preheat grill and brown marinated tofu on both sides, basting with marinade. Cook noodles according to package directions. Drain, pour cold water over noodles, and drain again. Add sesame oil and mix. Season noodles with any remaining marinade. Serve tofu and noodles warm.

Difficulty

Older Adults

If you have older or disabled relatives living at home, review emergency procedures with them. If you need special transportation or assistance, try to arrange these in advance. If a relative lives in a care facility, discuss emergency preparedness with the staff and plan accordingly.

In many catastrophes, a quiet emotional virus starts to take hold, feeding off the fear and strain of the individuals struggling to make headway and stay balanced. Emotional viruses are created by individual immaturity and group stress. As with other viruses, an emotional virus can be highly infectious. But there are ways to resist it.

Many researchers have studied what qualities help people display strength and resilience. They have discovered the following common factors:

- Contribution — The sense that our role is worthwhile.
- Recognition — The feeling that we are recognized and appreciated.
- Clarity — Knowledge of precisely what is expected of everyone.
- Self-expression — The feeling that we are free to question the way things are done.
- Challenge — Appreciation that our work is challenging.
- Supportive management — Confidence in the competence of our managers, and a feeling that we are being supported by them and they are concerned about our welfare.

Ask people in crisis — say, for instance, someone whose house has just been repossessed — to recall previous crises in their lives. Remind them that horrible events — car crashes, illnesses, family deaths, job losses — have occurred in their past. Once they can remember such an example, ask, "How did you cope? What did you do?" In this way you discover — and help them rediscover — the coping skills they already have and the hidden strengths they have yet to draw upon. Their personal assets might be a reliable friend, their strong family ties, or a deep bank account. Their assets might be very different from yours, but they are the assets that person should be turning to now, knowing that they were effective in saving them once before.

Building a Winning Team

"Entrainment" is a term used in physics to describe the tendency of systems to synchronize to allow maximum efficiency. When a team of people is entrained, they are able to unleash much more energy and innovation than they do when the team is incoherent, its goals and values fuzzy, and its communication frustrated or mired in bickering. Entrained teams have a high degree of internal self-management and coherent and sincere communication. Entrained teams function at high levels of creativity and collaboration.

The best strategy for survival is not to go it alone. Start organizing your team. Train yourselves. Capitalize on your collective assets. Improve your odds.

Survival Gear

Contrary to the impositions of the whiz-
bang-blinded and the gadget-addled among us, living
off the land is not about projects, or systems, or organizations,
but about shovels and buckets and hoes, and it is not even so much
about skills or techniques, as it is about habits.

— Dmitry Orlov, 2005

A major part of surviving a disaster of any type is being adequately equipped. There are tools and supplies that may help you get through an emergency. Some, like a water filter, candles, and batteries, are for meeting the most urgent immediate needs. Others, like books on campcraft and gardening, are for longer-term survival.

The sooner you put yourself into post-change mode, the more time you have to acquire valuable tools and skills. If you visit any farmer, it is likely you will find that somewhere, out in a shed or a barn, he or she has a tool that is almost never needed. But when it is needed, it is invaluable. Start accumulating those kinds of tools as a neighborhood cooperative. Even better than a complete set of the Beatles' recordings on vinyl is a full set of *Mother Earth News* or *Organic Gardening*. Most of us will not have the storage space or budget to seek out single-purpose obscure farm tools, keep them in good repair, and be able to use them. It's like putting a hot-dog cooker, fondue pot, and waffle iron in your kitchen instead of a heavy frying pan. So go for the accessible, multipurpose items whose proper use is relatively obvious (shovels, buckets, and hoes). In a pinch you can use a shovel instead of a post-hole digger, but not vice versa.

Before you rush off to the outdoor survival store, though, you need to have a plan. Finding your way to safety when you have been thrust into sudden danger involves a calm mind, advance preparation, skill,

---

DISHES

CREAMY BALSAMIC MILKWEED
Serves 6 to 8

5 pounds fresh harvested young milkweed leaves and stalks (about 4 dry gallons or 15 liters)
¼ cup raw pecan pieces
4 cloves garlic, peeled
¾ cup local cold-pressed oil, divided
½ cup lemon juice
2 tsp salt
½ tsp dry mustard
¼ tsp ground black pepper
1¼ tsp shoyu
3 Tbsp balsamic vinegar

Wash and trim milkweed after gathering it from the wild or purchasing it at a local farm market. Bring water to a boil in a 5-quart pot and boil milkweed for 5 minutes, then drain in colander. Bring fresh water to a boil and return milkweed for second cooking, boiling until soft and tender, about 15 minutes, then drain (if milkweed tastes bitter, a third boiling is recommended). Meanwhile, combine pecans, garlic, ¼ cup oil, and lemon juice and blend until completely pureed. Add remaining ingredients and blend until smooth and creamy. Serve milkweed as stewed green with creamy vinaigrette as dressing.

Difficulty
🐜🐜🐜🐜🐜

Risk of Death	
Type of Injury	**Lifetime Risk**
Deaths due to accidental injuries	One in 37
Nontransport accidental injuries	One in 70
Transport accidents	One in 77
Intentional self-harm	One in 122
Assault	One in 214
Intentional self-harm by firearm	One in 216
Other and unspecified personal injury	One in 226
Car occupant	One in 242
Falls	One in 269
Accidental poisoning	One in 281
Assault by firearm	One in 331

courage, and luck. You can begin acquiring all of those right now, except perhaps the last. You may not be able to improve your luck, but you can improve your odds.

Threat Analysis

What is the most hazardous thing that could happen to you or your family right now, today? While you can't rule out being blown up by a volcano, struck by a meteor, or crushed by an airplane falling out of the sky, the chances of any of those happening are remote, so stop worrying. If you can get a weather report, you might be able to rule out hurricanes, tornadoes, being struck by lightning, or being lost in a blizzard as well.

After the high-probability category there comes a grey area of what are called "low-probability high-risk" events. Even though they are rare, the consequences are so dire that it is worth making some plans. In this category are nuclear plant meltdowns, bombs going off in crowded areas,

God Bats Last

Ten unexpected endings we might not be able to prevent (adapted from www.livescience.com):

1. Earth crashes into the sun. Something comes out of nowhere and randomly knocks Earth in precisely the right direction. Earth's final resting place: a small globule of vaporized iron sinking slowly into the heart of the sun.

2. Earth is eaten by von Neumann machines. A von Neumann machine is any device that is capable of creating an exact copy of itself given nothing but the necessary raw materials. It is possible that by the mid-21st century, someone will have created one of these machines that subsists almost entirely on iron, magnesium, aluminum, and silicon. Loosed, it would replicate geometrically and eat up the whole planet in short order.

3. Earth is pulverized by impact with a marauding object. Either a very large (moon-sized) or a very fast (10^{12} ton at 90 percent of the speed of light) object can reduce Earth into small chunks of rock, scattered haphazardly across the greater solar system.

4. Earth is meticulously and systematically deconstructed by an alien lifeform. The lifeform launches the Earth, as cached resources, into space a bit at a time, or simply eats it in place and then leaves in search of another planet.

5. Earth is sucked into a giant black hole. The nearest black hole to our planet that we know of is 1,600 light-years away in the direction of Sagittarius, orbiting V4641. There is no assurance that there are not similar objects migrating in our direction.

killer storms, terrorist attacks, toxic industrial accidents, and the like. Even though we know that none of these are entirely preventable, we also know from experience that good disaster planning can save lives.

People who live near the coast have to be prepared for tsunamis. Those who live in snow-covered mountains must think about avalanches. Forest dwellers need to prepare for the eventuality of fire. Those in the desert need to anticipate unexpected droughts. It all depends on where you live.

In a major metropolitan area, the population is nearly completely dependent on the supply chain — the urban infrastructure — for food, water, and other basic needs. It would do no good for the entire populations of New York, Mumbai, or Jakarta to walk out of their cities in search of food, because any that existed in the surrounding countryside would be quickly used up.

For this reason, government planners typically choose to "shelter in place" for most urban disasters, rather than attempt an evacuation. If

6. Earth is destroyed by vacuum-energy detonation. The volume of space enclosed by a lightbulb contains enough vacuum energy to boil every ocean in the world. All you need to do is figure out how to extract this energy and harness it in some kind of power plant and then allow the reaction to run out of control. The resulting release of energy would easily be enough to annihilate all of planet Earth and probably the sun too.

7. Earth is blown up by a matter/antimatter reaction. A ball of 2.5 trillion tons of antimatter collides with Earth. The resulting release of energy turns Earth into a second asteroid belt around the sun.

8. Accidental creation of a microscopic black hole. A superaccelerator or other device accidentally jams large numbers of atomic nuclei together, creating sufficient neutronium to generate a microscopic black hole with a certain threshold mass, roughly equal to the mass of Mount Everest. The tiny black hole then oscillates back and forth through Earth, held by Earth's gravitational field, until eventually it comes to rest at the core, where it sits and consumes matter until the whole Earth is a singularity of almost zero size, happily orbiting the sun as normal.

9. Earth is gobbled up by strangelets. The Relativistic Heavy Ion Collider in Brookhaven National Laboratory, Long Island, New York, successfully creates and maintains a stable strangelet, which proceeds to absorb the entire Earth into a mass of strange quarks.

10. Earth suffers total existence failure. All atoms making up the planet suddenly, simultaneously, and spontaneously cease to exist. Vishnu awakens.

DISHES

TOFU NAPOLEON
Serves 6

Crust
1 pound extra firm tofu, drained and crumbled
¾ tsp sea salt
¼ tsp ground pepper
2 Tbsp nutritional yeast
¼ cup raw pine nuts
2 tsp lemon juice
1½ tsp red miso

Filling
1 red pepper
1 green bell pepper
1 yellow bell pepper
½ pound shiitake or wild mushrooms
1 medium onion
¾ cup water
1 tsp olive oil
½ tsp ground coriander
½ tsp ground cumin
¼ tsp sea salt
1 bunch spinach, washed, stemmed, and chopped

Topping
2 Roma tomatoes, sliced
¼ cup raw pine nuts
1 Tbsp finely minced parsley

Crust
Preheat oven to 400°F. Process ingredients until smooth and creamy. Spoon into a rimmed baking sheet to about 3/8-inch thickness and bake for 20 to 25 minutes. Remove and cool.

Filling
Dice peppers, mushrooms, and onion. Transfer them to a large skil-

you are going to stay where you are and survive, you still need to plan. Some governmental agency may come to your aid, but it's better to be more self-reliant — or neighborhood-reliant.

The change that is coming as we leave the petroleum era is not likely to rapidly throw industrial nations like the United States, Australia, Sweden, or Brazil into chaos and anarchy, although, because of multiple fault lines, that possibility cannot be entirely dismissed. What is more likely is a gradual erosion of public services and individual options.

At the same time, a world population of over 6 billion people is not suddenly going to shrink just because the price of rice goes up. The largest part of that population is under the age of 25, and those people will be bringing new children into the world for many more years to come.

If you couple the expanding human population with a steady erosion of public services, including food, water, waste management, medicine, and transportation, it is fair to suggest that we may experience some rough patches ahead. There is also no telling how severe the fevered revenge of global warming might be.

Whether you plan to shelter-in-place or develop a bug-out strategy for your family, you will need to acquire some essential survival gear.

A Short-Term Survival Kit

First, let's pack a short-term survival kit. This package is easy to carry around in a small backpack or in a car, and it will keep you alive for three to five days in any emergency. Within three to five days you should be able to —

- Get help in a natural disaster situation.
- Get to your main supplies.
- Scrounge up something more substantial.

Nitro-Pak (www.nitro-pak.com) sells 72-Hour Kits that contain food, shelter, and light for 72 hours (three days). Another good source is Survival Incorporated (www.survivalinc.com).

A short-term survival kit should provide the following items:

1. Food and water — You should have at least 2,000 calories of food and one quart of water per person per day. Supermarkets sell single-serving cans of chili, stew, beans, and soup. Two 2-quart military canteens will provide a four-day supply of water. It's a good idea to have iodine tablets and a water filter, which are available in most sporting goods

stores or the camping section of big department stores. You can also purchase a Katadyn® portable water maker or some water-purification tablets.

2. Shelter — Make sure you have a "space blanket" and a rain poncho. Both of these can provide overhead cover and warmth and are as small as a deck of cards when packed. It is good to set aside a complete change of clothing for each family member, with blankets or sleeping bags, plastic sheeting, and duct tape.

3. Heat and Light — A candle will not only provide light, but will also keep you warm when you bring it inside the space blanket with you. Matches are *very important*. Waterproof camping matches are best, although you can get inexpensive book matches and waterproof them by coating them with nail polish or candle wax. Cigarette lighters are useful. Other handy light sources are light sticks, hand-crank flashlights, Mini-Maglites,® and LED headlamps.

4. First Aid — Start with this list, which can be kept in small quantities for the three-day kit, or gathered in larger amounts and packed into a large tool box for longer survival periods:

- Acetaminophen or ibuprofen, or both, for aches, colds, fevers, or flu.
- Adhesive bandages, gauze pads, adhesive tape.
- Allergy pills or antihistamines.
- Aloe lotion or ointment for burns.
- Antacids for heartburn.
- Aspirin for pain, inflammation, and suspected heart attack.
- Bacitracin, neosporin, or other antibiotic salve for wounds.
- Bandages and gauze — several sizes.
- Blood pressure cuff (and batteries, if required, or stethoscope if not).
- Calamine lotion or oatmeal for poison ivy and other rashes.
- Cold remedies.
- Compression bandage — in case of sprains, strains, or pulls.
- Cough drops and/or cough syrup.
- A container of disposable disinfecting wipes.
- Sterile eye drops such as boric acid solution.

Tofu Napoleon cont.

let and add water, olive oil, coriander, cumin, and salt. Cook until soft and onion is transparent. Add spinach and sauté, stirring frequently, for 2 or 3 minutes, until spinach is wilted.

Cut the tofu crust lengthwise into 3 equal sections. Then make 4 crosswise cuts to produce 12 pieces. Take 6 pieces and place one on each of 6 dishes. Cover crust with filling and top with remaining crust, laying it at an angle so half the filling is exposed and part of the crust is resting on the dish.

Topping

Broil tomato slices and pine nuts for about 2 minutes, watching carefully so you don't burn them. Arrange tomato slices artfully over top crust, sprinkle with pine nuts and parsley, and serve.

Difficulty

DISHES

CHICKPEA PATTIES WITH HUMMUS

8 patties

Hummus

1 pound cooked or 15-ounce can garbanzo beans, drained, liquid reserved
¼ cup tahini
½ avocado (optional)
3 Tbsp lemon juice
3 Tbsp reserved garbanzo liquid
½ tsp sea salt or kosher salt
Dash of paprika
Sprig of parsley

Patties

2 pounds cooked or two 15-ounce cans garbanzo beans, drained
¼ cup whole-wheat flour
1 Tbsp shoyu
1 tsp onion powder
¼ tsp garlic powder
1 tsp paprika
1 tsp dried parsley
½ tsp cumin
¼ cup local cold-pressed oil

Hummus

Combine all the ingredients and blend until the consistency is smooth and creamy. Spoon into a serving bowl and garnish with a dash of paprika and parsley.

Patties

Mash beans. Mash in flour and seasonings. Wet your hands and shape the bean mixture into flat patties. Heat a skillet, add oil, and fry patties until golden brown. Serve with hummus.

Difficulty

- Hydrogen peroxide for wound cleaning or as an oral rinse.
- Hemostats.
- Iodine.
- Lip balm containing sunscreen.
- Moleskin to prevent blisters.
- Petroleum jelly.
- Single-edge razor blades.
- Small, sharp scissors.
- Snake-bite kit with instructions.
- Rubber-bulb syringe for clearing infant airways.
- Water-resistant sunscreen.
- Thermometer.
- Toilet paper, liquid soap, disinfectant, bleach, plastic garbage bags, zip bags.
- Toothache kit.
- Triangular bandage.
- Tweezers for removing splinters.
- Items required by your family members: sanitary napkins or tampons, disposable diapers and baby wipes, incontinence products, infant medicines and nasal syringe, insulin syringes, etc.
- First-aid booklet or guide.

5. A Swiss Army knife or a Leatherman-type multi-tool — You might also want to include some parachute cord, safety pins, sewing needles and thread, dental floss, and rubber bands. If you wear glasses, include a backup pair. If you wear contacts, include a set of fluids and containers for disinfection without heat.

6. Include copies of all prescriptions. Ask your doctor for an emergency supply of each item to put in the kit. Note expiration dates of all medications on the outside of the kit. An "Epi Pen" for allergies to insect stings expires after one year; nitroglycerine pills may only be good for one month.

7. Communications — a whistle, air horn, or signaling mirror can draw attention if you are disabled. A battery-powered AM/FM, shortwave, or weather-band radio will keep you in touch with the outside world. Two-way, CB, and ham radios all extend the range and capabilities of home and community organization.

On the outside of the kit, write a short list of items to collect from other places before evacuating in an emergency: refrigerated medications, pets, blankets, etc. Don't forget to include your wireless communication devices, and charging cords.

For those considering a bug-out strategy involving extended wilderness living, a more advanced survival kit would be needed.

Tools for Farming, Food Preparation, and Storage

I've compiled this next list from looking around a lot of houses, barns, and open-air markets in the rural US, Europe, and less-industrialized countries, and by consulting some of the mail-order catalogs favored by my Amish neighbors. While not complete, it provides an over-the-fence glimpse of the tools those most experienced in self-sufficiency favor.

Slipknot.

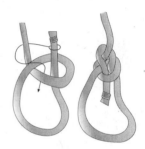

Bowline knot.

Carrick bend knot.

Sheet bend knot.

- 1-inch corner chisel
- 15-in-1 ratchet screwdriver
- 3½-ton wagon jack
- 5-gallon round buckets with rigid lids
- 8-pound splitting maul
- Adze
- Anti-cribbing spray
- Anvils
- All-purpose axe
- Bark spud
- Blacksmith's tongs
- Block and tackle
- Breast drill
- Buck saw
- Buckets of various sizes
- Burlap feed sacks
- Calf feeder pail
- Camp stove and butane tank(s)
- Canning jars and lids (pint, quart, gallon)
- Cant hook
- Carpenter's brace
- Carpenter's hatchet

- Carving set
- Chafing dish and fuel
- Chicken crates
- Chipping hammer
- Clinch cutter
- Collapsible shovel
- Comealong puller
- Cooper's in-shave
- Corn huskers
- Corn sheller
- Crosscut saws
- Crowbar
- Curved drawknife
- Cutting nipper
- Diatomaceous earth
- Drill brace bit set
- Egg crates
- Egg scale
- Fencing tool
- Filter disks
- Foot-mount corn knife
- Froe
- Galvanized steel utility can
- Gigantic auger bits

DISHES

CHUTNEY

Serves 6

1½ cups sugar or equivalent
sweetener
¾ cup cider vinegar
½ cup chopped onions
½ cup raisins
2 Tbsp gingerroot, peeled and
minced
1 tsp salt
1 tsp black mustard seed
½ tsp ground cardamom seeds
½ tsp ground red pepper
2 pounds apples, peeled, cut in
1-inch chunks
1 lemon, thinly sliced, slices
quartered

Combine all ingredients except fruit
and bring to a boil in a large
kettle. Add fruit, cover pan, and
cook, stirring occasionally, until
fruit is tender but firm when
pierced with a fork. Ladle into hot
sterile jars and seal. Peaches,
pears, mangoes, and other fruits
can also be used.

Difficulty

- Gimlets
- Grain scoops
- Grain/corn/cereal hand mill
- Half-moon goat-milking pail
- Hand gouging adze
- Hanging scale
- Heat sealer for plastic bags
- Hoof nipper
- Hoof rasp
- Hoof trimmers
- Horsehair brush
- Hoses and spare repair parts
- Ice tongs
- Incubator thermometer
- Kerosene-powered incubator
- Large stainless milk strainer
- Livestock canes
- Log carrier
- Log roller
- Log-jack
- Machete
- Maximum-minimum recording
  thermometer
- Metal files
- Milkhouse broom
- Mortising and framing chisels
- Mylar bags and liners
- Nail puller
- Non-hybrid garden seeds
- One-leg milking stool and strap
- One-man crosscut saw
- One-man fence stretcher
- Oxygen absorbers
- Peavey
- Pick and shovels
- Plastic bags, mesh bags, baskets, and crates
- Black and clear polyethelene
  rolls

- Post hole diggers
- Post popper
- Quart measures
- Rakes, hoes, trowels
- Revolving leather punch
- Rope-making machine
- Rope
- Rubber feed pails
- Scoop with chains
- Scythe peening kit
- Scythes
- Seed-starting trays
- Sewing awl
- Sharpening tools
- Sheep shears
- Shoulder yoke
- Sisal twine
- Skidding tongs
- Slate shingle ripper
- Slater's hammer
- Small milk tote
- Small poultry waterer
- Spoke pointer
- Spokeshaves
- Spring-bottom oil can
- Stainless steel can plunger
- Stainless steel milk cans
- Stainless steel milk pails
- Steel hay hook
- Steel troughs
- Straight drawknives
- The split and kindling set
- Traditional mallet
- Two-man crosscut saw
- Universal wafer thermostat
- Unker's medicated vet salve
- Volcano stove and charcoal
- Warrington hammer
- Washbasin

- Water-bath canner
- Water glass (liquid sodium silicate)
- Watering can and misters
- Well wheel
- Wheelbarrow

- Wheelhorse cultivator
- Wire egg basket
- Wooden hay forks
- Wooden snath
- Work gloves

Useful Household Tools and Supplies

All those Amish tools impractical for you? Here are some more basic tools to consider acquiring:

- 12-volt car batteries, distilled water, and electrolyte
- Binoculars, night scope
- Chlorine bleach, calcium hypochlorite, hydrated lime
- Clothesline, clothes pins
- Grease
- Hand-crank spout pump
- How-to books and textbooks
- Narrow (well-gauge) water bucket
- Non-electric washing machine
- Pick and shovel
- Portable water containers
- Rope and string
- Sharpening tools, WD-40®
- Shoulder yoke
- Sleeping cots

- Solar shower
- Toilet paper and paper towels
- Torches, solder, flux, soldering irons
- Washtubs, washboard, detergent, ammonia (When water is in short supply, soak clothes overnight in a bucket of water with a few ounces of ammonia. They will not require rinsing; just wring them out and hang them up.)
- Water-filter pump and filters
- Water-purification tablets
- Water-storage drums (black)
- Welding and brazing tools and welding rod
- Well wheel

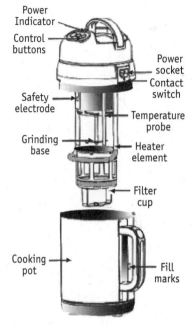

Soymilk maker.

Essential Bicycle Gear

- Adjustable wrench
- Air-cooling helmet
- Box wrenches
- Car rack
- Chain-link pusher
- Comfortable seat
- Freewheel removal tool
- Hand-driven tire pump

- Heavier gloves for winter
- iPod®
- Light gloves for summer
- Lightweight frame
- Lubricating oil
- Padded handlebars
- Padded-seat shorts and pants
- Panniers
- Sandpaper

DISHES

BOMBAY CHUTNEY

Serves 6

1½ Tbsp oil
½ tsp cumin seeds
¼ tsp mustard seeds
½ tsp turmeric
2 green chiles, stemmed and diced
1 onion, finely chopped
1 eggplant, diced
1 large potato, peeled and cut into bite-size chunks (about 1½ cups)
Salt to taste
¼ cup plus 2 Tbsp water
3 Tbsp arrowroot flour
½ tsp tamarind paste

Warm oil and add cumin seeds, mustard seeds, and turmeric. After mustard seeds start splattering, add chiles and onions and cook until golden brown. Add eggplant, potatoes, salt, and 2 Tbsp of water and simmer. In a small bowl, mix flour and tamarind paste in ¼ cup water, blend, and add to the above mixture. Simmer on low flame until potatoes are tender. Serve hot.

Difficulty

- Screwdriver
- Self-drying windbreaker
- Socket wrenches
- Spare tires and tubes
- Sunglasses
- Tube patch kits
- Wheel spoke tool
- Wicking sport shirt(s)

There is an old saying, "there are three kinds of people; one who watches things happen, one who makes things happen and one who says 'what happened?'" We do have an alternative to just sitting back and allowing a deeply uncertain future to simply unfold. Our collective dependence on fossil fuels leaves us very vulnerable, and indeed is largely responsible for the instability we see in the world today. To quote Jan Lundberg of the Sustainable Energy Institute [now Culture Change], "real peace in a petroleum-fuelled world means rejecting petroleum dependence in all ways possible."

— Rob Hopkins, 2005

Change Your Ride

*During 2000–25, oil
use is officially forecast to grow by 44 percent in
the United States and 57 percent in the world. A fifth of that
global increase is to fuel the US, which by 2025 would use as much oil
as Canada, Western and Eastern Europe, Japan, Australia, and New Zealand
combined. As the richest nation on earth, we can afford it. But five, soon
seven, billion people in poor countries, whose economies average more than
twice as oil-intensive, want the same oil to fuel their own development.*

— Amory B. Lovins, E. Kyle Datta, Odd-Even Bustnes, Jonathan
G. Koomey, and Nathan J. Glasgow, 2004

Because cars and trucks use more than half of the petroleum consumed in many industrial countries, it would be only natural to think that is where the biggest problem will be. The "End of Suburbia" scenario popularized by a film of the same name is based on this premise. In reality, the issue of personal transportation may be one of the easier pieces of the Peak Oil puzzle to slide into place.

Retooling

According to Rocky Mountain Institute, an energy-security think tank in Colorado, about 85 percent of a car's fuel is lost to heat and noise and only 6 percent is actually consumed in acceleration. What that acceleration is moving is 99 percent cargo weight (mostly steel and alloys) and 1 percent driver weight. Of the 1 percent that is doing something useful in a single-passenger trip to the grocery store, a third is used to heat the air the car pushes aside, a third heats the tires and the road, and the remaining

In present-day transportation worldwide the four biggest petroleum users are light trucks, heavy trucks, airplanes, and automobiles, in that order.

DISHES

BOSTON BAKED BEANS
Serves 6

4 cups cooked or 2 cans pinto or
navy beans
¼ cup molasses
¼ cup brown sugar
¼ cup tomato paste or ketchup
(much sweeter)
2 Tbsp mustard paste
1 tsp onion powder
½ tsp garlic powder

Combine all ingredients in a deep
casserole and bake in a wood-fired
oven until bubbling hot.

Difficulty

third actually rotates the wheels before it is also turned into heat by braking. That is a lot of inefficiency, waiting like Spindletop, the famous Texas oil gusher, for some wildcat automotive engineers to drill into.

Over the past quarter-century, automakers have been lazily experimenting with ways to improve gas mileage but feeling no special pressure to get it done. Slowly, some of these ideas have been making their way into the marketplace. The hybrid-electric cars introduced by Honda and Toyota in the late 1990s were originally developed for the Austrian army by Porsche in 1900. In the late 1970s you could buy a set of plans from *Mother Earth News* and, with a lawn-mower engine, a starter motor, and a few batteries, squeeze 200 miles per gallon from a Datsun station wagon. I know those plans worked because I did it. My friends and I added solar cells and made a lightweight "hypercar" (to borrow Amory Lovins' term) that we showed off at the "Appropriate Community Technology" pavilion at the 1982 World's Fair.

Still, even as commonsensical as hybrid-electrics are, as recently as 2003 the big three Detroit automakers had concluded that these vehicles were too costly to be worth producing in volume and instead continued designing ever-more powerful and unsafe light trucks disguised as cars. They seemed determined to build cars that would halve the 1 percent of the gasoline performing purposeful work.

By the beginning of 2005 it was apparent that Japanese automakers had eaten Detroit's lunch. The Dinosaur Three, those same carmakers that put the squeeze on the Clinton government to soft-pedal global warming, are now either in, or teetering on, bankruptcy, unable to sell their gasguzzling behemoths, while Honda, Nissan, and Toyota are sprouting new factories like daffodils in the spring to keep pace with skyrocketing demand for their steadily improving and greenhouse-gas–conscious hybrids.

Eager to showcase the mileage capability of their Insight hybrid, which hit showrooms in 1999, Honda invited writers from *Car and Driver, Popular Mechanics, AutoWorld,* and other trade magazines to drive from Columbus to Detroit, about 200 miles. The team that averaged the combined highest speed and best fuel economy would win a $5,000 donation to its favorite charity. The stock Insight was rated at 61 miles per gallon in the city and 70 miles per gallon on the highway, but the magazines were invited to trick it out to boost performance. Using a Ford Excursion to break wind, NASCAR-style, *Car and Driver* got 121.7 miles per gallon at 58 miles per hour, beating *Popular Mechanics'* 83.4 miles per gallon at 59 miles per hour. While drafting SUVs is not a fuel-saving strategy that can be taken seriously, it does provide some ideas about future highway designs that join cars into moving lines like migrating geese, using synchronized wireless networks. Imagine driving to, say, Detroit and being passed by a high-speed caravan of hybrids. Your dashboard display asks, "Join network?"

Ron Gremban, an electrical engineer and committed environmentalist, spent several months and $3,000 to customize his Toyota Prius. In the trunk sits an 80-miles-per-gallon secret — a stack of 18 brick-sized batteries that boost the car's mileage with an extra electrical charge so it can burn even less fuel.

University of California engineering professor Andy Frank built a "plug-in hybrid" from the ground up in 1972 and has since built seven others, one of which gets up to 250 miles per gallon. They were converted from non-hybrids, including a Ford Taurus and Chevrolet Suburban. These plug-in hybrids get more than 100 miles per gallon by operating on new, more powerful lithium-ion batteries for the first 20 to 60 miles. If their gas contained an 85 percent ethanol blend, the vehicles could get up to 500 miles to the gallon. Former CIA head James Woolsey testified before a government committee in 2005 that small innovations such as these could produce 1,000-mile-per-petroleum-gallon performance immediately, without any long lead time for research.

Are electric-assist drives charged from the utility grid cheaper than gasoline? It depends. A gallon of gasoline weighs 6.15 pounds (2.79 kilograms). Multiplying that by the net energy content of 44 megajoules per kilogram gives you 122 megajoules per gallon of gasoline, or the equivalent of 34 kilowatt-hours of electricity. If you pay 10 cents per kilowatt-hour, you can buy the equivalent of a gallon of gasoline for $3.40. At 20 cents per kilowatt-hour that same gallon costs $6.80. However, you are storing your electrons in a leaky tank, so you better use them fast. Even expensive lithium batteries can waste 10 to 20 percent of their stored power in the charging/discharging process.

Solatec is a new company that sells rooftop-mounted solar panels for hybrid vehicles that can double or triple fuel mileage, depending on whether the car is used for short-distance or long-range travel and on the length of time it is parked during daylight hours. Once you've installed the panels, the electricity is free.

Whether you use solar assist or not, today's hybrids are only the first generation of what is coming from those clever Japanese engineers (and soon their even-more-clever Chinese and Indian competitors). Future hybrids will get ten times the fuel savings of today's hybrids. Hence — and pay attention here because this point is important — the price of oil would have

Busdriver Klaus Burgermeister accidentally picked up a hybrid Smart that unhappily got hooked onto his rear bumper while his city bus made its usual route. For more than two miles the bus pulled the Smart while the driver inside waved frantically through his sunroof, trying to get Burgermeister's attention. This is the best gas mileage ever recorded by a hybrid.

to go above $600 per barrel (nearly ten times present levels) before it would substantially affect the viability of suburbia. I'll revisit this point later.

Commercial Vehicles

Turning to trucks, the same picture emerges. At the annual meeting of the Association for the Study of Peak Oil in Lisbon in 2005, Volvo rolled out its concept for a new generation of trucks that will be *1,700 percent* more fuel efficient than current models, with 1 percent of the greenhouse gas emissions. Volvo has partnered with Mack Trucks to produce the power trains, and with a consortium of European companies to produce the special new fuel, known as dimethyl ether (DME). We'll look at DME in greater detail later in this chapter.

Air Travel

Rapid changes of design will be essential if the air travel industry is to avoid rapid decline as jet fuel tops $90 per barrel. Like the dinosaurs of Detroit, air carriers have run a cumulative net financial loss for many years, and half of the top ten are now operating in bankruptcy.

Foreign Fords

As other industries have learned the hard way, WTO-governed global competition works both ways, and it's dangerous to underestimate the dynamism of Chinese manufacturing. Chinese industry is supported by a strong central policy apparatus rooted in five millennia of history, and is enabling the world's most massive construction boom in at least two thousand years. Already, too, homegrown Chinese fuel-cell cars are rapidly advancing in several centers, raising the likelihood that Chinese leaders' aversion to the oil trap will be expressed as leapfrog technologies not just in efficient vehicles but also in oil-free hydrogen fueling. In a few decades, a mighty Chinese economy's automakers might have taken over or driven out the Big Three and even bought major Japanese automakers.

In case 1.4 billion Chinese moving rapidly to make something that beats your uncle's Buick isn't enough of a threat, there's also India's younger, smaller, but rapidly maturing auto industry. It's only $5 billion per year, but is growing by 15 percent a year. Quality has improved so rapidly, on a Korea-like trajectory, that in 2004, Tata Motors is exporting 20,000 cars to the UK under the MG Rover brand. India "may be better placed than China is to become a global low-cost auto-manufacturing base." A billion Indians, with an educated elite about as populous as France, have already transformed industries from software to prosthetics, using breakthrough design to undercut U.S. manufacturing costs by as much as several hundredfold. India's domestic car market, like China's, is evolving under conditions that favor an emphasis on fuel efficiency.

— Amory B. Lovins, E. Kyle Datta, Odd-Even Bustnes, Jonathan G. Koomey, and Nathan J. Glasgow, 2004

*The average driver may be able to absorb fuel costs
for a few years more, but not the average flier. Within a year
— or two, or three? — affordable passenger flight will be history.
What will that mean in real life? Airfares will skyrocket. Schedules will
be pared to the bone. If you're not rich, and if your lifestyle includes hopping
planes when you choose — you're grounded. As airlines fail and the surviving
carriers cut back, flights will be fewer, especially to smaller cities. Some areas will
lose service altogether unless the government mandates that every city of under
half a million people must get, say, two flights a week. Conventions and conferences
of every description will be beyond the means of any but the wealthy. The average
person won't be able to jet to the wedding, sick bed, or funeral of a loved one. Even
if you can scrounge the money for a ticket, there may not be a flight. Music and
film festivals that can't be sustained locally will be a thing of the past (unless and
until rail service is restored). Families will think twice about letting their kids apply
to colleges hundreds or thousands of miles from home. Family members who live
scattered all over the country will see one another rarely, if at all (again, unless
and until rail service is restored). None but the rich will vacation in far-off
places — and "far off" will come to mean any place beyond two tanks of gas
.... Tourism as we know it, an industry merely decades old, will not survive.
Nor will such minor luxuries as next-day delivery. Mega-airports and mega-
hotels will become ghostly caverns, monuments to a failure of foresight.*

— Michael Ventura, 2006

Still, there is a two- to three-fold "efficiency gap" in airplane design, meaning that instead of averaging about 100 miles per gallon per passenger (at ten times the speed of automobiles), commercial jets could be getting 200 to 300 miles per gallon per passenger. The more efficient planes have not been built, not because they aren't better, but because the industry is broke. Security mega-paranoia and higher fuel costs won't help.

Brazil's aircraft manufacturer, Embraer, is now building an ethanol-fueled crop-dusting airplane, the Ipanema, that will fly on AvAlc (aviation alcohol), which is currently three to four times cheaper than aviation gasoline (AvGas). Richard Branson has already announced plans to run all Virgin Atlantic's jets on ethanol.

Refueling

Alternative fuels will provide the next big change in car, truck, and airplane design. There are five major alternatives that we can expect to see at the pump in the near future:

DISHES

PHILADELPHIA BEAN STEAKS
Makes 8 patties

Cheezy Sauce
½ cup white flour
½ cup nutritional yeast
½ cup oil
3 cups water
1 tsp sea salt

Patties
1¾ cup cooked or 15-ounce can of kidney beans, drained
2 cups cooked rice or oatmeal
¼ cup finely chopped onion
2 Tbsp tomato paste
1 tsp dried oregano
1 tsp poultry seasoning or sage, thyme, and marjoram
½ tsp sea salt
Dash of pepper

Cheezy Sauce
In a heavy pan, heat flour and yeast until you can almost smell it (about 3 to 4 minutes). Pour in oil, then stir in water and salt. Cook until thick and bubbly.

Patties
Mash the beans. Mash in the rice or oatmeal, onion, tomato paste, and seasonings. Wet your hands and shape the bean mixture into 8 patties, about ½ an inch thick. Heat a skillet and brown patties in a little oil. Serve with hot Cheezy Sauce.

Difficulty

DISHES

GRILLED TEMPEH STEAK
Serves 6

1½ pounds tempeh
1 green onion cut into 1-inch lengths and finely slivered

Marinade
¾ cup rice vinegar
¾ cup shoyu
6 cloves garlic, minced
1½-inch piece ginger root, peeled and minced
½ tsp five-spice seasoning
4 Tbsp olive or other local cold-pressed oil
3 Tbsp blackstrap molasses
Freshly ground black pepper to taste

Score tempeh on both sides, making shallow diagonal cuts about ¼-inch apart. Cut tempeh into 6 portions and spread out in one layer in a baking dish. Combine marinade ingredients in a bowl and pour over tempeh, turning to coat both sides. Marinate in refrigerator for 24 hours or longer, turning pieces several times.
Preheat barbecue and grill tempeh 5 to 7 minutes on each side or until well striped. Remove to a serving platter and garnish with the slivered green onion.

Difficulty

- Ethanol
- Biogas
- Methanol
- Biodiesel
- Dimethyl ether
- Hydrogen

Ethanol

Ethanol (EtOH) is what people in my neck of the woods call moonshine. It's produced by fermenting plant material. Today most of it comes from corn and other cereal grains, or beets and other sugar crops, that are also eaten by people. And that's part of the bad rap that ethanol gets when we start to talk about replacing the world's supply of petroleum. If we used ethanol to power our cars, critics say, we will make cornflakes too expensive for people in Botswana.

Things are changing, however, because we now know how to make ethanol from the waste products of food processing and from cellulose, which is not corn, but cornstalks, yesterday's newspapers, sawdust, and a host of other "waste" materials. And after the waste product is fermented, it can still become fertilizer — sometimes even an improved fertilizer because distillation has broken down complex carbohydrates and made a better food for plants.

Ethanol can be blended with gasoline to a level of 10 percent without requiring changes in vehicle fuel systems. It is already blended to 25 percent in all gas sold in Brazil. According to David Blume, author of *Alcohol Can Be A Gas,* "If the US matched Brazil's 25 percent content for all our gasoline, we would not have to import a single drop of oil from the Middle East!"

Blume points out that we feed more than 80 percent of our corn to cattle. Cattle did not evolve to eat grass or the seed of grass but, rather, woody biomass. As a result, cattle digest only about 20 percent of the starch in corn. The rest goes to waste. But when corn is fermented to make alcohol, which breaks up the starch, the resulting mash is much more digestible for animals, and the available protein actually increases meat or dairy output by 17 percent.

In Brazil, a major producer of cheap alcohol fuels, about 40 percent of the cars have been adapted to run on up to 96 percent alcohol and 4 percent water. They are built with a small software programming change that automatically makes the adjustment. Brazil builds several million of these vehicles per year, including the same familiar Ford and Dodge pickup trucks you can buy farther north without the nifty Brazilian computer code. If fed the same software, virtually all modern automobile computers made since 1980 will readily adjust to run on alcohol mixtures with little vehicle modification (a fuel pre-heater for cold mornings is useful), while dropping emissions 70 to 90 percent. David Blume has shown that some vehicles' computers are already smart enough to be able to use any mixture of alcohol and gasoline, even though the cars aren't sold as flexible-fuel vehicles. Volvo 850s and the Toyota Prius are two examples of cars smart enough to adjust to any mixture. General Motors recently announced plans to reduce its flex-fuel offerings to its seven heaviest passenger cars — the ones that look like armored assault vehicles — in the 2007 model year, but the genie is out of the bottle. Aftermarket kits costing about $300 make it possible to operate almost any car as a dual-fuel vehicle at the flip of a switch.

Iogen Corporation, a Canadian company partnering with Shell Global Solutions, has developed a cellulose-based fuel called EcoEthanol. Once it scales up its commercial facilities, Iogen expects to produce 45 million gallons per year — and since US law prohibits importation of ethanol, China stands ready to buy its entire output at the going price. Japan's JGC Corporation, like other companies that see opportunity, is going around the import law by building a plant in California that will make 20 million gallons of ethanol each year from scrap wood and sawdust.

E3 Biofuels is building an ethanol still with a similar yearly output at a cattle feedlot in Mead, Nebraska. It will be powered by methane from the cattle manure. Panda Energy has three 100-million-gallon ethanol plants in Kansas, Colorado, and Texas, but E3 is promoting its smaller system as "closed loop." The 30,000 cattle at the Mead feedlot eat the distillers' grain right at the site. A slatted floor allows the manure to drop onto a collection surface, where it goes into an anaerobic digester that breaks the manure down into fertilizer and methane gas. The plant will use about 7 million bushels of locally grown corn to produce its 20 million gallons of ethanol a year. Rather than scaling up, E3 Biofuels hopes to build 100 more small plants in the next 15 years.

If you want to read up on the cellulose-to-ethanol process, or on how to grow and distill your own fuel, the indispensable guide is David Blume's *Alcohol Can Be A Gas*. Blume foresees a future in which midsize moonshine stills will convert local wastes to ethanol at a neighborhood, village, or county level, providing skilled jobs for locals and making regions more self-reliant.

Blume is fond of pointing out that the largest crop in the United States by weight is not corn or soybeans but grass clippings, and, moreover,

DISHES

RED BEANS AND RICE

Serves 4 to 6

1 pound uncooked red kidney beans
2 cups rice
2 cloves garlic, chopped
½ cup chopped celery
1 large bay leaf, crushed
1 medium onion, chopped
½ cup olive or other local cold-pressed oil
½ tsp sea salt
2 tsp chili powder
2 Tbsp parsley, chopped

Separately soak both the red beans and rice in cool water before cooking.

Beans
Place beans in cold water in a 4-quart pot. Add garlic, celery, bay leaf, onion, and oil and bring to a boil. Reduce heat and simmer for about 2 hours. Add water as needed, stirring occasionally. Add salt, chili powder, and parsley and continue cooking over low heat for about 1 hour or until tender.

Rice
Line the steamer basket insert of a pasta pot with fresh corn husks or soaked dried corn husks (used as Mexican tamale wrappers). Spray the corn husks with oil to prevent sticking. Drain the soaked rice and spread it evenly over the husks. Fill the pot with water to come to just under the steamer basket insert. Put the steamer basket insert into the pot, cover, and bring to a boil over medium-high heat. Steam the rice for at least 20 minutes. Serve beans over steamed rice.

Difficulty

DISHES

CUBAN BLACK BEANS

Serves 4

Black Beans

2 pounds black beans
1 tsp sea salt
1 bay leaf
½ tsp kombu
1 tsp oil
2 red or yellow bell peppers, diced
2 large yellow onions, diced
2 medium tomatoes, diced
3 cloves garlic, minced
2 cups cold-pressed oil
½ cup sugar or equivalent sweetener
1 cup diced pimentos
½ cup dark rum
Vinegar to taste
1 Tbsp dried parsley

Yellow Rice

2 Tbsp oil
2 tsp cumin seed
¼ tsp crumble saffron thread
2 cups unconverted long-grain rice
4 cups water
¾ tsp salt

Black Beans

Soak black beans overnight. Drain and add to pressure cooker with water 2 inches over top of beans. Add sea salt, bay leaf, kombu, and 1 tsp oil. Cook at 15 p.s.i. for 45 minutes. Do not drain any remaining fluid. Add all remaining ingredients to beans and simmer for 2 to 4 hours. Beans should make their own broth. Add liquid as necessary to prevent drying out or burning, but keep broth thick. Garnish with parsley and serve over yellow rice.

that clippings yield 180 gallons per ton when processed into ethanol. Green gold. Golf-course tea.

After watching gas prices peak after Hurricanes Katrina and Rita, Bill Sasher had a business idea. Dogwood Energy, Sasher's Tennessee creekside assembly warehouse, is five miles from the distillery that makes Jack Daniels whiskey. In 2005 he began building small stills for homebrew ethanol. A bushel of a fermented starch crop, mixed with yeast, water, and sugar, is allowed to sit for a couple days, then strained and heated to boiling to make 2.6 gallons of 190-proof ethanol. After all is said and done, it costs about 75 cents to make a gallon of ethanol in one of Sasher's stills. E85 produced this way costs about a dollar per gallon at 2005 gasoline prices. Each machine stands about six feet tall, fits in a garage corner, and retails for $1,400. Sasher also sells his blueprints to homeowners who are handy with tools and want to build one themselves for less than $1,000. Owners still need a (free) federal permit to make fuel, but at Dogwood Energy, phones are ringing off the hook.

Methanol

Methanol (MeOH) made from wood and coal is also known as synfuel, and although it has a long history as a last-resort fuel in hard times (it fueled Wehrmacht trucks in 1944), during the Carter, Thatcher, and Reagan years it enjoyed something of a renaissance as the coal industry's gala response to OPEC hegemony. After nearly three decades of research and billions of tax dollars, synfuels are nearly forgotten because they are incredibly expensive, dangerously toxic, deadly to touch or inhale, and ecologically devastating to produce. Moreover, wide use of synfuels would greatly accelerate global warming. Still, ask a coal industry spokesperson, and what's not to like about methanol? Apparently the European Union, the US, and Canada agree, because they have thrown billions down the methanol rat-hole over the past five years and plan to throw billions more.

Biogas

Methane, or biogas, should not be confused with methanol or biodiesel. Methane, CH_3, is produced naturally by the decomposition of organic materials and by deep Earth vents. It is a greenhouse gas, and although it is less plentiful than CO_2 in the atmosphere, it produces global warming 20 times faster. That is, unless it is burned as a fuel, which changes it to carbon dioxide, hydrogen, and water. Carbon dioxide and water are also greenhouse gases, but they are 20 times less harmful, and since most biologically produced methane would go into the atmosphere anyway, burning it is one way to dampen the greenhouse effect.

It is not difficult to harvest methane. Indeed, farmers in many less-industrial countries have been doing it easily for a long time. Although CH_3 is most often produced by pig and cattle farms, it is possible to harvest it from human wastes and kitchen compost on a small scale as well. Every ten dry cubic feet of biomass produces four to six cubic feet, 5,000 BTU, of gas. A two-burner stove uses 20,000 BTU per hour, so it takes a lot of biomass to deliver a year-round supply of gas for the average kitchen. One kitchen I visited in Egypt was able to produce enough gas for 30 minutes per day from the humanure and kitchen scraps of six residents.

While methane is a practical alternative home-cooking fuel in many settings, it is currently impractical as a fuel industry for cars, trucks, and airplanes. The energy density is simply too low (we'd need a lot of land or ocean surface to produce necessary quantities of methane), the production process too slow and inefficient, and the storage requirements too problematic for highly mobile applications. Nonetheless, it is lower-tech than ethanol or biodiesel, puts human and animal wastes to good use, and reduces global warming, so some people, especially pig farmers, may want to give it a try in their trucks and tractors.

David Chynoweth has studied many different crops and feedstocks, including kelp (macrocystis), sorghum, sargassum, napier grass, poplar, water hyacinth, sugarcane, willow, laminaria, municipal sewage sludge, logging wastes, animal wastes, and miscellaneous cellulose. His conclusion is that low-temperature biological gasification can convert all of these products to

Cuban Black Beans cont.

Yellow Rice
In a 3-quart saucepot heat 2 Tbsp oil until it is hot but not smoking and sauté cumin seed 10 seconds, or until it is fragrant. Stir in saffron and rice and sauté 1 to 2 minutes, stirring to coat rice. Stir in water and salt and boil rice, uncovered and without stirring, until surface of rice is covered with steam holes and grains on top appear dry, about 8 to 10 minutes. Remove from heat, cover, and let stand 5 minutes. Fluff rice with a fork before serving.

Difficulty

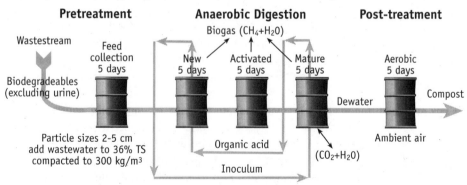

Sequential batch anaerobic composting system (from Chynoweth et al. 2003). This simple methane-digesting process developed by David P. Chynoweth at the University of Florida uses four to six 55-gallon plastic barrels with screw-on lids and some plastic tubing.

Energy Potential of Methane from Solid Wastes and Biomass	
Resource	EJ/yr*
Municipal Solid Waste	1.5
Sewage Sludge and Sludge-Grown Biomass	0.8
Biodegradable Industrial Wastes	0.4
Crop Residues	4.1
Logging Residues	0.3
Animal Wastes	0.4
Energy crops	
a. land-based	22.0
b. marine	>100.0
Total (excluding marine)	29.5
* one exajoule = 1 quad = 1015 BTU Figures given are only for the USA.	
Source: D. J. Chynoweth, Renewable Biomethane from Land, Ocean, Wastes, and Outer Space, 2003	

methane economically at a variety of scales and that methane will take an appropriate place among our future energy fuels.

It is worth mentioning that methane is also a form of natural gas that may or may not be organic in origin (some deep "abiogenic" methane was formed by the cooling of the planet). Some of this is transported in pipelines and tankers and is used to heat buildings, generate electricity, make fertilizers, and produce synfuels in dirty factories in Qatar, Nigeria, and Egypt. While the world may have 450 million boe (barrels of oil equivalent), or two gasoline years, of methane reserves still in the ground, for the sake of climate change, it is best left there.

Biodiesel

Diesel is another technology that has been with us almost as long as the internal combustion engine. Diesel engines are most efficient at high power, which is what has made them ideal for railroad trains and long-haul semi-tractor trailers. The diesel Volkswagens and Mercedes that started showing up in driveways after the first OPEC embargo three decades ago were a low-power use, and they suffered from poor fuel economy and frequent repairs. Using old-style engines to move the heavy steel weight of a car was such a mismatch that engine efficiency was cut in half. After 2000, the introduction of advanced engines and hybrid diesels gave us 100-mile-per-gallon vehicles. Substitute new composite materials for the steel frames, and add better aerodynamics and powertrain controllers, and diesel fuel consumption will steadily improve.

Biodiesel is a methyl ester produced by a chemical reaction between methanol (note my scathing review above) or ethanol and vegetable oil or animal fat. The main crops used to make biodiesel are rapeseed, soybeans, and palm trees. Rapeseed methyl ester (RME) is a fuel made from the same oilseed that gave us the Frankenfood known as Canola (short for "Canadian oil," a now-obsolete name the guys in white lab coats came up with, being gene-splicers, not ad-men). Frankenfuel biodiesel — obtained from genetically modified plants digested by genetically modified microorganisms — may cause the price of biodiesel to drop from today's $45 to $60 boe equivalent to a third or half that over the next decade. Of course, this assumes that none of the GMOs escape the lab to become self-replicating, omnivorous, and indestructible juggernauts that reduce the surface of the planet to bubbling grey goo before then.

In 2002, the city of Montreal converted 155 of its 1,000 city buses to run on biodiesel. In the first year these Biobuses consumed 550,000 liters of biodiesel, made of 24 percent vegetable oil, 28 percent animal fat and 48 percent used cooking oil. This included winter operations in temperatures of –5°F to –25°F. The Montreal project averted an estimated 1,300 tons of greenhouse gas emissions. Tailpipe emissions of air pollutants were also reduced so that the Biobus effectively cut urban smog.

Other Canadian cities are following the Montreal example. Brampton converted 200 city vehicles, including street vacuums and large graders used to shovel snow. Calgary and Halifax launched fleet biodiesel projects in 2004 using B20 (20 percent biofuel and 80 percent regular diesel). Toronto will use 5 to 6 million liters of biodiesel by the end of 2007, blended with petrodiesel in concentrations up to B50.

For a few hundred dollars, any diesel car or truck can be converted to run on biodiesel or the used-fish-fry equivalent known as "greasel." As long as there are more sources of used frying oil in your area than there are greasel-ready cars, this is a good strategy for cutting your gasoline bills to almost nothing. As more conversions happen and more uses are found for that old vegetable fat, home-brewed biodiesel can and likely will become a community solution to the high price of gas. For more on how to grow, process, and use biodiesel, see Joshua Tickell's book *From the Fryer to the Fuel Tank: The Complete Guide to Using Vegetable Oil as an Alternative Fuel*.

Putting aside the danger of mixing vegetable oil with hard-to-handle methanol, biodiesel has another dark side. Its largest source crop is soybeans, which are, not coincidentally, the largest single cause of rainforest destruction in the Brazilian Amazon. Brazil is now ramping up production of palm oil, which is native to the Amazon basin but not indigenous everywhere. Fuel production is taking land needed for climate regulation and turning it into another cause of climate change.

Between 1985 and 2000, the development of oil-palm plantations was responsible for nearly 90 percent of the deforestation of Malaysia. In Sumatra and Borneo, some 15,000 square miles of forest have been converted to palm farms, and a further 85,000 square miles are scheduled for clearance in Malaysia and Indonesia. As a result, the orangutan is likely to become extinct in the wild; Sumatran rhinos, tigers, gibbons, tapirs, proboscis monkeys, and thousands of other species could follow; and thousands of indigenous people have been evicted from their lands. According to Greenpeace, some 500 Indonesians were tortured when they tried to resist.

Before oil palms, which are small and scrubby, are planted, vast tropical forests, containing a much greater store of carbon, must be felled and burned. Having used up the dryer lands, the plantations are now moving

DISHES

COUNTRY SOYSAGE GRAVY
Serves 6

Soysage
7/8 cup water
1 cup TVP or fresh okara
1 tsp sage
1 tsp thyme
1 tsp onion powder
1 tsp sea salt
¼ tsp black pepper
2 Tbsp oil

Gravy
3 Tbsp oil
¼ cup unbleached flour
2 cups reconstituted dried milk, soup stock, bean juice, or almond milk
1 tsp salt
¼ tsp black pepper
1 tsp sage
1 tsp thyme
1 tsp onion powder

Soysage
Pour hot water over TVP or okara and let stand 20 minutes. Stir in seasonings and mash, then pat into patties or crumble. Heat a pan, add oil, fry until lightly browned.

Gravy
Stir oil and flour together in a 2-quart pan. Stir in liquid, salt, and pepper. Whisk until bubbly. Whisk in seasonings. Add browned soysage last. Serve over biscuits or potatoes.

Difficulty

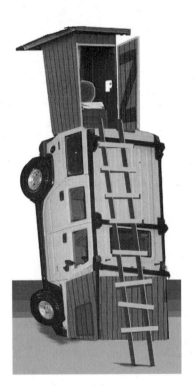

into the swamp forests, which grow on peat. Before they cut the trees, the planters drain the ground. As the peat dries, it oxidizes or burns, releasing even more carbon dioxide to the atmosphere (contributing, in recent years, up to 40 percent of all CO_2 emissions worldwide). Biodiesel, produced on this kind of industrial scale, is a global-warming nightmare.

> *To the extent that a shift away from ancient solar*
> *resources increases human consumption ... this shift could place*
> *additional burdens on the myriad species that depend on the sun's energy for*
> *life. By minimizing society's future energy demands and carefully selecting*
> *energy capture and generation technologies, we can limit human impacts on*
> *many other species.*
> — Jeffrey S. Dukes, 2005

Dimethyl Ether

Dimethyl ether or DME (CH_3OCH_3) is a biofuel made from many of the same plants that are used to make ethanol and biodiesel. The difference is that the plants are gasified into a product that behaves more like natural gas or propane before it is burned in a specially modified engine.

A new generation of nine-liter Volvo-Mack trucks are being built to run on DME because the Swedish engineers think it has the best "well to wheel" energy efficiency of any bio- or non-crude-oil fossil source. Although they are hoping to have the first DME trucks on the road in 2007, Volvo engineers also see potential for DME in fuel cells, in gas turbines for electric power stations, as a domestic heating and cooking fuel, and as a chemical feedstock.

The *China Securities Journal* reported in 2006 that China's estimated annual DME output from planned refineries was 500,000 tons. Water is China's principal constraint, since it takes three liters of water to make one liter of DME. Unlike ethanol or methane, DME is energy-dense and liquid at low pressure, handling like propane. Unlike methanol and biodiesel, it is nontoxic and biodegradable if produced from plants, rather than coal.

> *Building new whaling ships was a bad investment decision in 1850*
> *after the arrival of kerosene fuel, well before kerosene achieved even a five*
> *percent market share .... In our view, building new downstream oil facilities*
> *could be a bad investment during the onset of the new efficiency era (of which*
> *today's hybrid vehicles are a harbinger) and of competitive biofuels.*
> — Amory B. Lovins, E. Kyle Datta, Odd-Even Bustnes, Jonathan G. Koomey,
> and Nathan J. Glasgow, 2004

Hydrogen

Hydrogen (H_2) could be the petroleum of the future, but the kind of future that will be depends on how the hydrogen is produced and used. Hydrogen is a carrier fuel, taking energy that comes from other sources and giving it back as needed to operate machinery or produce heat. If we use solar power and renewables, such as ethanol, to produce hydrogen, and if we use it in nontoxic, recyclable fuel cells, it has already shown us some of its many advantages, including its use as a compact, high-energy fuel for transportation. However, if we produce hydrogen by burning coal, natural gas, or uranium, it could become a monster that will hasten the destruction of the environment and bankrupt the industrial world.

The best features of H_2 are its abundance (it can be derived entirely from water), simplicity (it can be produced by running electric current through water), and benign emissions (it turns back into water when oxidized).

The world is already producing 3 million boe per day of hydrogen — about the oil output of Kuwait at its peak before the first Gulf War. Unfortunately, nearly all of this is extracted not from water — which is still quite energy-expensive to crack, yielding at best about half again as much energy as went into the cracking process — but from increasingly scarce and expensive natural gas, which cracks much more easily but produces CO_2 and other pollutants as byproducts.

Hydrogen is four times bulkier than kerosene jet fuel, but is 2.8 times lighter, so it is possible to use H_2 as a fuel for commercial aircraft. The US Air Force tested liquid H_2 in a B-57 in 1956, and the Russians tried it in a Tu-154 in 1988. Tomorrow's H_2 plane would more likely be a fuel-celled hybrid-electric prop-drive that could, using present technology, be twice as efficient in energy cost as today's jets in the 100- to 400-passenger range. However, the lead time for developing lightweight, long-lived fuel cells is sufficiently long to make H_2 inferior to ethanol as a solution.

Research today focuses on making smaller, lighter, safer reformers and fuel cells for the many potential commercial applications. The major automakers are all actively involved in this effort, designing both large central H_2 generating stations and small reformers that can be distributed for local H_2 production at every gas station.

Engineers are also eyeing untapped wind sites. In North and South Dakota the wind potential — omitting human settlements, forest, agricultural, range lands, wetlands, parks and wilderness areas — could

DISHES

SOY HASH

Soybeans are at their most flavorful when cooked whole and in combination with seasonings that bring out their oil and sugars. This hash recipe uses boiled soybeans to advantage, showing how one of the least-expensive sources of protein can also be one of the best tasting.

Serves 6

1 cup soybeans
½ tsp sea salt
1 bay leaf
½ tsp kombu
1 tsp oil
½ cup flavored granule or chunk-style TVP
3 large potatoes, grated
1 small onion, chopped
1 Tbsp shoyu
¼ cup nutritional yeast
1 tsp sea salt
1 jalapeño pepper, deseeded, deveined and minced (optional)
2 Tbsp oil

Wash and soak dried beans for 1 hour or longer depending on the age of the beans. Drain and add to pressure cooker with water 2 inches over top of beans. Add sea salt, bay leaf, kombu, and 1 tsp oil. Cook at 15 p.s.i. for 90 minutes. Beans should be dark brown and soft enough to mash between your tongue and the roof of your mouth, not crunchy. Pour hot oily water from beans over TVP and let stand 10 minutes. Combine with potatoes, onions, shoyu, nutritional yeast, salt, and optional pepper. Heat iron skillet, add oil and hash mix, and fry until lightly browned and potatoes are tender.

Difficulty

produce 50 million tons of hydrogen and 200 million tons of oxygen (another very useful gas) each year. Even greater potentials can be found in Australia, China, Africa, and elsewhere. Moreover, the latent energy in these wind sites is dwarfed when we start looking into offshore tidal and wave power. Mother Nature has always held these out to us. Up until now, we have mostly ignored the offer. We preferred to play with fire.

I have seen one device that uses H_2 in a low-tech way to cut gasoline costs by a third. A small reformer in the car's luggage compartment, made from a used propane tank or beer keg with electrodes bubbling water, generates enough H_2 pressure in the tank to force a steady stream of hydrogen gas through a small tube into the carburetor or fuel injectors, thereby increasing the combustion and decreasing the amount of gasoline burned by 15 to 30 percent. The car's belt-driven alternator sends electric current to the electrodes, and as long as the driver refills the tank with water periodically, it works.

Commercial versions with names like Hydrogen Boost and HydroGen 2000 are available for around $750 and come with 100-percent-satisfaction guarantees. For $100 more, experienced technicians will even do the installation for you. The Hydrogen-Boost Gas Mileage Enhancement System (from Queensbury, New York) produces 1.5 to 2 liters of hydrogen and oxygen per minute. A fuel-heating system brings the fuel to a temperature that allows more of the injected fuel to vaporize, which increases engine power and also reduces hydrocarbons by 50 percent and cuts carbon monoxide at the tailpipe by 90 percent. Fuel mileage can improve from 15 to 100 percent after installation, depending on the type of car you drive and your driving habits.

To the best of my knowledge I never
had a security briefing which said what some of these
very serious but conservative petroleum geologists say, which is
they think that either now or before the decade is out that we'll reach
peak oil production globally. And with the rise of China and India and oth-
ers coming along, unless we can dramatically reduce our oil usage we will run
out of recoverable oil within 35 to 50 years. And that would mean in addition
to climate change we have a very short time in the life of the planet to turn
this around.

—Bill Clinton, 2006

Change Your Need

*The United States is the wealthiest
nation in the history of the world, yet its inhabitants
are strikingly unhappy. Accordingly, we present to the rest of
mankind, on a planet rife with suffering and tragedy, the spectacle of
a clown civilization. Sustained on a clown diet rich in sugar and fat, we
have developed a clown physiognomy. We dress like clowns. We move about a
landscape filled with cartoon buildings in clown-mobiles, absorbed in clownish
activities. We fill our idle hours enjoying the canned antics of professional
clowns. We perceive God to be an elderly comedian. Death, when we acknowl-
edge it, is just another pratfall on the boob tube. "Bang! You're dead!"*

— James Howard Kunstler, 2005

Okay, it's time to pause and take stock.

After seeing how easy it is to rehabilitate degenerate automotive designers and set them on a new path of righteousness and social responsibility, on pain of having their jobs exported to Shenzhen and Mumbai, we observe that the price of crude would have to reach $600 per barrel before soccer moms might feel the pinch as they schlep half the team to and from the practice field, which itself is an ethanol well.

Is this a good thing or a bad thing?

It's a bad thing.

What is the point, exactly, of finding techno-fixes that will let us continue to live in a burning house?

The personal mobility and consumptive lifestyles enjoyed in North America, Australia, and Europe simply cannot be transferred to another

DISHES

BAKED AUTUMN PUMPKIN

The best pumpkins for cooking are the small ones, three to four pounds — about the size of a cantaloupe. In this recipe you use a larger one as a serving bowl for buckwheat and traditional autumn seasonings, imparting its rich pumpkin flavor while baking. Because we are not dishing up the pumpkin, we are not concerned about the chewy, fibrous texture, so you can have your large pumpkins and eat them too.

Serves 6 to 10

Sour Cream
¼ pound silken tofu
Pinch sea salt
1 tsp lemon juice
Dash of rice vinegar

Pumpkin
One large (8- to 10-pound) pumpkin
1 cup water
½ tsp sea salt
½ cup toasted buckwheat
2 Tbsp oil
½ pound sliced mushrooms
4 stalks celery
2 medium onions
5 slices of whole grain bread, toasted and cubed
2 cloves garlic, minced
1 medium carrot, diced
1 red bell pepper, chopped
¼ cup hazelnuts chopped and toasted
⅓ cup hazelnut meal
⅓ cup raisins
⅓ cup dried cranberries
1 tsp dried sage, crumbled
1 tsp sea salt or to taste
½ tsp ground black pepper or to taste
2 to 3 Tbsp pomegranate syrup
Fresh seasonal herbs (parsley, mint, basil, sage, fennel, or cilantro) ☞

4 to 8 billion people already or soon to be living on Earth. It isn't just about petroleum, after all. It is about unrestrained human population and the consumer ethos that is killing every other species on the planet except cockroaches and bed lice.

At the current annual U.S. grain consumption of 900 kilograms per person, including industrial use, China's grain consumption in 2031 would equal roughly two-thirds of the current world grain harvest. If paper use per person in China in 2031 reaches the current U.S. level, this translates into 305 million tons of paper — double existing world production of 161 million tons. There go the world's forests.

— Lester Brown, 2006

Somehow it seems hard for many citizens of the First World to grasp this concept of parity, but how can we ask Chinese, Arabs and Africans to forego our excesses? Could it be that if they don't, then they too will become fat clowns wielding nuclear weapons while silently wiping every other animal from the planet, including, finally, the human animal too?

How about if we instead *imagine* a crisis brought on by Peak Oil, and rather than having the skunk works at Boeing, Amory Lovins' hand calculator, or Indian engineers save us, we actually begin to alter our lifestyles to orient ourselves toward survival?

In the worst-case scenario, it can't hurt us to be prepared. In the best-case scenario, we are all better off for having made the change.

This is a better way to approach the post-petroleum world.

We have to liberate the workforce from office-based jobs and let them work in their village, through the modern technology of emails and faxes and video conferencing. We have to address the distribution of food: much of the food in supermarkets today comes from at least a continent or two away. We need to return to local farms. And we have to attack globalization: as energy prices soar, manufacturing things close to home will begin to make sense again.

— Matthew Simmons, 2005

Stay Home

In a well-designed homestead, many of the comforts that you once found somewhere distant can be found, made, or substituted right where you are.

One way to stay home more is simply to work at home, or to work less elsewhere. Compressed work schedules and flextime can help reduce commutes to fewer days per week as you spend more time at a distant office when you are there, but you go there less frequently. Companies that have tried these programs have discovered there is less absenteeism, fewer late employees, and less use of sick leave.

Another way to stay home more is to insist on shorter workweeks. Who enshrined 40 hours as the standard for so many countries? Countries that have gone to 35- and 30-hour weeks have discovered a 30-hour workforce is healthier and happier.

Telecommuting eliminates the need to physically move yourself from home to work. It may cost you a little more for space, office equipment, and utilities at home, but you avoid the time and expense spent in repetitive travel.

> *Perhaps you have had the experience of running*
> *out of gas and having to push your car a few feet to get it off*
> *the road. That's hard work. Now imagine pushing your car 20 or 30 miles.*
> *That is the service performed for us by a single gallon of gasoline, for which*
> *we currently pay $2.65. That gallon of fuel is the energy equivalent of roughly*
> *six weeks of hard human labor.*
> — Richard Heinberg, 2006

Walk

In a well-designed community, home and work are within walking or biking distance of each other, and the trip is made pleasurable by winding footpaths through nature, greenways, and graded trails, some with stopping points at scenic vistas or at exercise or learning enrichment stations. Along the way there may be places where people can chat with neighbors, have a cup of coffee, read a book, or otherwise enjoy the sense of community they have created and regularly contribute to.

Regular walking is very important for your health. Obesity and related medical problems can be effectively prevented and/or cured by moving on foot on a daily basis. The widespread habit of taking the car for short grocery trips significantly contributes to both obesity and air pollution.

Over the last 40 years, Copenhagen has developed the Strøget, the world's longest pedestrian shopping area, thanks to the work of Danish architect Jan Gehl. Due to the influence of city planners like Gehl, pedestrian traffic is now officially encouraged in many parts of the European Union, and dedicated walking paths exist or are under construction in most large European cities, often in conjunction with bikeways, streetcars, and other light-transit options.

Baked Pumpkin cont.

Sliced persimmon or wedges of pomegranate

Sour Cream
Blend ingredients until smooth and chill.

Pumpkin
Scrub pumpkin well with a soft brush. Allow to dry. Using a heavy knife, cut a lid, about 5 to 6 inches in diameter, from the top of the pumpkin. Scoop out the pumpkin seeds and set them aside for future roasting. Combine water and salt in a 2-quart saucepan, cover, and bring to a boil over high heat. Add buckwheat, cover, and steam 15 minutes. Transfer the cooked buckwheat to a large mixing bowl.

Preheat oven to 375°F. Heat oil in skillet and add mushrooms, celery, and onions. Sauté, stirring frequently, until softened and lightly browned, about 8 to 10 minutes. Add the remaining ingredients and sauté 2 minutes to blend flavors. Add to bowl with the buckwheat and mix. Spoon the mixture into the prepared pumpkin and cover it with the pumpkin lid. Place on baking sheet.

Bake 45 to 75 minutes, until the pumpkin feels soft when pressed but before it collapses. Remove lid, move to serving platter, and garnish with dollop of sour cream, fresh herbs, and sliced persimmons or wedges of pomegranate. Ladle contents onto individual plates without cutting up the pumpkin.

Substitutions include yellow cornmeal, oatmeal, bulgur, or 7-grain cereal; local fruits, nuts, and berries.

Difficulty

DISHES

FETA SALAD SANDWICHES

Serves 4

4 ounces feta cheese, crumbled (about ⅔ cup), or crumbled tofu marinated in vinegar
¼ cup olive or local cold-pressed oil
3 Tbsp water
2 Tbsp soy mayonnaise
1 tsp fresh lemon juice
1½ tsp fresh oregano leaves or ½ tsp dried oregano
Sea salt and freshly milled black pepper
Baby spinach (a handful)
4 cherry tomatoes, thinly sliced
6-inch English cucumber or regular cucumber, seeded and thinly sliced (about 1½ cups)
1¾ cup cooked or 15-ounce can of chickpeas, rinsed and drained
½ cup fresh mint leaves
⅓ cup sliced olives
6 peperoncini (Italian pickled peppers), chopped
Four 5- to 6-inch pita rounds, cut in half

Blend feta, oil, 3 Tbsp water, mayonnaise, lemon juice, and oregano until smooth. Add salt and pepper to taste. Mix the spinach, tomatoes, cucumber, chickpeas, mint leaves, olives, and peperoncini with the feta dressing. Stuff the salad mixture into the 8 pita halves and serve.

Difficulty

The average Atlanta resident spends more than 12 hours a week stuck in traffic. These are prime hours that might be better spent with family, at leisure or in other meaningful activity. And after arriving home, many of these commuters are complaining about the speed and volume of traffic where they live and the long distances they must travel to get basic products and services. A growing number now want peacefulness where they live and an end to the sprawl they bought into.

— Dan Burden, 2001

Cycle

The bicycle is the world's most popular transport vehicle. Bike enthusiasts will tell you that, pound for pound, a person on a bicycle expends less energy than people using any other mode of travel. Of course, they're forgetting surfboards, kite-surfboards, sailboats, ice skates, skateboards, hang gliders, and sail-cars, but never mind. Bikes are still great. They are great whether they are upright or recumbent; one-, two-, three-, or four-wheeled; or hybridized with pedal assist.

Bicycles are so important to the future of urban transportation that bike riders should be paid for the example they set. Let's write our government officials and suggest they put a progressive tax on car engines above three liters in size and rebate that to cyclists, starting in alphabetical order.

If you plan to make a personal conversion from car to bike, it is best to do it in stages. Bicycling is a pleasurable and healthy experience, but it does require exertion, so you may need to condition yourself by building up from short trips to longer commutes. Good equipment and appropriate clothing helps, and both have advanced markedly in the past 20 years. With the right gear it is now possible to bike relatively comfortably in bad weather, over rough terrain, and with modest amounts of cargo. People who bike between home and work may have to carry or pre-position a change of clothes, and they might try to persuade their employer to put in showers and lockers, but the extra effort will accrue to their health. They will also save money, because cars and mass transit are both more expensive.

All too often, the world of the car is an unsafe world for the bicycle. This is changing. Take the German National Plan on Bicycles; by 2012 Germany will broaden its cycle tracks, increase interconnections between tracks, and create the D-netz of long-distance intercity tracks. The country will invest $100 million over ten years, with a target of 30 percent car-to-bike conversion, in the process reducing annual CO_2 output by 23 million tons per year.

The idea of bike-to-rail has been discussed for the past 30 years, but its implementation has been slow. Many people bike from home to the nearest rail station, but all too often parking bicycles or carrying them aboard is more of a hassle than it should be. Metropolitan areas need to encourage bike-to-rail. They should even pay people to participate (starting alphabetically).

Get a Horse

The traditional horse-powered vehicle has sustained speeds of 5 to 7 miles per hour with occasional bursts of 10 to 12 miles per hour. Even though this seems like a slow method of getting around, the number of horse-drawn vehicles has been steadily increasing in the US and Canada for the past 50 years.

Most people recognize the Amish. More than 100,000 of them refuse to use motor vehicles for religious reasons. They believe it is more important to maintain a close-knit family, church, and community than to get somewhere quickly. They see car culture as a disruptive, destructive force that is especially harmful in the hands of young people. Not to mention the car radio.

Style, speed, comfort, and convenience — all the attributes used to sell cars — are seen by the Amish as signs warning that we are on the wrong track. Hmmm.

The Amish are also opposed to insurance for moral reasons. They feel that written policies are proof one is expecting something bad to happen and is trusting in man instead of God. The Old Order does not want to share an unequal yoke with worldly insurance companies, which may behave in unchristian ways, especially when it comes to litigation, something insurance companies do a lot of, and something the Amish would rather not do at all.

Among the "plain people," children get their first experience driving a horse in the field, operating various farm implements. By age nine, an Amish child may be allowed to take the family buggy down a back lane, although he or she may have already used a goat or pony cart when younger. By 12, a boy will be an accomplished driver, and by 16 he will likely have his own horse and open buggy. As an adult, his buggy will have a top and possibly a second or third seat, depending on the size of his family. Of course, "adult" is a relative term because by age 12 the average Amish boy or girl will have more responsibility than most of their "English" neighbors have at twice that age.

The world's horse population is estimated at 75 million. China not only has the most people in the world, but also has the most horses — 10 million.

Horses are intelligent, caring, and courageous animals, but in the care of an untrained owner they are helpless to protect themselves and can become weak, dangerous, and a burden. While mules are smarter, harder working, more resilient, and more tolerant of abuse, the same advice applies.

Share a Ride

An alternative to owning a car, or using a ton of steel to move just one occupant, is ride-sharing. All that is required is willingness to share the trip and a method for riders and drivers to find one another. Hitchhiking is one variant of ride-sharing, but it is more random, and its safety and legality are problematic. Neighbors who commute on a regular basis to workplaces, rail stations, shopping centers, schools, or other destinations often arrange to carpool, sharing the costs, cars, and driving. But there are newer variants, and because they reduce urban smog and traffic, some are even subsidized by government.

Increasing numbers of cities, campuses, and rural activity centers are seeing ride-share boards pop up, with messages posted asking for or offering rides. In some green neighborhoods, residents are surveyed to discover their most common travel needs, and a computer program then matches potential ride-sharers.

We need to consume less; less packaging, less red meat, less fast food, less car, less house. Consuming less does not mean living below the poverty line, and it brings its own benefits; better physical fitness, healthier living, more investment in local community, a slower paced lifestyle, and more money (just selling your car can save you an average of $3,000 a year). Cultural bigotry demanded that the [Greenland] Christian Vikings starve rather than change to resemble their more adaptive heathen neighbors. We now face a crucially similar choice: do we keep the expensive trappings of our lives, in which we invest our money, effort, and social identities, and starve when we can no longer support them? Or do we merge "primitive" strategies of simplicity with our technological know-how to create survival tools that are better suited to the world as it changes around us?

— Sorcha Keepers, 2005

Share a Car

The average North American car is driven just 66 minutes a day, but fixed capital costs, licensing, insurance premiums, and depreciation don't respect that. North Americans spend about 15 percent of their household income on their cars, up 2 percent from 1990. Each year more than 20 million cars are made but not sold because they are beyond the financial reach of buyers.

Car-sharing, launched in 1987 in Switzerland and 1988 in Germany, came to North America via Quebec in 1993. As of December 2004, 15 US car-sharing programs claimed 61,781 members sharing 1,045 vehicles, and 11 Canadian car-sharing programs claimed 10,759 members sharing 528 vehicles.

If you drive fewer than 7,500 miles a year, car-sharing could be saving you thousands of dollars.

Online car-sharing networks offer a choice of vehicle types, from motor scooters to large trucks. You pay only when you use them. You reserve the vehicle by phone or Internet; use it for a few hours or a week. You pay per use and never have to worry about repairs, insurance, or monthly parking.

European Car Sharing is an umbrella organization for car-sharing groups with 68 member organizations in seven European countries. Car Sharing Canada is a similar umbrella group in Canada. There are organizations and federations in Israel and China — three in Singapore alone. The Swiss government's department of energy reports that when former car owners join car-sharing networks, the amount they drive is reduced by an average of 72 percent.

In Germany, where car-sharing enjoys federal support, growth rates are around 10 percent annually for the last decade. Some 80,000 people use car-sharing services in more than 250 German municipalities. In Berlin, a member of GreenWheels might pay three euros an hour for a compact car and ten cents per kilometer driven. If the client checked the car out for three hours and drove 40 kilometers (25 miles), the total bill would come to 13 euros (about $15.50 US). One would need to make more than two such trips each day for a year to pay the purchase price on Germany's least-expensive car, the VW Fox. Germany's largest car-sharing network offers discounted taxi and bus passes for its members and also provides home grocery delivery.

> *Thirty years from now there will be a huge*
> *amount of oil — and no buyers. Oil will be left in the ground.*
> *The Stone Age came to an end, not because we had a lack of stones,*
> *and the Oil Age will come to an end not because we have a lack of oil ....*
> *[Fuel cell technology] is coming before the end of the decade and will cut gaso-*
> *line consumption by almost 100 per cent .... On the supply side it is easy to*
> *find oil and produce it, and on the demand side there are so many new*
> *technologies, especially when it comes to automobiles.*
> — Sheikh Zaki Yamani, 2000

BREADS

BASIC BISCUITS
16 biscuits

2 cups white flour (or 1 cup white and 1 cup whole wheat)
3 tsp aluminum-free baking powder
½ tsp sea salt
⅓ cup olive or other local cold-pressed oil
½ cup milk, soymilk, or water

Preheat oven to 375°F. Stir dry ingredients together, add oil and milk, and mix well. Turn out on a lightly floured board, knead 5 times, and pat down to ½ inch thick. Cut rounds with 2-inch biscuit cutter or a glass (or cut squares with knife). Put on baking sheet and bake 15 to 20 minutes or until golden brown.

Variations
Cheese biscuits: Add ½ cup grated soy cheese or ¼ cup nutritional yeast to dough.
Fruit biscuits: Add 1 Tbsp honey and ½ cup dried fruit (raisins, currants, blueberries, cherries) to dough.

Substitutions
Corn flour, coconut milk.
For 1 tsp of baking powder: Use ⅝ tsp cream of tartar plus ¼ tsp baking soda **or** two parts cream of tartar to one part baking soda plus one part cornstarch **or** 1 tsp baker's ammonia.

Difficulty

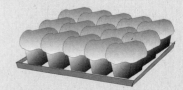

BREADS

DROP BISCUITS (STOVE-TOP, OVEN, CAMPFIRE)

16 biscuits

Use the same ingredients as for basic biscuits (p. 149), but add 2 Tbsp more milk or water and drop dough onto oiled baking pan surface from the mixing spoon. Place pan on coals or stovetop. Cover pan and cook until done. If baking over campfire or on wood stove, cover with foil to keep out ash. On stovetop, you may need to flip biscuits halfway through.

Variation

Add cheese or nutritional yeast or dried fruits, as described for basic biscuits (p. 149).

Difficulty

In the United States, Flexcar (www.flexcar.com) memberships are available in Seattle, Portland, Washington DC, Los Angeles, San Diego, San Francisco, and Chicago. Zipcar (zipcar.com) is available in Boston and eight other cities. Do a web search for "car sharing" to find a service in your area.

Use Mass Transit

Rapid transit was devised in about 1834, when New York engineer John Stephenson invented the horse-car that could run on tramways — flat rails laid in the streets. Within a short time, Vienna, Berlin, Paris, London, Liverpool, and Glasgow had horse-trams running. The history of mass transit is similar in many parts of the world, despite differences in the size and layout of various cities. The pattern is usually one of boom and bust, as the benefits of mass-transit were alternatively overshadowed by the traffic congestion it created. In an 1892 issue of *Scribner's Magazine,* Thomas Curtis Clarke described this pattern in Boston in the late 19th century.

> Boston jogged along for many years with slow, infrequent, and shabby horse-cars. The lines were owned by different corporations, and people could not change from the cars of one line to those of another without paying extra fare. This, naturally enough, did not encourage travel nor the growth of the city. But as neither streets nor cars were uncomfortably crowded, some wise men of Boston said: "Behold, how much better off we are than those wretched New Yorkers!"
>
> Eminent citizens went to the Statehouse and opposed the grant of more rapid transit facilities, on the ground that it was better and healthier to walk than to ride. They did not stop to consider that this would mean the increase of the crowded tenement system with all its horrors.
>
> But in an evil hour for the slow people, the seven different horse-car systems who had attempted to carry the people, were consolidated into one, called the West End Company.
>
> The first benefit was single fares. Then came more frequent cars. Then the electric system was introduced. At first it was attempted to run the car motors by wires placed in conduits. It was found that this led to all sorts of delays due to the loss of current from induction and grounding. The small boy became an important factor. He soon discovered that by dropping a forked wire into the slot after dark, which should straddle

the conductor and touch the sides, he could short-circuit the current, and produce a most beautiful display of green sparks. This also had the effect of stopping every car on that division, which was still more delightful, and makes some of us wish that similar opportunities had been offered to us in our boyhood.

The city authorities of Boston wisely gave permission to replace the conduits by overhead wires and trolleys .... Since then all has gone well.

The simplicity and economy of the system has allowed its extension into the outlying districts, until there are now 245 miles of single track, of which 81 miles is now electrically equipped, and all soon will be. This is the longest system of any [US] American city except Philadelphia, which has 340 miles of single track.

The number of passengers carried has increased from 92,000,000 in 1887, the year of consolidation, to 119,000,000 in 1891. The population has increased in the same time from 425,000 to 451,000. This gives the yearly number of rides per inhabitant, 263.

Inner-city rail, or "light rail," is still a very efficient way to move large numbers of people while consuming less energy, if used to capacity, than private vehicles or buses. When you add in a well-designed bike-to-rail system, you can extend the reach of each node — every station — farther out, to encompass the distances that bicycles can cover. Adding taxis and light buses gives flexibility for non-cyclists and for those times when a bicycle is impractical.

Taxis and Buses

As we saw in Step 8, neither taxis nor buses have to be petroleum powered. They can be recharged directly by sun, tide, and wind when parked, or powered by renewable biofuels. Taxis and buses have their essential niche in any transport scheme, whether urban or rural, industrialized or not. Even on the most remote atolls of the South Pacific, if the population is large enough there will be a small jitney, either gas or electric, to carry people and commodities around.

Cuba's "special period" began when Mikhail Gobachev delicately explained to Fidel Castro that the Soviet Union could no longer supply cheap products transported halfway around the world because the Soviet

Union was in the process of imploding after the disaster of Chernobyl, the billions of rubles wasted chasing the chimera of Star Wars space shields, the leakage of MTV and the cyberworld into Russian homes and cafes, and sheer bureaucratic exhaustion. Castro, in turn, told the people of Cuba that henceforward they would have to tighten their belts.

From 1989 to 1992, Cuba lost 85 percent of its trade. It lost 85 percent of its fertilizer and 93 percent of its pesticides. The gasoline available for agriculture dropped by half. In ten years, Cuba went from having more tractors and combines than the Central Valley of California to having 1,000 yoke of oxen. By 1994, agricultural output had dropped to half its 1990 level. Per capita daily calories in the Cuban diet plunged by 36 percent, which was the equivalent of the whole population going from three meals per day to two. The average Cuban dropped ten pounds. Cubans literally tightened their belts. Then they punched holes in them so they could tighten them more.

Spontaneous home gardening, organized food rationing, and emergency food distribution to the most vulnerable prevented the Cuban population from experiencing the mass famines suffered in that other former Soviet client, North Korea, at the same time.

From 1995 to 2001, by changing its agriculture, Cuba recovered 90 percent of its caloric intake. It converted from high-input, fossil-fuel-dependent farming to self-reliant organic gardening and urban permaculture. Urban gardens today produce 60 percent of the vegetables consumed in Cuba and more than 8,000 medicinal plants.

Cuba also revolutionized its public transportation systems. To transport people in cities, private cars were replaced by bicycles, pedal-rickshaws, horse-drawn cabs, and light trucks. Between cities, giant "Camels," semi-trailers retrofitted to seat 300 people, moved travelers more efficiently than the smaller 60-passenger buses that existed in the petroleum age.

Ten years ago Cuba, showing the resilience and creativity of an independent-spirited people, became the first post-petroleum nation. While it still uses some petroleum today, notably from Venezuela, it has demonstrated the value of a well-educated populace (96 percent literacy), the viability of organic agriculture and permaculture, and the importance of government intervention to establish a safety net for those least able to make rapid major changes in their lives.

> *C'est l'imagination qui gouverne le genre humain.*
> *(The human race is governed by its imagination.)*
> — Napoleon Bonaparte, c. 1800

Imagine Sustainability

We live on a finite object hanging
in space, a small, water-covered sphere with 58
million square miles of land sticking up through the water.
The ten percent of that land that is considered arable supports
the world's nearly 6.4 billion people. But it doesn't support them
equally. The average person in the U.S. uses 24 acres of land, five of which
are devoted just to supporting their car use. If everyone on the planet lived
at that standard of living, we would need five Earths to support them all —
four for the people, one for their cars. An average person living in the Southern
Hemisphere lives on 2.5 acres. It can be argued that adding one car in the U.S.
is the equivalent in resource use of adding two people in the world's South. If
all of the 6.4 billion of us on the planet were to live the same lifestyle and
all the available productive land were used, each person would use 4.5
acres of land. The poor of the South would nearly double their stan-
dard of living; the average [US] American would have to cut
back to less than she currently spends on her car.

— Sorcha Keepers, 2005

On a planet with 6 billion fellow beings with opposable thumbs, fourth-level tools, and an appetite for expansion, anyone concerned with the survival of their progeny must at this point be asking some fundamental questions.

What is sustainability? Ultimately nothing in the physical universe sustains, so, like the emperor's favorite fashion, the Geist of our current Zeit has no clothes. The quest for sustainability is ultimately futile. There is no there to get to.

What we really must try to accomplish with "sustainability" is a more or less steady-state economy in which we destroy nothing, reuse and recycle, and try to keep the natural world, which provides our every need, healthy and robust. In this way, we hope to sustain our puny existences for their natural span, retain some cultural heritage to pass on to the next generation, and prejudice the choices of our descendants as little as humanly possible.

Standing in opposition to this is our modern Nemesis, technology, wielding the sword of righteous retribution that justice demands for our ignorance and hubris. We stole fire from the gods. They want it back.

In 2001, Bill Joy published a lengthy screed about the trajectory of recent technology in *Wired* magazine. Remembering Finagle's law, "anything that can go wrong, will" (the fact that this is commonly known today as Murphy's law illustrates the point), he recounted our overuse of DDT and antibiotics and the emergence of super-resistant viruses and bacteria, and went on to describe our forays into genetics and the building blocks of life. He said, "The cause of many such surprises seems clear: the systems involved are complex, involving interaction among and feedback between many parts. Any changes to such a system will cascade in ways that are difficult to predict; this is especially true when human actions are involved."

For Joy, the most frightening scenarios were those that arose from the unintended consequences of his own life's work. Co-founder of Sun Microsystems, Joy was designer of three microprocessor architectures. He wrote that "the nuclear, biological, and chemical (NBC) technologies used in 20th century weapons of mass destruction were and are largely military, developed in government laboratories. In sharp contrast, the 21st century GNR [geno-, nano-, robo-] technologies have clear commercial uses and are being developed almost exclusively by corporate enterprises .... The new Pandora's boxes of genetics, nanotechnology, and robotics are almost open, yet we seem hardly to have noticed. Ideas can't be put back in a box; unlike uranium or plutonium, they don't need to be mined and refined, and they can be freely copied. Once they are out, they are out."

The four horses standing lathered and snorting at the edge of our global village bear riders carrying 21st century technologies into the post-petroleum era. The Four Horsemen are Bio, Robo, CO_2, and Nuke.

"Bio" wields the threat of chemical and genetic terror, whether in the form of escaped nanobugs, genes gone haywire, unmonitored or unlisted toxic waste sites, or myriad other time bombs. With replicating genetic assemblers, we are just one accident away from reducing all forests to photovoltaic-generating crabgrass.

> *I watched as the Lamb opened the first of the seven seals.*
> *Then I heard one of the four living creatures say in a voice like thunder,*
> *"Come!" I looked, and there before me was a white horse! Its rider held a bow,*
> *and he was given a crown, and he rode out as a conqueror bent on conquest.*
>
> — *Revelations 6:1–2*

"Robo" could simply be the inability to produce enough reliable electricity to propel elevators to the upper floors of high-rise buildings, or it could be the threat of unimpeded access to weapons of mass destruction via the Internet. Robotics need not be mechanical; it can be mere mathematics, like a formula for high explosives, or photovoltaic-generating crabgrass.

"CO_2" is the petro-binge hangover we have bequeathed to the next hundred generations of Earth's inhabitants. That would include spreading desertification in mid-continent regions, greater storm damage and erosion in coastal areas, and a dazzling array of new pestilences and diseases brought about by leaking toxins and pharmaceuticals, ecosystem destruction, and out-migrations of organisms from disturbed niches.

Instead of providing reliable, abundant energy that is "too cheap to meter," our nuclear power investments represent perpetual requirements for vigilance lest they either poison us by random genetic engineering or fall into the hands of zealots with the ability to turn them to the Dark Side.

"Nuke" is where our techno-hubris gets bitten back. Everywhere Nuke exists, the ability to end life on this world is placed in the fickle hand of fate.

What is needed in response to these threats is, first, a foreswearing. We must abjure the sources of these threats and forsake all benefit from their use. And then, as quickly as we can, we need to obtain the fruits offered by these demons from more benign devas, lest we wander in search again to places from whence nothing good can come.

We need to design with nature as our ally, not our opponent. Nature is our champion, and she will, given space and time, protect us from our Nemesis.

Energy-Intensive Building

Most housing in the industrial world today is industrial. Steels, alloys, hydrocarbon-based plastics, cement, and mechanically grown and processed

Dr. Strange meets Eternity, from "If Eternity Should Fail," Strange Tales No. 138, November 1965, marvelmasterworks.com © 1965 Marvel Comics.

plant products comprise the building blocks of our homes, offices, cities, and transportation and utility infrastructure. A simple lightbulb may contain bauxite and tungsten mined in Bolivia, processed into aluminum screws and fine wire in China, and assembled in Africa using coated glass from Argentina before passing through a distributor in Marseilles and then on to a shopping center in Quebec. The higher costs of fossil fuels; the depletion of bauxite and tungsten mines; the need to pay fair wages for labor in South America, China, and Africa; and the availability of local alternatives will combine to change this business model.

The embodied energy in building materials is greatest in aluminum (71,926 kilowatt-hours per ton), then steel, glass, plastic, cement, bricks, and timber. By the end of the last ice age, our ancestors had learned to char timbers to increase their pest and rot resistance. When we learned to make "artificial stone" by firing clay in simple kilns, we were able to emerge from the caves and build kivas in canyons. For many thousand years we could divide human habitat between permanent, mostly agricultural, settlements made of mud-brick and stone, and more temporary, lightweight, and transportable settlements made of wood, bone, plant fiber, and skins.

When we start to think about sustainability, we have these two strategies. Permanent settlements look to their surroundings and devise defenses against predictable threats. If they are on the coast, they may have to shield themselves from hurricanes and tsunamis. In river basins they have to plan for flooding. If they are forested, they have to consider lightning and fire. In some areas, a village might be expected to protect its occupants against tornadoes, earthquakes or volcanoes. In each of these cases, the design of the built environment reflects the essence of the particular location.

A lightweight building strategy also prepares for known catastrophes. The plains tepee withstood the 1811–12 New Madrid earthquakes better than the wooden homes of frontier St. Louis. Mongolian yurts thwart Gobi dust storms using a Bernoulli effect, channeling winds harmlessly around a cone of enclosed space. The lightweight strategy relies on mobility, too. When the hunting is bad, the grazing bare, or the seasons changing, it's time to hit the road.

The Maya are perhaps the only still-extant culture to have survived at least two and possibly three major climate changes. The first came around the first century CE. Partially in response, the Maya developed the Long Count calendar to help them foretell any unwelcome repeat of an experience that destroyed many great cities, some 500 years old, and brought starvation to untold thousands of people.

*Nature has many
thresholds that we discover only when
it is too late. In our fast-forward world, we learn
that we have crossed them only after the fact, leaving
little time to adjust. For example, when we exceed the sustainable
catch of a fishery, the stocks begin to shrink. Once this threshold is
crossed, we have a limited time in which to back off and lighten the catch.
If we fail to meet this deadline, breeding populations shrink to where the
fishery is no longer viable, and it collapses. We know from earlier civilizations
that the lead indicators of economic decline were environmental, not economic.
The trees went first, then the soil, and finally the civilization itself.
Our situation today is far more challenging because in addition to shrinking
forests and eroding soils, we must deal with falling water tables, more frequent
crop-withering heat waves, collapsing fisheries, expanding deserts, deteriorating
rangelands, dying coral reefs, melting glaciers, rising seas, more-powerful
storms, disappearing species, and, soon, shrinking oil supplies. Although
these ecologically destructive trends have been evident for some time,
and some have been reversed at the national level, not one has
been reversed at the global level.*

— Lester Brown, 2006

The Long Count calendar tracks the movements of the night sky and the changing of the seasons, as the Gregorian calendar does, but it adds a few interesting twists. One twist has to do with sets of potential outcomes, and it involved a parallel universe of calendars. Which calendar was used depended on empirical evidence drawn from observation of nature. For example, if a Mayan saw that certain birds or insects were appearing at new times of the year, or that jaguars were drinking from different sources of water, he turned the calendar to a new page to account for it. In this way, the signs and omens of impending climate change would not be missed.

Following their complex calendar, the Maya changed water sources, grew different crops in new locations, and relocated entire populations away from the paths of storms and floods. This strategy of mobility rescued their culture in the Classic period (600 CE) as they abandoned cities in central Mexico, including Teotihuacan, in order to build cities in fertile areas farther to the east.

City populations swelled in the late Classic period, in large part because the Maya began to forget their light, mobile strategy and to cover their entire region with elaborate new cities and dense supporting

BREADS

FLOUR TORTILLA
Makes 4 tortillas

1 cup white flour (or half white and half whole wheat)
2 Tbsp local cold-pressed oil
½ tsp aluminum-free baking powder
¼ tsp sea salt
Water

Mix ingredients; stir in enough warm water to make a dough that holds together, about ⅓ cup. Knead a few times and divide into 4 balls. Cover with a towel to rest 15 minutes. Flatten into 8-inch rounds using a tortilla press, rolling pin, or your hands. Lay out in a sweeping motion (so that one edge touches first) on a hot, ungreased pan or griddle. Turn as soon as blisters form, 15 to 30 seconds. Remove when it rises and cover with a towel to keep it warm and flexible.

Difficulty

BREADS

IRISH SODA BREAD
Makes 2 loaves

4 cups all-purpose or whole-wheat flour
1 tsp aluminum-free baking powder
1 tsp baking soda
1 tsp sea salt
2 tsp grated orange zest
1 tsp caraway seeds
¼ cup butter or margarine, softened
1 cup dried currants or golden raisins
¼ cup of honey
1 to 1½ cups buttermilk or sour milk at room temperature, or substitute rice milk or almond milk, soured with cider vinegar
1 egg or equivalent flaxseed substitute
2 Tbsp milk or soymilk
Sprinkle of salt
Caraway seeds

Preheat oven to 350°F. Combine flour, baking powder, and baking soda. Add salt, orange zest, and caraway seeds. Mix butter into flour mixture by hand until the dough resembles coarse crumbs. Mix in currants or raisins. Set aside. In a medium bowl, combine honey with 1½ cups buttermilk and mix into flour mixture until dough is sticky. Turn out onto a floured surface and knead 1 minute. Cut dough in half, shape into 2 round loaves, and place on greased baking sheet. Using sharp knife, score ½-inch-deep lines down centers. Create glaze by beating the egg with 2

populations. Intensive farming fed their high numbers in the short term, but their vulnerability grew apace. Sediments drawn from ancient lakebeds show that the second Mayan decline corresponded to widespread deforestation and eroded, exhausted soils.

Climate evidence suggests that a long drought period began soon after 800 CE, and large site abandonments took place until 830. The Maya retreated into the Yucatan, the highlands of Guatemala, and the coasts of Belize, but, weakened and factionalized by fights over diminishing resources, they became sitting ducks for incursions by other nations and, eventually, the arrival of the Spanish conquistadores.

Still, the resilient spirit of the Maya, who number today about 8 million, ultimately gave them all they needed to survive into the present. They are now engaged in a political struggle to gain fair treatment and respect in the modern states that cover their homeland. From the standpoint of being prepared for climate change and the post-petroleum era, they are more ready than most. Despite the huge tourist industry of the "Mayan Riviera," the Yucatan is a net exporter of food and energy. Mexico supplies most of the fresh vegetables imported into the United States. These are people who know how to grow food.

It is difficult to imagine a bug-out strategy for villages and population centers today, whether we are talking about Guatemala or Newark. For one thing, there are no empty lands to bug-out to. Humans cover the planet, in some places to a density of several people per square foot, arranged vertically. The fact that the land was already occupied didn't stop Europeans from pushing Native Americans ever westward, but each nation that was bumped had to turn around and bump the nation west of itself. Try that today and you would be bumped from behind.

The other, less-mobile, survival strategy is to build more wisely. I was recently speaking (about, what else? Peak Oil) in a large church in New York City, and as I waited my turn for the podium, I stared around at the walls and ceiling, three stories high. The previous building on this site would have been made of fired brick and/or quarried stone and, given the seismic stability of the Manhattan bedrock, would have lasted as long as its wooden roof was maintained. Sometime in the past 30 or 40 years, the more sustainable structure had been torn down and replaced with architecture that reflected the capabilities of late-20th-century engineering and materials. The walls were now steel-reinforced concrete, as was the roof, and suspended from the roof were shelves of cement, lowered into the space below the ceiling to dampen echoes in the great hall.

As I sat there peering up, I tried to imagine how long those suspended cement baffles would last. The steel inside them would not rust quickly in the dry atmosphere of the church, but the cement itself was just lime, sand, and stones. It would remain very strong for 50 years, and then it would slowly begin to embrittle from the outside in. Eventually, perhaps after another 50 years, larger and larger pieces would begin flaking off. In a future century, how would it be repaired? It would have taken between 2,000 and 3,000 degrees of heat to bake that cement in a large kiln, and to erect this large church and raise those baffles into place required very large machinery — massive cement mixers and very tall cranes.

In the minds of today's city planners, 50 years is a long time. All through the past half-century, old landmarks have been routinely taken down to make way for newer edifices, no matter the structural condition of the originals. Today's new buildings are often designed to have a much shorter life span than their predecessors. The United Nations building in New York is a good example of designed obsolescence.

Not so long ago, a big city building would have been expected to stand for much longer than 50 years. In many parts of Europe it was normal to plant a forest of oak trees when a new roof was put on a great cathedral or university hall. Five hundred or a thousand years later, when the roof had to be replaced, those trees were ready to serve, and another new forest was planted in their place. In Japan, large Shinto temples are designed to be taken apart, timber by timber, at regular intervals for inspection and replacement of any defective parts. This is thinking in terms of sustainability.

In most ecovillages you visit, the structures you see reflect their surroundings. In forested villages there will be timber and stone buildings with living roofs. In dryland villages they may be adobe and tile, or straw bale, bamboo, and thatch. In cities, builders might use a lot of "urbanite," or recycled metal, glass, and broken concrete. In many places there are rammed earth, cob, and earthbag buildings because the versatility of those styles makes them practical over a wide range of geographic zones. The point is the materials come from close at hand, typically right under your feet. Replacement materials come from the same place when it is time to take care of your buildings through routine maintenance.

Designers of natural buildings ask questions specific to their location. Where does the sun rise? Would we like it to enter our bedroom window as it rises, or perhaps enter through the kitchen and come into the bedroom later in the day? Should we put the living room where we can watch the

Irish Soda Bread cont.

Tbsp milk (for an egg-less substitute, whip 2 Tbsp flaxseed meal in ¼ cup water). Brush loaves with glaze and sprinkle lightly with salt and caraway seeds. Let stand for 10 minutes. Bake 35 to 40 minutes. To test for doneness, turn the bread over and tap underneath. If the bread sounds hollow, it is fully cooked. Cool before slicing.

Difficulty

sunset? Where is the wind? Will we want to move a breeze through the house in the summer? What about precipitation? Are we at the bottom of a slope and thus need to build up our foundation to keep snow off our doorstep? How far should the roof overhang to shelter the walls from rain?

Once they have the basics of their plan in mind, they reach down into the mud and make a clay model. It doesn't have to be much more elaborate than a floor plan because, once they are begun, organic buildings have a way of changing shape in the hands of their builder-residents.

Building with nature is a more detailed process than I can adequately describe in this short book, but I've given you the idea. If you are living in a large, poorly insulated, air-conditioned building with no shelterbelt of trees and foliage, an insecure water supply, nowhere to dispose of your wastes, and either rising rents or a mortgage that is enslaving you, you need to start thinking about a complete makeover, or maybe moving to something more liberating.

- Insulate.
- Put the rainwater where it will do the most good.
- Replace, relocate, or rebuild, and use natural materials.
- Install solar collectors or attached greenhouses for heat, and reconfigure your furnace or room heater to use some fuel that is plentiful in your region.
- Get rid of that mortgage or rent payment, take permaculture and natural-building workshops, and find somewhere to build or live that will be more resilient through unpredictable times. Think ecovillage.

Elements of Design for Sustainability

1. Smaller is better — population foremost.
2. Use energy efficiently — from solar income.
3. Optimize materials — full cycle.
4. Landscape holistically, considering energy and food.
5. Design for maintenance and gradual renewal.
6. Plan for greywater capture and use.
7. Orient toward solar gain in siting and landscape.
8. Consider pre-existing foliage and protect topsoil.
9. Plan for access and transportation needs.
10. Avoid unhealthy and socially irresponsible products.

Adapted from *Ecovillages: A Practical Guide to Sustainable Communities* by Jan Bang.

*The most gloomy thought is the likelihood that we are unable
to stop emissions in time; think how difficult it could be for those large
nations, China, India and the United States, to overcome the social inertia
of their massive populations. Whatever happens, we have to give up fossil fuel as
soon as possible, because even when we are past the threshold of irreversible
climate change, the extent and rate of adverse change will still be affected by
what we do. Our aim should now be to try for the least hot future world.*

— James Lovelock, 2006

There are several dimensions to the "sustainability" issue:

- We want to sustain communities as good places to live, which offer economic, educational, and cultural opportunities to their inhabitants.
- We want to sustain the values of our society — things like individual liberty and democracy, family ties, and generational relationships with land and community.
- We want to sustain the biodiversity of the natural environment for the contribution that it makes to the quality of human life, for the contribution that it makes to ecosystems and all they support, and for its own inherent value.
- We want to sustain the regenerative ability of natural systems to provide the life-supporting "services" that are rarely counted by economists, but which we now know to be worth far more than the total gross human economic product. Regenerative ability, once lost, is nearly impossible to recover.

*Apparently, many of us feel that we can
always get what we want, if only our governing bodies develop the
right policies. We have no appreciation for the special-ness and uniqueness
of our current transitory historical period, during which we still have options,
and we mindlessly let this period lapse and thereby foreclose those options forever.
We don't understand that ruthless competition for resources is much more common and much more fundamental as a driving force of history than, say, our
cherished notions of democracy, human rights, and public welfare. We don't
realize that investing into the infrastructure alternative to "big, convenient,
safe cars" that we have such a strong love affair with today is what may save
our economy from total paralysis in historically very near future, allow it to
regroup, and thereby give our civilization a chance to fight another day.*

— Dmitry Podborits, 2005

BREADS

BEGINNER'S BREAD
Makes 1 loaf

1 Tbsp fresh baking yeast
2 Tbsp honey
1¼ cup water, divided
¼ cup oil
4 to 5 cups flour (unbleached white or half whole wheat)
1 tsp sea salt

Put yeast, honey, and ¾ cup warm but not hot water in a bowl. Let sit 5 minutes till bubbles form on surface. Add ½ cup warm water, stir in oil, and begin to add flour. When too hard to stir, stop adding flour and turn out on lightly floured and salted surface. Knead until smooth and elastic, about 10 minutes. Place in oiled bowl, turning to oil dough. Cover and let rise until double (about 1 hour). Punch dough down and place in a loaf pan. Let rise again for 45 to 60 minutes, until impression of finger does not spring back. Bake at 375°F for 15 minutes, reduce heat to 350°F, and bake about 40 minutes more. Tip out of pan to cool.

Variations
Rolls conserve heat because they bake in about 18 minutes. After initial rising, shape dough into 16 to 18 round rolls or breadsticks. Let rise again, bake. Add caraway, fennel, flaxmeal, sesame, or poppy seeds to dough, or make herb rolls by adding 1 Tbsp dried dill weed, basil, or oregano or a combination to dough while kneading.

Difficulty

BREADS

ONION FOCACCIA CROSTINI

Serves 6

1 cup olive or local cold-pressed oil, divided
2 large yellow onions, chopped or sliced
1½ tsp sea salt, divided
Pinch freshly ground black pepper
1 Tbsp dry yeast
1 Tbsp sugar or equivalent sweetener
1 cup warm water (about 110°F)
3 Tbsp kosher salt
3½ cups all-purpose flour
2 cloves garlic, minced
12 ounces hard cheese or vegan cheese, thinly sliced

Add 3 Tbsp oil to a large pan over medium heat. When hot, add onions, ½ tsp sea salt, and pepper. Sauté until brown but not burnt, about 15 minutes, stirring often. Cool to room temperature. Stir together yeast, sweetener, 2 Tbsp oil, water, and cooled onions and stand 2 minutes to dissolve yeast. Add kosher salt and flour. Mix until dough comes away from sides of bowl. Grease a clean bowl with 1 tsp oil. Add dough and turn to coat. Cover and place in a warm place until doubled in size, about 1½ hours. Grease a large baking sheet with 2 tsp oil. Turn dough out onto sheet. Punch down and press dough out to fill the pan. Brush with oil. Sprinkle with remaining salt and pepper. Lightly cover and let rest for 1 hour. Preheat oven to 350°F. Bake for 30 minutes or until golden.

The Problem of Growth

Interest rates and money supply are the tools capitalism uses to grow and resupply itself for successive stages of investment. Interest assumes the ventures being funded are profitable, skims a small portion of that profit, and uses that to induce further growth. Money supply grows or shrinks to keep growth stable and uniform. Over the past two centuries, this system has produced consistent growth — in jobs; houses and commercial buildings; machinery; food supply; expenditures for science, education, and culture; and the military. We have come to expect that. It is normal.

But normal isn't normal anymore.

What do we do when we can no longer grow the economy because we can no longer consume oil and gas at a 2 percent annual increase, but instead are having to cope with a 2 percent (or more) annual decrease in supply? How can capitalism function in a negative-growth scenario? What happens when there is little possibility of profit, interest, and net earnings to be reinvested?

In 1974, M. King Hubbert told a government committee that "money, being a system of accounting, is, in effect, paper and so is not constrained by the laws within which material and energy systems must operate. [But in] fact money grows exponentially by the rule of compound interest .... [T]he maintenance of a constant price level in a non-growing industrial system implies either an interest rate of zero or continuous inflation."

Hubbert provided this advice:

Since the tenets of our exponential-growth culture (such as a non-zero interest rate) are incompatible with a state of non-growth, it is understandable that extraordinary efforts will be made to avoid a cessation of growth. Inexorably, however, physical and biological constraints must eventually prevail and appropriate cultural adjustments will have to be made.

Easy for you to say, King. What cultural adjustments are appropriate for the single mom on food stamps? What about the corporation vice-president approaching retirement and moving into that condo in Barbados or Tenerife? What appropriate cultural adjustments will keep them in food? As the billionaire Texas financier Richard Rainwater points out:

We've got a lot of things going on simultaneously. The world as we know it is unwinding with respect to Social Security, pensions, Medicare. We're going to have dramatically increased taxes in the US. I believe we're going into a world where there's going to be more hostility. More people are going to be asking, "Why did God do this to us?" Whatever God they worship. Alfred Sloan said it a long time ago at General Motors, that we're giving these things during good times. What happens in bad times? We're going to have to take them back, and then everybody will riot.

Hubbert had a specific proposal for the national legislature, although it fell on deaf ears at the time. His idea was to issue "energy certificates" to everyone equally. All goods and services would be priced based on their embodied energy, and the certificates would be used to purchase all goods and services. The certificates would be non-negotiable and specific to a given individual. Hubbert said:

Contrary to the price system rules, the purchasing power of an individual is no longer based upon the fallacious premise that a man is being paid in proportion to the so-called "value" of his work (since it is a physical fact that what he receives is greatly in excess of his individual effort) but upon the equal pro rata division of the net energy degraded in the production of consumer goods and services. In this manner the income of an individual is in nowise dependent upon the nature of his work, and we are then left free to reduce the working hours of our population to as low a level as techno-logical advancement will allow, without in any manner jeopardizing the national or individual income, and without the slightest unemployment problem or poverty.

Hubbert went on to say that, based on the US population in 1974, the work required of each individual need be no longer than about four hours per day, 164 days per year, from age 25 to 45. Income would continue until death. "Insecurity of old age is abolished and both saving and insurance become unnecessary and impossible."

Gee, that sounds very promising! Where do I sign up?

What good are vitamins? Eat four lobsters!
Eat a pound of caviar! Live!

— Artur Rubinstein

Onion Focaccia cont.

Sprinkle the focaccia with garlic, cheese, and any remaining oil. Raise oven temperature to 400°F and broil about 3 inches from flame until cheese begins to seethe and soften, 3 to 4 minutes. Cut the focaccia into diagonal crostini. Serve hot.

Substitutions

Use a baguette, crusty whole-wheat or multigrain bread, fougasse, or baked pizza crust.
Use crumbled tofu with nutritional yeast in place of cheese.
Add sun-dried tomatoes, olives, pickled peppers.

Difficulty

Dr. Albert Bartlett, a physics professor, has been lecturing for more than 30 years on the subject of sustainability and what it really implies. He is quick to point out that you can't understand sustainability without first understanding some basic arithmetic.

Simple addition reveals that steady growth (a fixed percent per year) gives very large numbers in relatively short periods of time. For example, a population of 10,000 people growing at 7 percent per year will become a population of 10 million people in just 100 years. Indeed, anything increasing at a steady 7 percent will have created more of itself in the most recent ten-year period than had been created in total in all the decades that came before, whether it is electricity, automobiles, locusts or HIV-AIDS.

Bartlett gives the example of a bottle filled with bacteria. Bacteria grow by doubling, so one bacterium divides to become two; the two

Developmental Communalism

After the experience of the 20th century, when enormous experiments in state socialism produced oppressive, regimented, and environmentally destructive cultures and then imploded (in the case of the Soviet Union), rapidly evolved into market economies (in the case of China and Cuba), or were left isolated, famished, and destitute (in the case of North Korea), many observers would conclude that communism is the last thing anyone would voluntarily embark upon. And yet there may still be a place for the communal economic system. If history is replete with irony, a supreme irony may be that communism supplants market capitalism by the end of the 21st century.

Historian Donald Pitzer has coined the term "developmental communalism" to describe a phenomenon he observed in numerous settings over the past two centuries. According to Pitzer, when a small community begins forming around a shared philosophy or religion, it often encounters a predicable set of adversities — opposition of mainstream society, lack of access to starting capital, and the special burdens of its unusual faith, for instance. A strategy that has seemed to produce remarkable success in such circumstances has been adoption of communal economics — the shared purse. The early Christians, Mormons, Shakers, kibbutzim, and many other groups provide examples. There is something about sharing finances, much the way a single family does, that works exceptionally well in small to medium-sized communities of closely aligned interests and shared ethical values.

As a community grows in size and becomes more prosperous and diverse, history also shows that communal financial arrangements are often abandoned in favor of greater personal decision making. The kibbutz becomes a moshav. The hippie commune becomes a community land trust. And yet, when times grow hard or a population becomes aged and infirm, communal economies once again offer the allure of simpler management, efficient husbanding of limited resources, and fair allocation of burdens among community members. In a time of challenge and privation, such efficiencies become harder to ignore.

divide to become four; and so on. Suppose we had bacteria that doubled this way every minute. Suppose we put one of these bacteria into an empty bottle at eleven in the morning and then observed that the bottle was full at 12 noon.

First Question: When was the bottle half full?

Answer: 11:59, one minute before 12, because they double in number every minute.

Second Question: If you were an average bacterium in that bottle, when did you first realize that you were running of space?

Answer: At 12 noon the bottle is full. One minute before that it's half full. Two minutes before noon it's a quarter full, then an eighth, then a sixteenth. At five minutes before noon, when the bottle is only 3 percent full and 97 percent open space just yearning for development, it is unlikely you, being a bacterium, would realize there's a problem. If bacteria had human intelligence, you might see your predicament in the last ten seconds.

Last Question: How long can the growth continue as a result of this magnificent discovery?

Answer: Suppose the bacteria are very smart — even smarter than humans — and they go out in that last ten seconds and find three more bottles and get back with them before noon. At 12 noon, one bottle is full and there are three to go. At 12:01, two bottles are filled and there are two to go, and at 12:02 all four are filled and that's it. Game over. They'd need to find eight more bottles to go another minute.

So if we assume we are now at about 99 percent of the carrying capacity of the planet (or beyond), and we are still adding human population at 1.3 percent per year (our present rate), how long do we have to find another planet? Having found that other planet, how long before we need to find two more? And four more after that?

No one can really speak of sustainability without understanding this basic arithmetic. Herman Daly, former chief economist at the World Bank, has pointed out that the term "sustainable growth" is really an oxymoron, but that you can theoretically still have "sustainable development."

The Dismal Theorem

In 1971 the economist Kenneth Boulding presented his "Dismal Theorem." If the only ultimate check on the growth of population is misery, warned Boulding, then the population will grow almost without limit until it is finally miserable enough to stop growing. Technical solutions

BREADS

UNHURRIED WHOLE WHEAT AND OATMEAL BREAD
Makes 1 loaf

1½ cups liquid (milk, yogurt, water)
2 Tbsp sugar or equivalent sweetener
1 tsp yeast
4 cups fresh ground flour
½ cup rolled oats
1 tsp sea salt
2 Tbsp olive or other local cold-pressed oil

Heat liquid to 105°F, pour into large bowl, and add sweetener. Stir in yeast and allow to stand until bubbly. Stir in flour and oats until mildly thick. Allow to stand for 3 hours. Add salt and oil and begin to work dough, adding more flour. It should not stick to the bowl. Allow to rise for 1 hour, then knead on a lightly floured surface. Do not add too much new flour at this stage. When the dough is only slightly sticky, place it in a well-oiled pan and let rise 30 minutes. Bake in oven preheated to 350°F for 35 minutes, and test by tapping the bottom for hollow sound.

Variation
Cinnamon Raisin Bread: After dough has risen, roll it out into a rectangle. Spread with butter or margarine, sprinkle with ¼ cup brown sugar, 1 Tbsp cinnamon, and ½ cup raisins. Roll up tightly and put in loaf pan to rise.

Difficulty

BREADS

SKILLET CORN BREAD

Makes 8 wedges

1 cup yellow cornmeal
1 cup white flour
¼ cup sugar or equivalent
sweetener
4 tsp aluminum-free baking powder
¼ tsp sea salt
⅓ cup cold-pressed oil, divided
1 egg (optional)
1 cup milk, soymilk, water, or other
liquid
½ tsp oregano, dried or fresh and
chopped
6 ounces (10 Tbsp) cooked whole
corn kernels
1 fresh jalepeño or other hot
pepper, minced

Preheat oven to 375°F or have a
good hot campfire going. Mix
cornmeal, flour, sweetener, baking
powder, and salt. Stir in 1 Tbsp oil,
egg (if using), and liquid. Heat an
iron skillet and add remaining oil,
oregano, corn, and jalepeño. Toast
briefly and then stir hot ingredients
into the batter. Pour batter into the
oily skillet but do not stir. Cover
and place in oven or over coals and
cook about 30 minutes. Stick a fork
or toothpick into center to check
doneness. Turn out onto dish or
serve in skillet, cutting into 8
sections.

Difficulty

to encountered limits only enable populations to grow larger, which really only enables more people to live in misery than before.

But Boulding was not a complete pessimist. He also propounded a "moderately cheerful" corollary of the Dismal Theorem — if something other than misery and starvation can be found to keep a prosperous population in check, the population does not have to grow until it is miserable and starves. It can be stably prosperous.

Whether we can devise the means to be stably prosperous is the challenge of our time. Rationing Hubbert's energy certificates might offer a way to dampen fertility rates within individual families, but it could also increase misery in the process. Perhaps we can discover ways to change our growth-based cultures more cheerfully than that.

> *The raging monster upon the land is*
> *population growth. In its presence, sustainability*
> *is but a fragile theoretical construct.*
> — E.O. Wilson, 1997

> *I like to use what I call my bathroom metaphor: if two people live in*
> *an apartment and there are two bathrooms, then both have freedom of*
> *the bathroom. You can go to the bathroom anytime you want to stay as long*
> *as you want for whatever you need. And everyone believes in freedom of the*
> *bathroom; it should be right there in the Constitution. But if you have twenty*
> *people in the apartment and two bathrooms, no matter how much every person*
> *believes in freedom of the bathroom, there is no such thing. You have to set up*
> *times for each person, you have to bang on the door, "Aren't you through yet?"*
> *and so on. In the same way, democracy cannot survive overpopulation.*
> *Human dignity cannot survive. Convenience and decency cannot survive.*
> *As you put more and more people onto the world, the value of life not*
> *only declines, it disappears. It doesn't matter if someone dies, the*
> *more people there are, the less one person matters.*
> — Isaac Asimov, 1989

Quit Your Job

Girls, wine, weed, wild hats, Viva!
— Jack Kerouac, 1958

Actually, the workweek and benefits proposed by Hubbert are only about a third as cushy as those enjoyed by your average Incan during the Classic period of Andean civilization. The keys to the wealth of Tiwantinsuya (for that is what they called their empire) were not oil wells or gold mines but extraordinary plant- and animal-breeding prowess and the mita system. The mita was a public labor program created to deal with the indolence that might otherwise result from their success. Using the mita system, the Tiwantinsuyanicos carried topsoil from the river valleys to the highlands and filled the terraces with rich organic material. They built an all-weather highway system with more than 14,000 miles of 12-foot-wide paved roads, lined with stone walls, that was kept swept and free of rubbish. Their domain gradually expanded until it was larger in geographical spread than the Macedonian or Roman empires.

Because of their clever breeding of potatoes and corn, llamas and alpacas, it only took about 65 days a year for a Tiwantinsuyan family to farm for its own needs. The rest of the time was devoted to social diversions or to building bridges, roads, temples, and terraces.

There is no reason we can't all do as well as the inhabitants of Tiwantinsuya.

The principal challenge of the Great Change is not physical but mental (as it is in any survival situation). Collectively, societies that are heavily addicted to consumer goods and the pattern of waste that a con-

BREADS

HUSH PUPPIES

Serves 6 to 8

Use the same dough as for skillet corn bread, adding 1 tsp onion powder. Heat 2 cups oil in a deep pan until a tiny piece of dough sizzles a little when you drop it in. Shape dough into small balls, adding a little more flour if needed. Drop a few at a time into hot oil and cook until browned outside and cooked on the inside. Remove with a slotted spoon and drain on paper towel or cut brown paper bags. Serve in covered dish or paper-lined basket.

Difficulty

sumer culture creates will have to adjust.

The easy path is to downsize expectations and simplify lifestyles. This path requires us to give up certain ways of looking at the world in order to embrace other, more survival-oriented ways. The hard path is to try *not* to make this change, to somehow cling to the old ways as long as possible, which will entail huge — I would say cruel — efforts for diminishing yields.

> *Politically unrealistic? Ah, but here's the central epistemo-logical truth of our time. Never so suddenly ripped a chasm between what is "politically realistic" and reality itself than that opened up by climate change.*
> — Robert Newman, 2004

Creative Loafing

De-petroleolizing is not necessarily about working shorter hours and earning less, although that may become part of it. It is about making your daily activities something you control, not something that controls you. Carl Honoré, a leading spokesperson for the Slow movement, suggests some painless ways to slow down that will fit any budget:

- Walking instead of driving.
- Giving children more free time.
- Reading instead of watching television.
- Eating home-cooked meals with family and friends.
- Taking up relaxing hobbies such as painting, gardening, or knitting.
- Practicing yoga, tai chi, or meditation.
- Unplugging from technology.

> *The presence of the clock gave birth to the notion that time lies outside our bodies — that it can be tracked by a machine, and that we can sit and watch it "fly" by, tick-tock, as though it is something linear, containable, and separate from the organic, flowing process of life.*
> — Jose Arguelles, 2005

- Indulging in leisurely love-making.
- Simply resisting the urge to hurry unnecessarily.

Glossary of Surfspeak

Acid drop
Dropping into a wave and having the bottom suddenly fall out, followed by a sense of weightlessness and helplessness.

Burrito money
Pocket change. Usage: "I've just been doing some random gardening to earn a little burrito money."

Choiceamundo
The exhilarating feeling you get when you tube through a wave and flip over its back like an ocean pizza.

Delamination
Peeling skin from a really bad sunburn.

Eat it
To eat the sand or a piece of your surfboard; to get munched.

Floater
A move initiated by Cheyne Horan in 1983, where the surfer rides over the falling curtain of a breaking wave.

Gnarly
The kind of wave that can eat a surfer for breakfast and then use the board as a toothpick.

Go into Zen
When you relax and don't panic during a big wipeout, knowing the washing machine is about to go to spin cycle.

Hoon
Someone who tends to compensate for a lack of surfing ability with eye-catching performances in the car park.

Ice cream headache
A piercing pain in the head resulting from ducking under freezing cold water while paddling out.

Surfer among the ruins, from "The Origin of the Silver Surfer!" Silver Surfer No. 1, August 1968, marvelmasterworks.com © 1968 Marvel Comics.

Mack
To eat enthusiastically and without inhibitions, usually after a surf session. Usage: "Let's mack."

O-double
Being in tune with the ocean, regardless of the activity — surfing, sailing, scuba diving, body surfing, living in close proximity to the beach, or whatever.

Passmodious
Really tired.

Pet the cat, petting the cat
The motion of a surfer who crouches down and strokes the air or water to get through a section.

Rubber arms
The feeling you occasionally get in your arms when you're paddling for an unusually large wave and you're not quite sure you want it.

Soul barney
A surfer in his or her 30s and 40s.

Vibe
The atmosphere created by and how people relate to each other.

— From *The Story of English*, www.pbs.org

BREADS

GRILLED FLATBREAD FOR CAMPFIRE AND FIREPLACE

Serves 6

1 Tbsp baking yeast
1 Tbsp sugar or equivalent sweetener
1¼ cups warm water, divided
¼ cup olive or other local cold-pressed oil
4 to 5 cups flour (white or half whole wheat)
1 tsp sea salt or kosher salt

Put yeast, sweetener, and 1 cup warm but not hot water in a bowl. Let sit 5 minutes till bubbles form on surface. Add ¼ cup warm water, stir in oil, and begin to add flour. When too hard to stir, stop adding flour and turn out on lightly floured and salted surface. Knead until smooth and elastic, about 10 minutes. Place in oiled bowl, turning to oil dough. Cover and let rise until double (about 1 hour). Punch dough down and return it to the bowl. Let rise again for 45 to 60 minutes, until impression of finger does not spring back. Divide into 6 balls and roll one at a time to an even ⅛-inch thickness. Place rounds on greased baking sheet, brush tops with olive oil, and cover all with a damp cloth. Let them rest in a warm place for 30 minutes or so. To cook, place 1 round of dough on grill over hot coals, oiled side down. Brush top with oil. In 2 to 3 minutes, when grill marks appear on underside, turn bread over with tongs. Cook 2 to 3

You can go rent a good surfer movie like *Blue Crush* or *Step into Liquid* and it lays out the whole new sense of timelessness. When the waves aren't running high enough, surfers work, building boards or flip-

The Slow Food movement began in Italy in 1986 as a response to the opening of a McDonald's in Piazza Spagna in Rome and was launched as an international movement in Paris in 1989 .... The movement has about 100,000 members in more than 100 countries around the world, but its ideology has an even broader appeal. Slow fooders, as followers are sometimes called, respond to the rush of the modern world by intentionally enjoying life, especially food, and by making deep connections to people and places.

— *UU World*, a publication of the Unitarian Universalist Church

ping burritos. Otherwise, "productivity" is measured by how close one came to a perfect ride.

The Slow movement — the Japanese call it "Slow Life" — grew out of the Slow Food movement in Italy, the Slow Cities idea in Holland and France, and the Slow Sex campaign in Italy and Germany. There is now even a Slow Roads movement emerging in response to inconsiderate over-paving. In North America, Slow advocates have dedicated October 24 of each year as "Take Back Your Time Day," symbolizing the 350-hour difference in work time between the US and many parts of Europe. According to European law, if Usanians had not taken any time off by October 24, they should be entitled to nine weeks' vacation — the rest of the year.

Carl Honoré says that "the Slow philosophy can be summed up in a single word: balance. Be fast when it makes sense to be fast, and be slow when slowness is called for. Seek to live at what musicians call the *tempo giusto* — the right speed."

Slow Food founder Carlo Petrini adds, "If you are always slow, then you are stupid — and that is not at all what we are aiming for. Being 'slow' means that you control the rhythms of your own life. You decide how fast you have to go in any given context. If today I want to go fast, I go fast; if tomorrow I want to go slow, I go slow. What we are fighting for is the right to determine our own tempos."

An Italian ecovillage on the French border, Torri Superiori, is representative of the emergence of *de croissance soutenable* (sustainable contraction), which holds that that material wealth will never purchase happiness but will only inflict "affluenza," and that lower levels of consumption, properly managed, yield a higher quality of life. This idea is spreading quickly in Italy and France, where the 20th century nearly extinguished the distinctive southern European *joie*.

Consumption and production are two sides of the same coin. We have to scale back both, but without giving up happiness and comfort. Actually, we want to *increase* happiness and comfort. But how do we ele-

> *The ride itself is such a bitching*
> *deal, so rewarding, it becomes so important to*
> *you that it becomes the object around which you plan the*
> *rest of your life and everyone else is planning their life around*
> *money and the acquisition of money.*
> — Steve Pezman, 2002

> *And all of a sudden a bunch of guys come along and they go, screw the*
> *money, I'm having all the fun I could possibly have .... All I know is once you*
> *get into it, there's an adrenaline, a stoke, and that high is so addictive that*
> *once you have a taste of it, it is very difficult to not want more.*
> — Greg Noll, 2002

> *I haven't missed a swell in 55 years. I'm still as excited about surfing*
> *as I've ever been. I mean I literally run to the water with my*
> *board hooting and laughing and giggling.*
> — Micky Muñoz, 2002

vate serotonin for people with type-A, multitasking lifestyles without actually producing or consuming anything?

Fifty years ago in Sri Lanka, Dr. Ari Ariyaratne founded a social justice movement called Sarvodaya Shramadana, which translates roughly as "awakening of all through sharing." A student of Gandhi and a devout Buddhist, Ariyaratne believed that the poor people of his country could overcome their difficulties by themselves, without waiting for the help of governments or international development agencies. He focused on peoples' real needs and got them working together in an organized way.

Ariyaratne compiled a list of ten basic human needs that would guide Sarvodaya's goal of a "no poverty, no affluence" society:

- A clean and beautiful environment.
- A clean and adequate supply of water.
- Basic clothing.

Grilled Flatbread cont.

minutes more until cooked through. Keep warm. You can sprinkle flatbreads with seeds and herbs just before baking. They may also be cooked on a griddle or frying pan or oven-baked in a free-form loaf like a long baguette

Difficulty

DESSERTS

DECADENT CHOCOLATE-PEANUT BUTTER-BANANA CREAM PIE

Serves 6

Pie

1 pound silken tofu
1 small banana, cut into coarse chunks
½ cup maple, cane, or other syrup
1 tsp vanilla extract
½ tsp oil
½ tsp lemon zest, minced
1 prepared graham cracker pie crust
⅓ cup chunky peanut butter
1 small banana, sliced

Topping

2 ounces unsweetened or bitter-sweet chocolate (2 squares)
½ cup soymilk or equivalent
¼ cup light brown sugar
2 tsp oil
1 tsp vanilla extract

Garnish

½ cup dry roasted peanuts, chopped

Pie

Combine tofu, coarse chunks of banana, syrup, vanilla, ½ tsp oil, and lemon zest and blend until smooth and creamy. Spoon peanut butter into prepared pie crust and spread to the edges with the back of a spoon. Arrange banana slices over the peanut butter. Pour creamy filling over banana slices and smooth to the edges. Protect with a dome-shaped cover or tented aluminum foil and refrigerate for several hours or overnight.

- A balanced diet.
- A simple house to live in.

- Basic health care.
- Simple communications facilities.
- Basic energy requirements.
- Well-rounded education.
- Cultural and spiritual sustenance.

Sarvodaya used this list of ten basic needs to determine the weakest segment of any community, whether it was the sick and elderly, the children, or single mothers. Then it worked to improve the standing of that group. By limiting the list to real needs, poverty could be alleviated more easily than if the list attempted to embrace the whole range of human desires — or Western standards of material consumption. Ariyaratne's genius was also in placing material and spiritual needs on an equal footing.

Ariyaratne formed a core group of trainers to motivate villagers to undertake a broad range of improvements, from roads to latrines, preschools to cottage industries. Once one village reached a level of adequate subsistence, it was asked to "give back" by adopting another, needier village. "Shramadana" means voluntary public giving. Everyone in the movement is expected to give back by helping others less fortunate than themselves. Today Sarvodaya has grown to nearly 1 million people in over 15,000 vil-

Instead of going through the agonizing process of losing and rediscovering one's identity in a post-collapse environment, one could simply sit back and watch events unfold. If you are currently "a mover and a shaker," of things or people or whatever, then collapse will surely come as a shock to you, and it will take you a long time, perhaps forever, to find more things to move and to shake to your satisfaction. However, if your current occupation is as a keen observer of grass and trees, then, post-collapse, you could take on something else that's useful, such as dismantling useless things.

— Dmitry Orlov, 2005

lages, and it is the single largest developer of ecovillages on Earth.

Dismantling Useless Things

What are the most valuable trade skills for the transition and afterward? While the picture of what will emerge is still too unclear to give a definitive answer, it seems likely that, at least for a while, most of the trade skills of the past decades will continue to be useful. We will need people who can build soil and reseed the desert the way the early kibbutzniks did. We will still have to build and repair machines, so there will be ample need for engineers, draftspeople, machine workers, and mechanics. All of the crafts will still be in demand, with employment available for everyone from carpenters and plumbers to boat-builders and bambuseros.

We can hope that there may be a rebalancing of the scale used to assign professional worth, so that an hour of a schoolteacher's time will be worth as much as an hour of a merchant's time, but time is becoming less important as a measure of things. Personal satisfaction is the better measure.

Many relative assignments of worth have fallen out of kilter as we moved farther from our natural world realities into speculative realms of what the market will support. These markets are changing, and as we move away from the endless-growth paradigm and into alternative economies that are more aware of their limits, assignments of relative worth could and should change.

One livelihood that consumes little by producing little (in a strictly material sense) is that of the artist, although I use that term with caution. Life is art. Science is art. We are all artists, at least in the design of our personal life paths. And yet, there will be a great need and great

> *No city child should grow up without*
> *knowing the beauty of spring in the country or where*
> *milk comes from, how vegetables grow and what it is like to play*
> *in a field instead of on a city street. No country child who knows these*
> *things should be deprived, however, of museums, books, music and better*
> *teachers because it is easier to find them and to pay for them in big cities*
> *than it is in rural districts. With more leisure time, we are discovering that the*
> *arts are a necessity in our lives, not only as a method of self-expression, but*
> *because of the need for enjoyment and occupation which requires apprecia-*
> *tion of many things which we could never hope to understand when we*
> *toiled from dawn till dark and had no time for any aspirations.*
> — Eleanor Roosevelt, 1936

opportunity for artists in the narrower sense of the term, for people drawn to visual arts, performing arts, music, and creative explorations of these kinds. We are entering an era devoted to art.

Decadent pie cont.

Topping

Melt the chocolate squares in a 1-quart saucepan over very low heat, whisking 3 or 4 minutes. Add the soymilk, sugar, 2 tsp oil, and vanilla and stir well to combine thoroughly. Set aside until ready to serve the pie.

To serve, put each slice of pie on a dessert dish, drizzle warm topping over the top, and sprinkle with chopped peanuts.

Difficulty

Permaculture

"Integrated farming," "no-till," and "ecological agriculture" are ideas that have been bandied about for many years, and they mean different things depending on whom you ask. They are all an attempt to move away from the heavily mechanized method by which humans presently get their food and to work more with the plan nature has been using. However, some of these techniques use lots of chemicals or lots of labor to accomplish what machines did. That is not the direction we want to go.

In the late 1960s a Japanese farmer, Masanobu Fukuoka, devised a more trouble-free pattern of polyculture and mixed perennials that he called the One-Straw Revolution. A decade later, refined and expanded by two Australian ecologists, Bill Mollison and David Holmgren, Fukuoka's cultivated ecology became what we know today as the design science of permaculture.

The word "permaculture" was initially a contraction of "permanent agriculture," but the two Aussies soon used it to more accurately describe "permanent culture."

Permaculture undertakes the harmonious joining of humans and their built environment — taking into consideration microclimate, annual and perennial plants, animals, soils, and water — to create stable, productive communities. As in intentional communities, the emphasis is on building relationships. The outcome, when it works, is the provision of human needs by nature's daily labors. Gravity, the rotation and orbit of the planet, and the biological bounty accumulated over 3 billion years supply us in abundance, if we merely learn how to harness the flow.

Practically speaking, permaculture uses methods such as swaling, mulching, and trellising; husbanding animals to recycle nutrients and

Permaculture is a design system for agricultural systems and landscapes ... it is a thinking tool. It is also a process for reclaiming our place in nature. Part of the problem in the current psychology that prevails in our culture is that we are separate from nature and not constrained by its limits. Clearly energy peak and descent will smash that mistaken view once and for all. What is also necessary is to realize that we are not some contradiction of nature — a destroyer of it — but that we have a place in it and can reclaim that place.

— David Holmgren, 2005

DESSERTS

SPICY ORANGE PUMPKIN MOUSSE
Serves 6

Pumpkin Stuffing
One 3-pound pumpkin, butternut, or winter squash
2 cups ground almonds or hazelnuts
1 cup maple, cane, or other syrup
½ cup orange juice
1 tsp orange zest
1¼ tsp ground cinnamon
½ tsp nutmeg
½ tsp vanilla extract
¼ tsp ground ginger
¼ tsp ground cardamom
Pinch sea salt
3 Tbsp flaxseed meal
6 Tbsp water
¼ cup dried cranberries

Orange Ginger Sauce
⅓ cup maple, cane, or other syrup
2 Tbsp light brown sugar
¼ cup lemon juice
1 Tbsp finely grated ginger
½ tsp ground cinnamon
½ tsp ground orange zest
1 cup and 1 Tbsp water
2 Tbsp cornstarch

Stuffed Pumpkin
Preheat oven to 375°F and bake the pumpkin or squash on an oiled baking sheet for 50 to 60 minutes or until it feels soft when pressed. Cut in half, remove the seeds (reserve them for toasting), and scoop the flesh out into a large mixing bowl. Add the ground almonds, syrup, orange juice, orange zest, cinnamon, nutmeg, vanilla extract, ginger, cardamom,

control weeds; and successional planting to encourage food forests, protect wildlife, and supply the needs of construction. Low-cost nontoxic buildings, sewage and greywater reedbeds, alternative credit unions, and ecovillages are all part of the permaculture portfolio.

Depending on who you ask, you'll hear all kinds of claims about what to expect from the economic effects of Peak Oil, but these times are so accelerated and so unprecedented that no single viewpoint can encompass all the implications. From cataclysm to enlightenment, from world war to world peace, from massive Earth changes and physical destruction to massive spiritual awakening to our inherent oneness, there are a multitude of views.

We don't yet even have a date for the peak and the resulting change; 2000, 2004, 2007, 2010, 2012, or 2030 all have their adherents. One thing is clear — we are right in the thick of change. And as this Great Change asserts itself, we will witness an old world dying and a new world being born.

Throughout this book I have repeated that I don't know what is in store for us in the coming years. We are at the tipping point. From this place we cannot see five years ahead. Like you, I can only make some educated guesses. Like yours, my guesses become more realistic the more I inform myself. We can hope that at the point where we now stand, a range of responses are still available to us. Personal and community preparation is the one thing we can be certain will help.

So get in shape. Take a permaculture course. Get out of debt. Buy what you need to feel prepared for anything. Sell the rest. Take up a challenging hobby that keeps you stimulated and having fun. Grow your own food. Store what you eat and eat what you store. Help your neighbors and get to know them better.

This moment on Earth, with all of its heightened energies, has never existed before. The opportunities and challenges of today's world are the product of all that has come before. Tomorrow's world is still ours to fashion.

The wise man knows when it is time to abandon the baggage.

— Chinese proverb

Spicy Mousse cont.

and salt. Mix well. Blend the flaxseed meal with water until thick and viscous, about 1 minute. Stir the flaxseed mixture into the squash and mix well.

Raise the oven temperature to 400°F. Spoon the mixture into an oiled casserole dish or springform pan. Sprinkle the cranberries over the top and lightly press them into the squash. Bake for 1 hour and 15 minutes, or until the mousse is firm when lightly shaken. Cool about 20 minutes and loosen the edges with a spatula. Remove the springform collar or turn out of the casserole onto a platter and either serve slightly warm or chill and serve cold.

Orange Ginger Sauce

Combine syrup, brown sugar, lemon juice, ginger, cinnamon, and zest with 1 cup water in a 1- or 2-quart saucepan. Bring to a boil over high heat, then reduce heat to medium and simmer until sugar dissolves. Combine the cornstarch with 1 Tbsp water in a small cup or bowl and stir to a thin paste. Add to the bubbling liquid and stir constantly until the sauce thickens, about 1 minute. Drizzle while warm over mousse.

Difficulty

Utopia by Morning

A medieval city was a very
picturesque object, with its narrow
and winding streets and overhanging houses,
and the tall cathedral towering above the market-
place. As nobody rode, except here and there "an abbot
on an ambling pad," or a noble lady on her palfrey, its area
was small, and had to be kept small, so that people could get
over it on foot. Hence the strong aversion, which we find expressed
in the literature and history of those times, to the growth of cities.
Even as late as in Charles II's days, Sir Christopher Wren, in making a
new plan for London after its great fire, proposed to move all the grave-
yards and arrange them in a ring around the city, for the express purpose of
preventing its enlargement.
People dwelt in all parts of these cities, and carried on their trades, manufac-
tures, and selling of goods under the same roofs where they ate and slept.
There are persons still living who have heard it said that the proper place for a
tradesman to live was over his shop. But with the changes caused by modern
inventions, the evolution of a city makes it more complex. Differentiation of
parts takes place. One part becomes the financial centre; another, that of
wholesale business; a third, that of manufactures; and a fourth, that of
retail shops; while the residence quarters are farther and farther removed
from the centre. These changes everyone must have noticed in almost all
cities, but few have paused to consider that this evolution of the modern
city comes from the extensive use now made of the sun's energy stored
up in coal, and utilized through machinery in all the innumerable

177

DESSERTS

CANDY FLOWERS

Gather any of these blossoms: apple, borage, carnation, chamomile, chive blossom, chrysanthemum, clary, daylily, dianthus, English primrose, geranium, hibiscus, hollyhock, impatiens, lavender, lemon, lilac, mimosa, nasturtium, orange, pansy, peach, plum, pot marigold (petals only), rose, sage, snapdragon, squash, tiger lily buds, or violet

4 Tbsp flaxseed meal
1/3 cup water
Superfine sugar

Whisk flaxseed meal in water, then use a brush to coat the flower petals. Roll petals in superfine sugar and sprinkle more superfine sugar on top. Lay petals on a cookie sheet to dry overnight.

Difficulty

processes of manufacturing, industry, and transportation. Cities depend upon coalmines. They have grown with their growth, and prospered with their prosperity: and if ever the mines become exhausted, the cities will dwindle with their decay; unless we learn to transform the energy of the medium which surrounds us into power.

— Thomas Curtis Clarke, 1892

Even without the looming threat of peak oil, a number of habitat redesign movements have been spreading around the world for the past 50 years or more. New urbanism, intentional community, ecocity, ecovillage, cohousing, city repair, communitarianism, and many other names have been used by the pioneers of these changes. It is clear from such conferences as United Nations Habitat II and the World Social Forum that millions of humans are becoming less and less satisfied with the patterns of settlement that might have made sense in an earlier era — although perhaps they made no sense even then. From the visible accomplishments of these contrarians it is clear that, with a little imagination, the rest of us could do a whole lot better.

What Is a Community?

The Latin word *munus* means "gift," as in "giving of one's self to others." The word *munere* refers to something prized, precious, and worth defending. Whenever people develop an attitude of caring for the wellbeing of the whole, community is present.

Resources, preferences, beliefs, and a multitude of other factors affect the degree of devotion individual members give to any community, but all members have some things they share in common. Together they agree, formally or informally, to sacrifice together to protect shared resources or values.

Whatever drives people to cooperate and collaborate in the first place is not quite as important as what makes them continue to associate. Resilient connections create viable and sustainable communities. Communities that succeed in making these connections tend to attract the attention of less-connected individuals, who may seek to join and add their resources, energy, and values.

While the modern worldview of linear progression may have no greater validity than the more ancient view of progress as cyclical, we can see that for at least the past 50,000 years, human settlements have progressed in ebbs and flows from small, separate clan hamlets toward more complex forms of social organization. Agriculture begat agrarian villages. Trade created prosperous towns and cities. Cities militarily expanded into city-states and nation-states. While huge areas of the Earth have confederated into empires and vast geographical dominions at various times, the entire planet has so far resisted creating a single governing authority. However, since the middle of the past century, we have even been building, in a deliberate way, the scaffolding needed to erect and manage that.

At the same time, as human institutions became ever larger and more complex, they also became more mechanical and less, well, human. While efficiencies of management drive us to consolidate and scale up our built environment, our spiritual, social, sexual, and artistic natures demand that we keep community relationships scaled down, personal, and more responsive to our soft inner sides. This conflict has created a need for balance in the patterns of our settlement designs.

It is apparent that under the pressure of the human population explosion, rapid industrial development, a personal transport revolution, and the digital entertainment era, spiritual needs and constructed habitats have been falling progressively farther out of balance for most people. The response has been a nascent habitat revolution.

The New Urbanists

Because more people now live within cities than outside them, the redesign of cities has become more urgent. The "garden city" concept has been batted around by urban planners for more than a century, but it has suffered setbacks from the same sources that have ruined rural communities — the car culture, finance, and human fecundity among them. New urbanists are those in the city-building business who simply won't give up.

Jane Jacobs epitomized the old guard. The author of *The Death and Life of Great American Cities*, *The Economies of Cities*, *Systems of Survival*, and *The Nature of Economies*, she wrote in *Dark Age Ahead* an obituary for contemporary city streets:

> Not all roads are community killers like those that have become so common in North America and in countries influenced by North American highway planning. Some roads are famous for fostering community-life, as they bring people into casual, pleasant and frequent face-to-face contact with one another.

DESSERTS

WHIPPED TOPPING

Serves 6

½ cup ice-cold water
½ cup nonfat dry milk, powdered soymilk, or equivalent
½ cup sugar
2 Tbsp lemon juice

Put water into an ice-cold bowl. Add dry milk and beat until stiff. Add sugar slowly while beating. Add lemon juice and beat only until well mixed.

Difficulty

🐦🐦🐦🐦🐦

Many an ordinary Main Street used to do these services, but Main Streets have proved easily transformable into bleak, standardized community killers.

Another kind of road, the boulevard, is capable of serving a district's full ranges of mobility: walks for pedestrians; lanes alongside them for bicyclers and roller skaters; lanes for public transit vehicles, and separate channels for automotive vehicles passing through and those heading for local destinations. Versatile boulevards are little known in North America, and those that do exist are seldom more than ghosts of what they could be, but elsewhere in the world, especially in places with Mediterranean cultures, boulevards are places to which people flock for a stroll when their day's work is done, to see the neighbors, get word of strangers, pick up other news, and enjoy a coffee or a beer and a chat while they take in the passing scene, including sidewalk play of children. People in cities and neighborhoods in much of the world understood their boulevards to be at the heart of their communities. A well-designed boulevard is always well provided with trees along its margins and medians, because a major concern of serious boulevard designers is to create environments welcoming to pedestrians.

Most of the patterns of design described by Jacobs have been adopted by the new urbanist movement. In redesigned cities they envision one or more walkable town centers (many may be needed in larger cities). The buildings frame the streets, and block lengths are short. Merchants take pride in their shops' appearances and may have their residences above or behind them. Great varieties of stores feature local products and services. There is unique and distinct personality or character to buildings, neighborhoods, and historic or cultural districts.

In the new urban design, neighborhoods are interconnected, giving a choice of many routes from residents' homes to the center. The most direct paths are walking routes. Sidewalks are wide, and most are buffered from streets by planting strips, bike lanes, and on-street parking. Most neighborhood streets have sidewalks on both sides. Bike lanes track principal avenues, and streets with higher traffic volume or speeds almost always have separate, protected, bike lanes. Where pedestrians predominate, traffic is dampened and calmed by strategic placement of bends and obstacles. Most streets have good handicap access to and from each block in all directions. People rarely have to walk more than 150 feet from their direct lines-of-travel to reach crossings or wait more than 30 seconds before being allowed to cross. Scenic objects or destinations anchor distant views.

Most children are able to walk or bicycle to school and small nearby parks. Most residents live within half a mile (or preferably within a quarter of a mile) of small parks or other well-maintained and attractive public spaces. Good public-space designs support and attract children, teens, people with disabilities, and senior citizens. Public restrooms, drinking fountains, and sitting places are common in many parts of town, especially downtown. It is safe to fall asleep or breastfeed a baby in public sitting places.

Homes and buildings are brought forward, relating to the street. Sidewalks are centered and surrounded with attractive edges — a planter strip to the street side, an edge or attractive transition to the private property. Residents understand and support urban infill, integral placement of mixed-use buildings, compact verticality, and mixed-income neighborhoods. The built environment is of human scale, with attributes that invite positive interaction and development of a local architectural vernacular. Historical and sacred spaces are respected and inform that vernacular.

Residents desire, and find ways to include, affordable homes in their neighborhoods and understand that small, local stores help create community as well as convenience. Most people live within walking distance of grocery, pharmacy, hardware, bank, medical clinic, daycare, laundry, post office, and other essential services.

Streets, plazas, parks, and waterfronts are fun, festive, secure, convenient, efficient, comfortable, and welcoming places. Many "green" streets, with trees and landscaping, including immense heritage trees, may feature native species, drought-resistant plants, colorful materials, and native stone.

There are places to give public speeches and listen to open-air concerts. Street performers, brass bands, string quartets, small dance troupes, local theater groups, and serenading mariachi bands are alive and well. Public space is tidy, well-kept, respected, and loved. Public commons are surrounded by residential properties, and many eyes-on-the-streets, from front stoops and second-story windows, add security and even running commentary.

Designs of this kind are not community. Designs of this kind are the good soil from which community springs.

Two Child Model

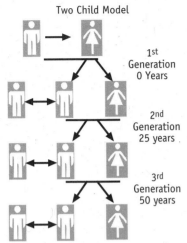

1st
Generation
0 Years

2nd
Generation
25 years

3rd
Generation
50 years

First generation dies (Age 75)
6 offspring survive. Population has tripled.

*Human fertility is presently 2.7 births
per woman, which doubles the population each century. India's rate is more
than 3 births per woman.*

One Child Model

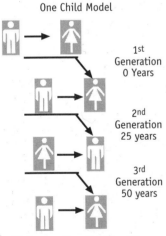

1st
Generation
0 Years

2nd
Generation
25 years

3rd
Generation
50 years

First generation dies (Age 75);
3 offspring survive. Population has
increased by up to 50% in 75 years.

*In 1979, China instituted its One Child
policy, and fertility fell to 2.5 births per
woman in rural areas and about 1.2 in
urban areas. Nonetheless, population
continued to expand and the policy is
no longer universally enforced.*

*Village life is about growing food, but
it is also about much more. It is about the sense
of security that comes from knowing what you need and
how to help yourself to it. And it is about the profound experience of beauty that only comes from direct, daily contact with
nature. Finally, it is about the sense of eternity, of the timelessness
that comes from knowing that nothing ever has to change unless you
want it to: great empires may rise up and crumble all around you, but
the village will abide.*

— Dmitry Orlov, 2005

Ecocity

The ecocity movement kicks new urbanism up a notch. Ecocityists are
dedicated to reshaping urban landscapes for the long-term health of biological systems, humans included — but without unduly weighting the
needs of bipeds. They want to return biodiversity — including fish, frogs,
and dragonflies — to the innermost hearts of cities by reopening paved-
over creeks and wetlands, returning agriculture to back lots and planter
strips, and giving nature a longer leash.

Ecocity is about growing food in de-paved streets and producing
electricity from solar alleys. It is about adding greenhouses to rooftops,
terraces, and window boxes for heat and kitchen gardens. It is less about
rerouting cars and trucks within cities, and more about eliminating the
need for them altogether.

One leading edge of the ecocity movement is City Repair, which
began in Portland, Oregon, by taking back intersections for pedestrian
mixed use, installing bike paths, putting up community bulletin boards
on street corners, and even painting street crosswalks with bright colors
and designs.

The ecocity movement, whose principal proponent for many years
has been Richard Register of Berkeley's Ecocity Builders, has now found
a powerful supporter in the People's Republic of China. China has the
unprecedented problem, remotely approached only by neighboring India,
of finding housing, food, and useful employment for a population that
will add another 2 billion people in the next 30 years — 18,265 additional
people per day, a small city every week, a city the size of Vancouver or
Sydney twice each year. With the natural systems that nourished their
ancient civilization now threadbare and seriously imperiled, it is not
hard to imagine why the Chinese are interested in ecocities.

*In Kinsale [Ireland] in 2021 there
are fewer cars and fewer fossil fuel resources, com-
muting long distances to work is no longer possible. Back
in 2005 nobody enjoyed being stuck in traffic, struggling to
find a parking space, the endless costs of owning a car and the problems that can arise. With the introduction of sustainable integrated
transport design within the town, starting first with traffic calming and reduction and leading on to a healthier and more localized lifestyle for all within
the area, Kinsale is now a far more pleasant and efficient place to live. Over the
years since 2005, as the town became more self-reliant, the need for private car
ownership steadily reduced. Kinsale residents gradually came to see that while it is
important for everyone to have access to a means of travel and that goods needed
to be moved from one place to another, this no longer necessitated every family
owning their own car. Transport in Kinsale now consists of a wide mixture of
choices, from easy safe ways to get around by bicycle, car sharing clubs and
lift sharing bulletin boards, improved public transport and more efficient short
distance vehicles. Plans for a light railway between Cork and Kinsale are well
underway. The benefits are clear for all, and people still occasionally
look back with horror on those summer days 16 years ago when the
streets were clogged with fume pumping cars and coaches.*

— Rob Hopkins, 2005

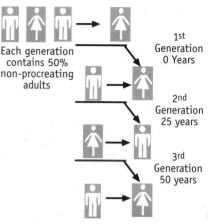

Half Child Model

Each generation contains 50% non-procreating adults

1st Generation 0 Years

2nd Generation 25 years

3rd Generation 50 years

First generation dies (Age 75);
3 offspring survive.
Population has decreased at least
25% in 75 years.

*If population is to decline without
catastrophic intervention, at least half
of us must pass through life without
producing children.*

Bartlett's Third Law

Albert Bartlett's Third Law holds that the response time of populations to changes in the human fertility rate is the average length of a human life, or approximately 70 years. This is called "population momentum."

Let's suppose that the White House science advisor and author of the ten-year comprehensive *Strategic Plan for U.S. Climate Change* has four children (I don't actually know how many children he has; this is just an exercise). How many grandchildren will he and his wife have if each child has a family the same size? Sixteen. If you add the number of children to the number of grandchildren, you have 20, or ten times the population of the two parents, in about 40 years. If the science advisor and his wife live to be 80 or 90, there is a good chance they will see their great-grandchildren. How many? Sixty-four. So now 84 descendants from the original two parents, plus the parents themselves, are on Earth, consuming resources.

At current US rates, each child will produce 18,000 tons of CO_2 per year. If you sum that from the time the parents were born to the time they die at age 90, assuming generations are 25 years apart on average, it works out to 36,720,000 tons of CO_2, which is a whole lot of global warming. Fortunately, the science advisor also heads up the White House's planning for the first manned colony on Mars.

Creating Walkable Communities

- Build for everyone.
- Create many linkages.
- Streets must have multiple uses.
- Sidewalks must be comfortable.
- Streets must be crossed with ease.
- Keep urban traffic dispersed and low speed.
- Keep traffic moving.
- Build green streets.

- Build bike lanes.
- Build compact intersections.
- Provide handicap access.
- Build public space.
- Build with proper size and scale.
- Provide mixed uses and mixed incomes.

— Dan Burden, 2001

If one thinks of an ecocity as a collection of self-sustaining ecovillages, it is possible China can accomplish an ecocity transition more easily than many Western countries. In China, each residential quarter is administrated by a subdistrict. For example, every district of Beijing (e.g., Chaoyang District) has many subdistricts (e.g., Panjiayuan Subdistrict), and every subdistrict administers many communities (e.g., Panjiayuan Subdistrict administers twelve adjacent communities). Every community has a residents' committee that represents the local interests to the subdistrict. In a structure like this, the learning curve can be negotiated rapidly, and when one ecovillage succeeds with a greywater management plan or a rooftop wind farm, all the others can quickly adopt similar plans. This is happening in some parts of China as I write, with active central-government support.

Intentional Community

*Hoping for our decision-makers to
lead us through this crisis would be an instance
of the blind leading the blind. Forget about them; they
surely have forgotten about us. Begin talking to your neighbors
and building awareness in your community. Organize to create community gardens, community markets, and community bicycle marts.
Work with your neighbors on taking your neighborhood off the grid.
Develop a local currency or a system of barter.*

— Dale Allen Pfeiffer, 2005

Suburbs at present are leisure deserts;
there is not much to do. The alternative neighborhood
would be full of familiar people, small businesses, common proj-
ects, animals, gardens, forests and alternative technologies and therefore
full of interesting things to do. There would be many festivals, drama clubs
and celebrations. Consequently people would be less inclined to go away at
weekends and holidays, which would reduce national energy consumption.

— Ted Trainer, 2003

Countercultural experimentation is an ancient tradition, flourishing most often when mainstream culture becomes authoritarian or when hard conditions impel it. Beginning in the second century BCE, some 4,000 Jews decamped from Jericho, Gezer, and Jaffa to live and work together in an Essene commune on the coast of the Dead Sea; in the Middle Ages, St. Benedict established elaborate rules for architecture, agriculture, and civil order in his monasteries, and monks flocked to join. In the 11th to 13th centuries, the Cathars rebelled against Catholic corruption and formed populist communes in the Languedoc region of France. In the mid-17th century, the Levellers and Diggers spurned the wealth and power of English society and formed open communes on public lands. In the early 1700s, Anabaptists, Inspirationists, and other cultural dissidents wandered through, and eventually left, Europe to escape military conscription and religious intolerance. They formed communal societies in other parts of the world, many of which are still in existence today. Practical and prosperous socialist initiatives inspired by the visions of Fourier, Owen, and Ruskin crisscrossed Europe and migrated to North America and Australia. The 19th century witnessed the popularity of Oneida, Amana, the Shakers, and the Mormons. At the turn of the 20th century, many of the lessons learned by these groups were transplanted into the thin soils of Palestine by the kibbutzim, then taken from there to Japan and returned again to Europe and the Americas in a post-war communal revival.

Correctly diagnosing war as a disease of our collective mental health, the pacifists of the 1940s were determined to retrace steps and discern root causes of humanity's penchant for self-destruction in hopes of then fashioning cures. They created communities of deeply shared values, most importantly nonviolence. They drew upon the work of Robert Owen and John Humphrey Noyes and added the influence of Tolstoy, Gandhi, Odum, Borsodi, and Fritz Lang. With sustained connections, mediated conversations, methodologies of inclusion, and full transparency, the intentional

DESSERTS

KEKCHI MAYA COCOA BALLS
Makes 12 balls

3 ounces (about ⅔ cup) cacao nibs or unsweetened chocolate
1 Tbsp piquin chiles or dried chipotles, ground
1-inch stick of cinnamon, coarsely chopped
½ tsp allspice berries
1 tsp sea salt
1 tsp vanilla extract

Heat a griddle, cast-iron skillet, or Mexican comal over medium heat. Add the cacao nibs and dry-roast for 2 minutes, until fragrant, turning constantly with a wooden spoon or spatula. Turn out into another container and set aside. Add the peppers, cinnamon stick, and allspice berries to the griddle and roast the same way, stirring, for 2 minutes. Scrape into a big marble mortar, spice mill, or coffee grinder. Add salt and grind to a fine powder.
Combine the spice mixture, vanilla, and roasted cacao and process into a warm, sticky paste. Scrape out onto a work surface and shape into 12 small balls. Let sit until thoroughly dried. Store in a tightly sealed jar. When ready to use, grate over any dish.

Difficulty

DESSERTS

APPLE CRANBERRY TARTS

Serves 6

1 Tbsp butter or margarine
½ cup brown sugar
½ cup apple juice or cider
6 medium apples, peeled, cored, and thickly sliced
½ tsp ground allspice
1 tsp ground cinnamon
⅔ cup fresh or frozen cranberries
Peel of 1 lemon, grated to zest
2 Tbsp diced crystallized ginger
6 small pie shells

Preheat oven to 375°F. Melt butter over medium-high heat, using large iron skillet. Add brown sugar and stir until sugar starts to caramelize, 3 to 4 minutes. Stir in apple juice. Stir until liquid starts to thicken. Add apples and stir every few minutes until soft and coated with caramel, about 10 minutes. Stir in allspice, cinnamon, cranberries, and zest. When cranberries begin to pop, stir in ginger. Cook until no liquid remains, 2 to 3 minutes. Remove from heat and divide into pie shells on ungreased cookie sheet. Place pies on middle rack of oven and bake 15 minutes or until shells begin to brown. Remove and cool. Garnish with whipped topping or sour cream and serve warm.

Difficulty

communities of the 1960s and later decades explored emotional trust, intellectual freedom, and new social terminologies as they gradually developed a higher capacity for critical thinking and problem solving.

As these communities matured and were replicated with improvements, they began to strike a balance between inclusion and exclusion and between normal human needs for both social contact and privacy. They also began to develop a balanced distribution of responsibilities for daily work amongst individuals, families, village, and greater world. Economic collectivity, important in the formation stages of many communities, became less essential as they matured, and Latter-Day Saints, kibbutzim, and hippie communes alike decollectivized when their members came to appreciate the value of a shared purse at the family or household, rather than community, level. Ample evidence of their success is found in members' own pride in their communities' resilience, safety, and well-being.

In a recent study, David J. Connell of the University of Northern British Columbia looked at sustainability indicators for North American intentional communities. Drawing on surveys of more than 600 communities over nearly 20 years, Connell was intrigued to discover a correlation between community success and food — both growing it and eating it. Communities that ate three or more meals together each week had greater success than those that dined together less frequently. Those that ate together more frequently also grew more of their own food, and the percentage of its food a community grew correlated directly to its longevity and sense of success.

Surviving alone in the wilderness is for movies. Even cave men lived in small groups and depended on the group to survive. Nations are just bigger groups. Peak oil will not be the death of us all, there will be survivors. To survive peak oil and life, you are going to have to be surrounded by good, honest, trustworthy people — people that help each other out.

— Chris Lisle, 2005

Cohousing

In the late 1960s, a new type of community called cohousing emerged in Denmark and spread to Germany and North America. Cohousing attempted, without all of the social commitments and mumbo-jumbo of intentional communities, to overcome the alienation of modern high-rises and subdivisions where no one knows their neighbors. There are now several hundred such communities completed or in development across the United States, Canada, and Europe.

In cohousing, smaller, more affordable private dwellings surround extensive, well-appointed common facilities. The common house may include a large dining room, a kitchen, lounges, meeting rooms, recreation facilities, a library, a laundry, a dispensary, guest rooms, workshops, and children's spaces. The typical cohousing community has 20 to 30 single-family homes along a pedestrian street or clustered around a courtyard. The physical design itself encourages and facilitates community.

The principal elements demanded by cohousing residents are a resident-managed participatory process, a non-hierarchical shared decision-making process in which it is rarely or never necessary to resort to voting, a physical design for the village that creates a strong sense of family, easy access to multifaceted common facilities, and no shared community economy — it's pay as you go, and it's affordable.

> *The problem of poverty is not the lack of money per se; it is the inability to obtain needed resources. Geodesic greenhouses, bicycles, and superadobe housing can make vast numbers of people self-sufficient in food, transportation and shelter, and reduce their subsistence costs nearly to zero. With their basic needs comfortably met, people who would otherwise live in abject poverty would be freed to pursue fulfilling work, education, leisure, and community development — lives of full citizenship.*
>
> — Sorcha Keepers, 2005

Ecovillage

Drawing upon the experience of both intentional communities and cohousing, yet another movement emerged in the early 1990s to carry the habitat revolution beyond its human-centered origins and give it greater biological community membership.

Ecovillages sit upon a three-legged stool of social/spiritual, economic, and ecological sustainability, according equal worth to each leg lest the stool wobble. It is ecological sustainability that tends to define ecovillages and separate them from other patterns of settlement, and, indeed, most ecovillages either protect nearby natural reserves or have large wilderness areas set aside for the primary use of Gaia. However, the recognition of the need to incorporate social/spiritual and economic sustainability has added implications that are seldom fully appreciated.

DESSERTS

CAROB NUT BONBONS
Makes about 20 candies

1 cup prunes, chopped and pitted
½ cup chunky peanut butter
¼ cup maple or other syrup
¾ cup dry milk or powdered soymilk
2 Tbsp carob or sweetened cocoa powder
¼ cup raw pistachios or salted peanuts, coarsely chopped

Combine the prunes, peanut butter, syrup, milk powder, and carob and mix well. Put chopped nuts into a separate bowl. Take 1 tsp of prune mixture at a time and roll into small balls. Roll in chopped nuts and place on serving dish. Serve immediately or chill for the following day.

Variation
Spread nuts along one side of a 12- by 12-inch piece of waxed paper, about 2 inches from the edge. Spoon peanut butter mixture onto the nuts and roll waxed paper into a tube. Twist the ends to seal. Wrap to retain moisture and chill for several hours. To serve, unwrap and cut into slices about ¼- to ⅜-inch thick.

Difficulty

DESSERTS

STRAWBERRY RHUBARB COBBLER

The first food plants of spring are a welcome sight, and ever since edible rhubarb spread to Europe and North America in the 1830s, pies and cobblers have been a delightful remedy for the privations of winter.

Serves 6

Filling
½ cup (3½ ounces) sugar or equivalent sweetener
1 Tbsp cornstarch
Pinch cinnamon
Pinch sea salt
1 pound fresh rhubarb stalks, trimmed and chopped
3 cups (15 ounces) fresh strawberries, rinsed and picked over, or 18 ounces frozen strawberries
1½ tsp grated lemon zest
1 Tbsp fresh lemon juice

Biscuit Topping
1 cup unbleached flour
2 Tbsp coarsely ground cornmeal
¼ cup and 2 tsp sugar or equivalent sweetener
2 tsp aluminum-free baking powder
¼ tsp baking soda
¼ tsp sea salt
4 Tbsp (½ stick) unsalted butter, melted
⅓ cup buttermilk or unsweetened almond milk
½ tsp vanilla extract
⅛ tsp ground cinnamon

Filling
Preheat the oven to 375°F. Stir the sweetener, cornstarch, cinnamon,

In 1991, Robert and Diane Gilman defined an ecovillage as a:

- Human-scale.
- Full-featured settlement.
- With multiple centers of creative initiative.
- In which human activities are harmlessly integrated into the natural world.
- In a way that is supportive of healthy human development and can be successfully continued into the indefinite future.

Ecovillages attempt to provide housing (often in the cohousing model), income-producing work, and enriching social life, all in the context of a traditional villagescape. "Full-featured" distinguishes ecovillages, which are likely to have shops, schools, clinics, one or more churches, a cemetery, and other normal accouterments of village life, from strictly residential enclaves. In creating an economically self-reliant community, ecovillagers are forced, by definition, to select livelihoods that are as harmless to the environment and their social values as are their housing, sources of energy, and sources of food. To achieve these high goals, founders typically rely on permaculture design in planning, looking to nature and native communities for advice. They also make efforts to build energy-efficient and nontoxic houses; organically grow much of their own food; redirect waste into productive uses; and adopt sustainable social norms.

Hierarchy, paternalism, process rigidity, social rank, sexism, and many of the forms of cultural organization accepted as normal in mainstream society are viewed as unsustainable practices by ecovillagers. This obliges them to come up with alternative forms of self-governance. Humor helps. Indeed, the absence of humor would be another form of unsustainability.

Most ecovillages limit their size, or divide governance into smaller councils, in order to ensure that each member can influence the community's direction. Consensus decision-making is common.

Ecovillages are a worldwide movement, with as many as 20,000 villages belonging to the Global Ecovillage Network (www.gen.ecovillage.org). The earliest continuously existing ecovillage is Solheimer, near Selfoss, Iceland, which was founded in 1930. The United Nations has recognized the accomplishments of many well-known ecovillage projects, including Findhorn in Scotland (1962), Lebensgarten in Germany (1985), and Crystal Waters in Australia (1988). Ecovillages exist in rural and suburban areas and also within large cities. In 2000, the 100-household Munksgaard Ecovillage near

Copenhagen, Denmark, won first prize in a Danish competition for the best sustainable design for the 21ˢᵗ century.

Ecovillages are the newest and most potent kind of intentional community, and in the vanguard of the environmental movement that is sweeping the world. I believe they unite two profound truths: that human life is at its best in small, support-ive, healthy communities, and that the only sustainable path for humanity is in the recovery and refinement of traditional community life. In my view, ecovil-lages, and the larger social movements of which they are an integral part, are the most promising and important movement in all of history. Its success is crucial for the long-term viability of the human venture.

— Robert J. Rosenthal, 2001

I confess a certain softness toward the ecovillage model, having spent my past 35 years living at The Farm, a proto-ecovillage in Tennessee. From 1992 to 2004, I traveled as an emissary for the ecovillage movement to hundreds of experiments on six continents. Along with fellow "Johnny Ecovillageseeds" Diane Gilman, Max Lindegger, Declan Kennedy, Lucilla Borio, Liora Adler, Jonathan Dawson, May East, and others, I saw some truly amazing successes but also witnessed more than a few failures. It is not easy being ahead of your time, even if you have the wind of inevitabil-ity at your back.

So why do so many ecovillages crash and burn? I often receive letters from would-be ecovillagers who want to know how best to create their own experimental town, often in scenic places like Costa Rica or New Zealand. Sometimes they have already bought some land and moved their family onto it in hopes of attracting others to join them in the building process.

I have to sigh. The sad fact is that most ecovillages — by some esti-mates 90 percent in the past decade — fail, and not because they are short of ideas, money, or good advice, but because they are short of mem-bers. Too many people want to start ecovillages rather than join existing ones. Is it that they think the existing ones don't have the same values they do? Are they worried that their design sketches might not be appre-ciated? Why do they think their dreams are so different from those of others? With thousands of choices out there, I don't think it is a matter of mismatched values. I think it is about ego.

People who are unwilling to set aside the supremacy of their own pre-conceptions and listen to, and maybe even try out, the ideas of others

Cobbler cont.

and salt together in a large bowl. Add rhubarb and strawberries and mix gently until evenly coated, then add lemon zest and juice and mix. Transfer the mixture to a large pie plate, position on a rimmed baking sheet, and bake until the filling is hot and bubbling around the edges, about 25 minutes.

Biscuit Topping
Combine the flour, cornmeal, ¼ cup sugar, baking powder, baking soda, and salt in one bowl and mix. In a smaller bowl, whisk the melted butter, buttermilk, and vanilla. In a third small bowl, mix the remaining 2 tsp sugar with the cinnamon and reserve. Just before the rhubarb comes out of the oven, combine the contents of the first 2 bowls and mix well. Pinch off a dozen equal pieces of biscuit dough and place them on the hot rhubarb filling, spacing them at least half an inch apart (they should not touch). Sprinkle each mound of dough with cinnamon sugar. Bake at 425°F until the fill-ing is bubbling and the biscuits are golden brown on top and cooked through, 15 to 18 minutes. Cool the cobbler on a wire rack for 20 minutes and serve.

Difficulty

Battle in another realm, from "The Return of the Omnipotent Baron Mordo!" Strange Tales No. 114, November 1963, marvelmasterworks.com © 1965 Marvel Comics.

are unlikely to adjust well to the life of any small and intimate community. Sustainable community is not about dominance. It is about listening. And after everyone has listened to everyone else, usually the best choice emerges on its own merit.

> *By all rights this founding of a new peace is a spiritual mission and at the same time an economic mission, an environmental mission, and a humanitarian mission. It will require a collaboration of individuals and cultural organizations working together to succeed. Its sign of success will be the renewal of local communities around the world.*
>
> — Susan Witt, 2001

Developing Consensus

The process of fair and nonviolent self-governance is one of the skills that any new community has to acquire in its formative years. It must be able to make this its regular, normal, and unremarkable practice, and even make it fun. After that, teaching non-boring and nonviolent self-governance is one of the skills that sustainable community has to give back to the rest of the world.

Tree Bressen of the Walnut Street Co-op in Eugene, Oregon, has been assisting intentional communities, nonprofits, and other organizations with group process since 1994. Pages from her website, www.treegroup.info, are available for copying and distribution free of charge. According to Tree, the consensus process is a powerful tool for bringing groups to decisions that are inspired and effective. However, like many tools, using consensus requires a particular set of skills that must be learned. Groups who try to apply it without learning those skills often end up frustrated.

The search for agreement relies on every person in the circle bringing his or her best self forward to seek unity. Members of the group need not all think the same way, have the same opinion, or support the same proposal in a unanimous vote. Rather, what is being earnestly sought is a "sense of the meeting," the essence of what the group agrees on.

How many times have you seen a meeting bog down in details to the point of exhaustion? The ability to distinguish when an item is small enough to send to a committee or manager can save everyone countless hours of frustration and boredom. In consensus process, the person who is tasked with making these distinctions is called the facilitator. Good facilitation is at the core of any successful group process.

The facilitator is responsible for keeping meetings on track, soliciting input from quieter members, and summarizing what's been said. Facilitation is an art and a skill, a science and an intuition. If your group is inexperienced in facilitation, consider bringing someone in to give a workshop or sending a few people off for more training. Rotating everyone through the role helps minimize power differences in the group. If the least-skilled members get more practice, it brings the level of the whole group up a notch. Being thrust into the facilitator role makes people better meeting participants too. At the same time, it makes sense to call upon skilled facilitators for more challenging or controversial topics.

During the meeting, if the group is nearing consensus, the facilitator states the sense of the meeting and then has a note taker read out the proposed minute, because it's the minute that will actually serve as the record of what was agreed to. Those who forget their own history are condemned to repeat it.

Tree Bresson says, "In a culture where we're taught that every person must struggle for themselves and we can't get ahead without stepping on others, consensus is a radical, community-building alternative. Consensus teaches that no one can get ahead by themselves: our success with the method depends utterly on our ability to work with others. Competition is no longer the root of experience; instead, we honor and integrate the diverse life surrounding us. Consensus is interdependence made visible."

Every group has conflicts, and they aren't even a bad thing. Conflicts show that people care enough to be invested and to go for what they want. Without people who care and push forward, communities wouldn't get built and maintained. However, conflicts are often uncomfortable, both for the participants and for people watching. People in conflict can sometimes behave unscrupulously, using coercion and threats, intimidation, economic leverage, emotional abuse, gender or other privilege, minimizing, belittling, distorting, denying, or blaming to get their way. In isolation, shielded from consequences, they can come to believe these methods are the most effective.

The problem with letting individuals get away with outrageous conduct is that it lowers the level of discussion; people end up listening to an exchange of taunts between bullies instead of a reasoned exploration of solutions to real problems. Problems persist, and continue to get worse, until people find more successful ways to truly discuss them. This is as true at the UN or in any government as it is in your family, workplace, or personal relationships.

Dr. Strange meets Baron Mordo, from "Face-to-Face At Last With Baron Mordo!" Strange Tales No. 132, May 1965, marvelmasterworks.com ©1965 Marvel Comics.

Solution-oriented behaviors include transparent and open-ended negotiation, equal-handed fairness, non-threatening language, economic partnership, respect, shared responsibility, trust and mutual support, responsible parenting, honesty, and accountability. If we want to see more of this, we need to teach and model this behavior to our children and elect officials who best embody this value set.

Growing up in a turbulent Detroit neighborhood, Marshall Rosenberg developed a keen interest in conflict resolution and the ways that new forms of communication could provide peaceful alternatives to the violence he saw. He studied clinical psychology and comparative religion, but his own life experience convinced him that human beings are not inherently violent. This insight motivated him to develop the process he calls Nonviolent Communication (NVC). Today Rosenberg travels to some of the most impoverished, war-torn states of the world. More than 180 certified trainers and hundreds of supporters teach his method.

Marshall Rosenberg, Tree Bresson, and others use many of the same techniques:

- Learn how to honestly express how you are feeling without blaming or criticizing.
- Empathically receive how others perceive you and your needs and values without hearing blame or criticism.
- Clearly request what you need without demanding.
- Empathically receive the requests of others without hearing a demand.

The Light of Truth, from "The Many Traps of Baron Mordo!" Strange Tales No. 117, February 1964, *marvelmasterworks.com ©1965 Marvel Comics.*

There are many more parts to the conflict-resolution paradigm, and Rosenberg, Bresson, Caroline Estes, and others have written books and publications that describe them in detail. Rosenberg sees changing the way we educate our children as key to achieving a culture of nonviolence, an end to war, and social advancement despite the limits of material resources, our history and tradition of force, and other impediments. Rosenberg writes:

I want to get the next generation of people around the world educated in a radically different paradigm, and with skills for creating structures that support the new paradigm. So, for example, we not only teach the kids in the school, we also set up Nonviolent Communication training with their parents, teachers, and administrators. And equally important is that the school is a reflection of the kind of government that we would like to see. It shows leaders as servants. Teachers are servants of the students; the administrators are servants of the teachers. Rewards and punishment are not used. The relationships among the student body are created as interdependent relationships, not as competitive ones. Tests are not given to determine grades. Tests are given to determine

Defending Against Warlords

Everybody likes to get organized, even gun nuts. But one thing people should not be doing in preparation for the transition is stockpiling guns and ammo. Not only is it a waste of money; it also adds to the overall danger and reduces your safety.

People are safest by simply living in non-threatening communities. Violence arises from many sources, but fear and anger are accelerants. By reducing those, you are safer.

Like most problems, the challenge of gangs of hooligans is best solved upstream of mob rule, at its origins, before it becomes unmanageable. Hooligans have always been with us. Gandhi advised his followers to befriend them and show them how to enjoy life in better ways.

Too often hooligans are the products of abuse in childhood, and the Great Change will now give us the opportunity to rethink how we raise our children and to do it more intelligently than is often the case today. That would have vast ripple effects. If we desire a more just, compassionate and Earth-sensitive future, that is where it begins.

Of course, there will be those who think differently and who continue to propagate the stereotypes of "rat-race," "dog-eat-dog," "survival of the fittest," "A Boy Named Sue," and so forth, into yet another generation of innocent and trusting souls. Armed gangs will attempt to gain unfair advantage by using force. There are, after all, an awfully lot of people in the world who have had modern military training, and it's easy to make beer.

In Akira Kurosawa's famous film *The Seven Samurai* (later Westernized as *The Magnificent Seven*), a village terrorized by marauding bandits recruits a group of Ronin, or unemployed samurai, to come save them. The Ronin organize the village for mutual self-defense and sacrifice their own lives in the struggle to defeat the bandits.

Don't imagine that there are Ronin you will be able to hire to do this for you.

One priority for any community should be to have well-trained security people — a constable, a sheriff, and deputies or a larger police force. This might even be a good use for some of your gun nuts, as long as they owe their first allegiance to the community and don't come to think that they are in charge. Support and nurture them. Give them help. Give them love. Keep telling them what good people they are.

Learn and practice nonviolence and instill it as a value in your children. This is not something you can master in a few short weeks and then forget about. It is something that you practice your entire lifetime.

DESSERTS

CHOCOLATE BRANDY CAKE
Serves 8

Cake Mix
1 tsp aluminum-free baking powder
1 tsp baking soda
¼ tsp sea salt
½ cup unsweetened cocoa
2¼ cups unbleached pastry flour or all-purpose flour
⅔ cup sauerkraut, rinsed, drained, and chopped
2 Tbsp flaxseed meal
1 cup warm water

Frosting
1 tsp vanilla
½ pound silken tofu
⅔ cup butter
3 ounces brandy or rum
2 tsp unsweetened cocoa
1 tsp instant coffee
1 cup sugar or equivalent sweetener

Cake Mix
Preheat oven to 350°F. Mix baking powder, baking soda, and salt. Add cocoa, flour, sauerkraut and mix well. In a large bowl, combine flaxseed meal with warm water and stir briskly. Add dry ingredient mix slowly to wet mix while stirring. When evenly mixed, pour the batter into a greased cake pan and bake for 30 minutes.

Frosting
Reserving 1 ounce of brandy, combine all ingredients and whip to a frosting consistency. Brush the cake with brandy before frosting.

Difficulty

whether the teacher has done his or her job. They're not tests of the students; they're tests of the learning process.

Anyone interested in creating sustainability memes — social conventions — that might allow humans to continue inhabiting this planet for additional generations will find alternative forms of education a worthy subject of study. Alternative schools run a gamut of styles, but most strive to improve the method and content of education. Many stress egalitarian and free-society values, creative solutions to old problems, and learning as a daily adventure. One of the best sources of information is the National Coalition of Alternative Community Schools (www.ncacs.org).

The pursuit of peace is not merely the pursuit of the absence of violence, because peace is never achieved until justice is achieved. And justice is not achieved until everyone's interests are addressed. So, you will never actually finish addressing everyone's issues. There will always be unfinished business. You can't achieve peace unless it is accompanied by constant striving to address the issues of justice. This means your job will never end.
— The Peacemaker of the Iroquois, 15th century

Small farms tend to be lonely places, and many, without access to diesel or gasoline, would become dangerously remote. You will need neighbors to barter with, to help you, and to keep you company. Even a small farm is probably overkill in terms of the amount of farmland available, because without the ability to get crops to market, or a functioning cash economy to sell them in, there is no reason to grow a large surplus of food. Tens of acres are a waste when all you need is a few thousand square feet. Many Russian families managed to survive with the help of a standard garden plot of one sotka, which is 100 square meters, or, if you prefer, 0.024710538 acres, or 1076.391 square feet. What is needed, of course, is a small town or a village: a relatively small, relatively dense settlement, with about an acre of farmland for every 30 or so people, and with zoning regulations designed for fair use and sustainability, not opportunities for capital investment, growth, property values, or other sorts of "development." Further, it would have to be a place where people know each other and are willing to help each other — a real community.
— Dmitry Orlov, 2005

Afterword: The Great Change

ike many islanders the world over, Cretans have a wonderful ability to blend nature into their stories. Take the tale of Icarus.

In the Cretan legend, Daedalus was a famous Athenian architect who was invited by Minos, King of Knossos in 2000 BCE, to come to Crete to build a labyrinth. When Daedalus finished, Minos decided that rather than pay him, he would imprison him in the labyrinth to see how difficult it really was to escape. Using wax and feathers, Daedalus built two sets of wings, one for himself and the other for his son, Icarus. They escaped the labyrinth and flew off toward Athens, but during the flight the foolish boy flew higher and higher until the sun melted the wax that held his wings together. He suffered, to use the terms of the nuclear power industry, an "energetic disassembly." Icarus fell into the Aegean and perished.

The ancient story was about hubris — it reminded its listeners that we should never leave the power of nature too far removed from our planning. Failing to observe the constraints of gravity, sunlight, and the frailty of material things, Icarus was certain to fall.

Today our world has begun to resemble something out of *Amazing Science Fiction*. Ancient pharaohs could not conceive of the wealth and power that the average Kuwaiti or Kiwi now takes for granted. But beneath the surface, our hubris is all too evident.

Nature has always sustained us. We inhabit a thin film of biological activity in the cold depths of space, many light years from any other star system. No other planet in our own solar system is hospitable to life. Our own planet's biosphere is thinner, by proportion, than the dew on an

DESSERTS

PENNSYLVANIA DUTCH PLUM CAKE

Serves 8

2 cups molasses
1 cup milk or soymilk
2 eggs, beaten, or substitute 4
Tbsp flaxseed meal whipped in ⅓
cup water
1 tsp nutmeg, grated
1 tsp ground allspice
1 tsp cinnamon
1 cup plum preserves or fresh ripe
plums, peeled
½ cup raisins
½ cup currants
½ pound chopped candied lemon
rind
About 2 inches of a vanilla bean,
split
A few black peppercorns
1½ cups pastry flour
2 cups butter, cut small
2¼ cups 80-proof brandy or cognac

Combine all except last 3 ingredients in large pot, bring to a simmer, and cook 1 hour. Preheat oven to 375°F. Add last 3 ingredients and stir well, then pour into baking pans and bake for 30 minutes.

Difficulty

apple. We are one large solar flare, one errant asteroid, one mutant gene, or one nuclear winter away from extinction.

Looking around, we should be amazed and reverential that we have been given paradise for the span of a lifetime. Instead, we are collectively polluting, overconsuming, and wasting it to death. By any reasonable index — diversity of species, soil productivity, fresh water, forest cover, carbon in the atmosphere, ice over the poles — we are squandering our inheritance at unprecedented rates.

James Lovelock, who, with Lynn Margulis, popularized the Gaia hypothesis, which posits that our planet's biosphere is a living and self-regulating organism, has recently come out with dire warnings of pending Earth changes. Lovelock says that "we are in a fool's climate, accidentally kept cool by smoke, and before this century is over billions of us will die and the few breeding pairs of people that survive will be in the Arctic where the climate remains tolerable."

If you give Lovelock's predictions credence, your grandchildren's survival boils down to one of three strategies: migrate away from the equator and plan to cope with the rising tide of millions of your fellow refugees; go mobile, follow the weather, and trust you will find safe places to set up camp when you need to; or shelter-in-place, nourishing your familiar ecosystems as best you are able, and build communities of like-minded people for shared defense, soil-building, and survival.

We are doubtless well beyond carrying capacity already. World population, which has already doubled twice in my lifetime, is headed for 8 or 9 billion by mid-century, even if fertility were to be held to sum zero: 1.4 births per couple. Half a child more and we are looking at 18 billion.

For thousands of years we have imagined the Earth as the source of fertility, nurturing humanity. To ancient Greeks, Gaia was Mother Nature. In the Americas her name combines Pacha (Quechua for "change, epoch") and Mama ("mother"). To the Norse she was Jord, the goddess of Earth, who entrusted her bounty to Idunn, the goddess of youth and springtime. In India she was Khali. Khali is a particularly appropriate goddess for our times because in her mad dancing, disheveled hair, and eerie howl there is a world reeling, careening out of control. The world is created and destroyed in Khali's wild dancing; redemption comes only when we realize that we are invited to take part in her dance, to yield to the frenzied beat, to find her rhythm.

Peak Oil may be the trigger for a global economic depression that lasts for many decades. Or it may not. It may plunge us into violent anarchy and military rule. Or it may not. But if Peak Oil doesn't wake us up to the precariousness of our condition, divorced from our roots in the soil and the forest, annihilating the evolutionary systems that sustain us and replacing them with brittle, artificial, plastic imitations, what will? What will it take?

We have gradually obtained more and more creature comforts since emerging from a world of ice 20,000 years ago. Since that time, our food supply, housing, mobility, and quality of life have gradually improved, extending our life spans and enabling us to have larger families. It was only a short time ago, two centuries at most, that we fell into our energy addiction and started down a path to ruin. Peak oil is an opportunity to pause, to think through our present course, and to adjust to a saner path for the future. We had best face facts: we really have no choice.

Peak Oil is a horrible predicament. It is also a wonderful opportunity to do a lot better. Let's not squander this moment. This will be the Great Change.

DESSERTS

CANDYLION
Makes 1 quart

1 quart just-picked dandelion blossoms, harvested from a pesticide-free area
3 cups water
½ cup sugar or equivalent sweetener (other than honey)
½ cup mild honey
3 Tbsp lemon juice

Immediately on harvesting, snip the yellow portions of the petals from the green calyxes (the outer whorl of sepals). Save the yellow parts, discard the green. Bring water and sweeteners to a boil, remove from the heat, and stir in the yellow petals. Cover and let steep for at least 1 hour. Strain the syrup through a fine sieve. Stir in the lemon juice and chill. Process the mixture in an ice-cream maker to make ice cream or blend with frozen yogurt to make candylion frogurt.

Difficulty

Appendix 1: First Aid

This information is only an overview and does not demand special equipment or training. It in no way represents definitive care or treatment.

In any health crisis, try to remain calm and in control. Others will take their lead from you. Just do one thing at a time and issue clear instructions without yelling or anger. A sense of humor helps a lot. Clear priorities to keep in mind:

- Don't rush to the rescue at the expense of your own life or health. Look for hazards such as downed wires, poison gas, traffic, fire, explosion, building collapse, etc., before you become a casualty too. Try to figure out what caused the injury before you get too close. If it's a car wreck, sniff for gasoline.

- Call for help! Your helpers can read these instructions to you, fetch supplies, dial the phone, get a car, get more help, summon the ambulance, or find a doctor.

- Decide early if it is safe to move the patient. You want to avoid all movement if the spinal cord might be compromised, which is possible in the case of a fall (any fall greater than the person's height can break their neck) or car wreck. Find a way to preserve the person's present position, stabilizing and supporting the spine without moving the head. Sometimes this is all you can do while awaiting rescue.

- If you expect medical help to be available soon, avoid medicating pain as long as possible as it can interfere with definitive diagnosis and treatment. There is also a risk of allergic reaction with all medications. Use "Comfort Measures" (see below) instead. If you do not expect an ambulance or hospital to help you, make pain management a high priority.

DON'T hurry. Be deliberate and thoughtful.

GET HELP for all medical emergencies. Your goal is to preserve life and limb until the professionals can take over.

If you care for children, an elderly person, or anyone in poor health, you may find a one-day CPR course and basic or advanced first aid training are good investments of your time. Prepare for situations you are likely to encounter in your home community, such as childbirth or heart attack, by assembling a home library, purchasing supplies, reading, and getting training.

Choking and Unconsciousness: Start with ABCs

If the patient can speak or cry, ABCs — airway, breathing, and circulation — are OK. If the patient is unconscious or choking, address these life-threatening problems first, regardless of any other problem.

Take your time and be sure! CPR doubles the chance someone will survive cardiac arrest, but it can cause injuries.

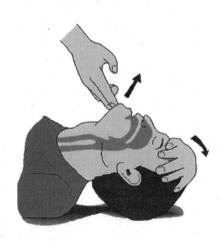

A for AIRWAY: Yell, tap their shoulder. Maybe they are drunk. Are they moving any air? Gently repositioning the head so the chin points up can open an airway. Perhaps the Heimlich maneuver is needed (see "Shortness of Breath," p. 204), or maybe they choked on food you can see at the back of their mouth. Look. Sweep with your hooked finger.

B for BREATHING: Still unresponsive? Does the chest rise? Can you feel breath on your face if you lean in close to their mouth? Listen hard! If breathing has stopped, pinch the nose and blow into the mouth just enough to lift the chest. (For infants, blow into mouth and nose.) Stop blowing when you see the chest rise. Repeat once. If the person is breathing, but with difficulty, try a position change — sitting up and leaning forward sometimes works best. Loosen the patient's clothing. Monitor him or her.

C for CIRCULATION: Is there a pulse? Feel for the neck artery beside the windpipe. (Feel yours first to get the position.) Concentrate intently while you count off ten seconds. If you are sure there is no pulse, tear off all clothing covering the chest. Press straight down, firmly, on the skin between the nipples with the heel of your hand (two fingers for an infant). With an adult, go two inches deep. With a small child, one inch. With a baby, half an inch. Release. Give the person 15 breaths, then do two more compressions.

Look, listen, and feel again. If the patient does not resume breathing on their own, keep breathing for them and continue chest compressions until you can feel a pulse; check every minute or two. Call for assistance between breaths. Drag the person to a phone. Continue until help arrives.

ABCs OK? Once the person can breathe and has a pulse, carefully seek other injuries, inspecting and gently touching front and back, head to toe. If you find severe blood loss, address it next. If an unconscious person is breathing and has a heartbeat but no apparent injuries, see if they respond to pain by pinching them hard.

Prevent and treat "Shock" (see below).

DON'T leave any person alone who has needed help with ABCs or shown signs of shock. Monitor them closely until they have seen a doctor.

GET HELP for every person who has trouble with ABCs.

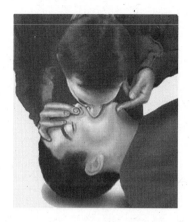

Shock

Shock can occur with any kind of trauma, even emotional trauma. Once shock sets in, it can kill, so don't wait for the person to become confused, irritable, pale, cold, nauseated, dizzy, or damp. If you notice these signs, get help urgently.

Prevention and treatment are the same:

- Keep the person lying down and immobile.
- Elevate feet and legs.
- Normalize body temperature. Prevent heat loss with a blanket if it's cold; keep them in the shade if it's hot.
- Keep the person comfortable and calm. Reassure them.
- Hydrate. If they are conscious enough to drink without choking and do not have internal injury, let them drink water, especially if there is severe blood loss or thirst.
- Monitor closely. Assign a buddy to hold the patient's hand, provide reassurance, attend to injuries, offer "Comfort Measures" (see p. 216), and inform you of changes.

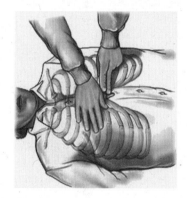

   DON'T let them get up too soon. Err on the side of caution.

   GET HELP for every person who shows signs of major injury or any sign of shock.

Wound Care

The rougher the living situation, the more important it is to provide assiduous wound care. Skin is the largest part of the immune system and any breach must be defended.

- Cleanse minor wounds thoroughly with plain soap and clean water (clean your hands first). Use a soft clean brush (like a toothbrush) to remove debris, or tweezers to extract splinters or glass shards.

DESSERTS

MOROCCAN CANDIED GRAPEFRUIT

Makes about 2 quarts

3 large, unblemished, yellow or pink grapefruit
Equal weight of sugar, or half part honey to one part fruit by weight
¾ cup water
3 Tbsp fresh-squeezed lemon juice

Using a vegetable peeler, remove and discard the thin outer layer of zest. With a fine grater, smooth the surface of the white pith. Immerse the fruit in a large bowl of cold water and soak 2 hours, then drain. In a large saucepan, boil the fruit for 10 to 12 minutes. Drain and repeat the process. Drain again and allow to cool. With a sharp knife, quarter the grapefruit. Carefully slice away and discard most of the pulp, leaving only ¼ inch of fruit along the rind. In a large pan over low heat, dissolve the sweetener in ¾ cup water and lemon juice, stirring occasionally until all grittiness disappears, about 15 to 20 minutes. Continue cooking, turning the rinds every 15 minutes and skimming off the foam. Using a sharp knife, pierce each rind in several places. After 2 hours the rinds will acquire a deep orange color and the syrup will turn light amber.
With a slotted spoon, transfer the rinds to a 2-quart glass jar. Pour the warm syrup into the jar through

- Pour peroxide into puncture wounds or deep cuts several times a day until they scab over.
- Keep all wounds clean and dry, no matter how superficial.
- Change dressings whenever they become wet or soiled.
- Apply cold compresses for pain. Consider using pain medication such as ibuprofen. Aspirin can interfere with clotting.
- If you must sew a wound closed yourself, sterilize a small sewing needle and a continuous piece of cotton sewing thread by boiling. Wear sterile gloves. Remove stitches in five days, after thorough cleansing of the site, by snipping and tweezing with good light. Do not leave any thread behind.
- Monitor for signs of "Infection" (see below).

DON'T assume a minor wound does not need attention. A small, untreated human bite could cause loss of a limb.

GET HELP for any wound that does not heal.

Infection

Look for the signs: pain (such as earache, or while urinating); redness, swelling, bad smell, discharge, or heat; fever.

- Garlic cloves and oregano oil are natural antibiotics and antivirals that the patient can eat or that you can apply to a wound.
- Antibiotic ointment may be applied on broken skin, but not in deep wounds.
- Most childhood ear infections clear up without antibiotics. It may help to avoid dairy products.
- Treat the symptoms: cold packs and fluids for fever and swelling; anti-inflammatories like ibuprofen for pain; fluids to prevent dehydration.
- Include in the diet as many immune-building foods as possible. For example, blueberries and shiitake mushrooms; cranberry juice is good for the urinary tract; live yogurt cultures are helpful for digestive and reproductive systems.
- Excellent hygiene is your primary defense. Expose clean laundry, blankets, cooking utensils, etc., to direct sunshine to help get rid of bacteria.

DON'T assume danger of infection is gone a few days after an injury.

GET HELP for even the most minor infection if the patient is very young, very old, or has any chronic health problem such as diabetes. Get help if an infection is not getting better with treatment. If there are red streaks on the skin, get help at once. Sometimes only antibiotics will work.

Moderate Bleeding

- Press HARD on the wound with a sterile pad and elevate the injury for a few minutes.
- Fasten the gauze with tape, but not so tightly that skin nearby gets cold or pale.
- If bleeding does not stop in a few minutes, proceed to "Heavy Bleeding" below.

    DON'T disturb a scab. Let it fall off on its own.
    GET HELP for any wound that seems large, deep, or infected.

Heavy Bleeding

If the above technique does not work:

- Position the patient to lie flat on the floor. Elevate the injured area above the heart.
- Apply VERY FIRM pressure directly on the wound with a dry, sterile dressing — such as gauze pads, a sanitary napkin, or the inside surface of a clean folded towel — and don't release. Lean with all your body weight.
- Slip more layers on top if needed, but do not move the layers next to the skin.
- When flow has stopped seeping through, have helper tape pad firmly in place while you maintain pressure. Add more pads on top if needed.
- Check temperature around the bandage. Skin should stay warm; nails must remain pink. If circulation is impaired, loosen the binding.
- If there is still bleeding through the pad, apply pressure instead at the spot in the groin or armpit above the wound where you feel a pulse. PRESS HARD on the pulse until bleeding stops. Do not release pressure until bleeding can be managed with direct pressure on the wound; this may mean leaning on the pulse until the person reaches a hospital.
- Treat for "Shock" (see p. 201) and push fluids if the person is able to drink and has no abdominal problems.

    DON'T delay medical care if any of these techniques were needed. And don't think "tourniquet" — it means sacrificing the limb.
    GET HELP for all instances of severe bleeding.

Moroccan Grapefruit cont.

a fine-meshed sieve to remove any trace of foam. Seal and store at room temperature for up to 6 months. Serve the wedges of candied grapefruit in a decorative bowl, chased with a demitasse of strong, black espresso.

Difficulty

DESSERTS

SHOOFLY PIE

Serves 8

Pastry Crust

1 cup unbleached all-purpose flour
1 tsp sugar or equivalent sweetener
½ tsp sea salt
½ tsp non-aluminum baking powder
4 Tbsp cold, unsalted butter, cut into ½-inch bits
3 Tbsp regular or tofu sour cream

Filling

1 cup all-purpose flour
⅔ cup light brown sugar
1 Tbsp cold butter
¼ tsp sea salt
1 cup light molasses
½ cup cold water
1 egg, lightly beaten (optional)
½ cup hot water
1 Tbsp baking soda

Pastry Crust

In a medium bowl, combine the flour, sweetener, salt, and baking powder. Add the butter and blend into flour as a very coarse mix. Chill the dough in the refrigerator for 15 minutes. Add the sour cream. Knead and squeeze the dough to incorporate any loose bits. Gather the dough together into a rough ball, flatten it into a 1-inch-thick disk, cover, and refrigerate at least 30 minutes. Before rolling, return dough to room temperature for about 15 minutes. Sprinkle the work surface and rolling pin lightly and evenly with flour. Beginning at one edge, press the rolling pin down onto the dough to flatten it, moving across the dough in increments. Then, moving from the

Chest Pain or Heart Trouble

Chest pain or pressure, pallor, difficulty breathing, weakness, fatigue, nausea, sweating, weak or irregular or rapid pulse, a feeling of impending doom: all are symptoms of heart attacks. Some people get back pain, indigestion, or pain radiating up the left jaw or down the left arm. Women are often misdiagnosed; they may just feel short of breath or have heartburn or extreme fatigue. If you suspect a person might be having a heart attack:

- Search for an identification card, alert bracelet, or doctor's telephone number.
- Look for nitroglycerine spray or pills. If you find them, use them under the tongue. Repeat every five minutes. Expect the person to report a headache.
- Help the person to a comfortable position, probably reclining with head and chest elevated.
- Send for an ambulance. Use the phrase "severe chest pain." Ambulances are usually the fastest route to definitive care. Transport the patient yourself *only* to avoid a delay in care.
- If the patient is conscious, he or she should chew one adult aspirin immediately, but eat or drink nothing else.
- Monitor pulse and breathing carefully until help arrives.
- Attend to the ABCs and address "Shock" (see p. 201).
- Remain calm and reassuring and stay with the patient.

DON'T ignore any cardiac symptoms, even if the patient is embarrassed or refuses help.

GET HELP for all suspected heart trouble, even when the patient is in denial.

Shortness Of Breath

If a person has difficulty breathing, life is in danger. Act fast.

- Go back to ABCs. Check for choking on food or secretions that could indicate a blocked airway. To perform the Heimlich maneuver, wrap your arms around the patient's waist from behind, form a fist with one hand and grab it with the other, and push in and up in a sharp motion to force the air out of the patient's lungs. A turkey baster will suction out mucus.
- Help the patient into a comfortable position, usually sitting up, maybe leaning forward.

- Send for help urgently. You want someone to bring oxygen if possible. Use the phrase "having trouble breathing" when you call the ambulance.
- See if the patient has an asthma inhaler and help them use it.
- While waiting, question bystanders and family. Get as much information as you can. Perhaps there has been exposure to chemical fumes or some other cause you can address. This may be heart trouble for which the patient has medication. If you suspect a gas leak, move everyone to open air.
- If breathing stops, start rescue breathing (see "ABCs," p. 200; "Shortness of Breath," p. 201).

DON'T take shortness of breath lightly, even if the person has experienced it before.

GET HELP for anyone whose breathing does not normalize quickly.

Special Situations

Chest Injury: Wounds that puncture a lung deserve special attention. If you hear or feel air moving from a torso wound, tape a piece of plastic bag or Vaseline-coated gauze over the hole. Release this if breathing gets worse.

Penetrations, Impalements: If there is a penetrating object, do NOT remove it. Use gauze or cloth as a pad around it; then tape it so it cannot move.

Amputations, Knocked-Out Teeth: Amputations and partial amputations are scary but usually don't bleed much. Gently bandage without interfering with circulation, and save all body parts (even skin) by wrapping in clean cloth and putting in a plastic bag, on ice, in a cooler. Preserve a lost tooth (handle gently) in a jar of milk on ice.

Eye Injury: Transportation is urgent. You can tape a paper cup over the eye to protect it, with moist sterile gauze underneath.

Necks and Spines: Neck and spine injuries can be life-threatening. Do not allow the patient to be moved or to move on their own; hold the head, neck, and torso in the exact position in which you found the patient, and have helpers assist you. If you must move a person with neck or back pain, strap them to a door or an ironing board. Use wads of towels to keep the head from rolling out of a straight line with the backbone. If a neck wound bleeds a lot, it may be tricky to hold pressure without affecting breathing.

Head Injuries: Your first priority is to keep the person breathing. Suspect their neck is injured and assume they will have airway trouble. There may be a lot of bleeding, but direct pressure will work.

Shoofly Pie cont.

center of the dough outward, begin to roll the dough, adding more flour as necessary to keep the dough from sticking. Roll the dough gradually in all directions, flattening as you go, to form a large circle about 14 inches in diameter; do not roll it thinner than 1/8 inch. To transfer the dough to the pie pan, place the rolling pin gently on one edge of the dough and roll the dough up over the pin. Reserve crumbs.
Sweet Pastry Variation: increase the sugar to 3 Tbsp and add 1/2 tsp pure vanilla extract or grated lemon zest.

Filling
Preheat the oven to 350°F. Combine the flour, brown sugar, butter, and salt. Remove 1/2 cup of the mixture and set aside. Transfer the rest to a medium mixing bowl. Add the molasses and cold water to the beaten egg and blend but do not beat. Set aside. In a small bowl, mix the hot water with the baking soda and blend into the molasses mixture. Add to the flour mixture and mix well. Pour into the pie shell and top with the reserved crumbs. Bake for 35 minutes. The pie will appear quivery but will firm up as it cools. Cool completely before cutting.

Difficulty

Toothache: If dental care will be delayed, make a rinse with two teaspoons of salt or one teaspoon of baking soda dissolved in a cup of warm water. Swish and spit until glass is empty; repeat when relief fades. A solution of half hydrogen peroxide, half warm water works too; hold in your mouth for a few minutes. A cavity can be stuffed temporarily with a wisp of cotton soaked in peppermint oil or clove oil, either of which can be rubbed on gums. Treat for infection if there is swelling or fever.

DON'T try to handle these injuries on your own.

GET HELP for any wound that is complicated or life-threatening or might impair a function, such as vision or mobility.

Suspected Fractures, Sprains, Dislocations, and Strains

Sometimes only an X-ray can tell the difference between fractures, sprains, and dislocations, and sometimes a severe sprain can be more disabling than a mild break, so most orthopedic injuries are treated the same way.

- Do not move the patient, unless you absolutely must, until the injury has been splinted.
- Attend to the ABCs and address "Shock" (see p. 200, 201).
- If skin is broken near the injury, apply a sterile wound dressing. Control bleeding and follow "Wound Care" instructions (pp. 201-202).
- Immobilize the injured area, and the joints above and below it, exactly as you find it (do not try to straighten or realign). Use clean towels, bedding, or clothing as padding around the injured area. Then tie on rigid items to prevent motion. Thick magazines or newspapers work well for children, or look for sticks, table legs, lumber, tent poles, curtain rods, whatever is handy. Use elastic bandages, bandannas, triangular bandages, clothing, and similar soft items to tie splints above and below the nearest joints, but expect swelling: do not tape too tightly or tie with string. Check that skin stays warm and nails stay pink.
- Strap an injured arm to the torso, or tie a damaged leg to the other leg, to further minimize motion. Tape fingers and toes to their neighbor.
- Keep any injured limb elevated; have the patient lie down. With a fractured hip, sometimes it is more comfortable to lie on the injured side.
- Remember "RICE" for all orthopedic injuries: Rest. Ice. Compression (elastic bandage). Elevation.
- When the thigh bone fractures, there may be excruciating pain until the limb is stretched back out straight. Treat the pain.

- Consider "Comfort Measures" and anti-inflammatories such as ibuprofen. Cold compresses will help. After the first day, alternate warm and cold compresses. Use a wheeled office chair as a home wheelchair.
- All these bandages plus swelling means it's easy to cut off circulation. Frequently monitor fingers and toes for warmth and color, and loosen bindings when necessary. The person should be able to wiggle the digits.

  DON'T bind a broken rib by wrapping around the body. ***DON'T*** try to walk on an injured limb. Do not allow crutches to touch armpits.

  GET HELP for any suspected fracture, any head or neck injury, if skin near injury site is broken, or if pain does not improve greatly within 24 hours.

Electrocution and Other Seizures

- Accidental electrification: Make sure you don't encounter the same fate.
- Get the power turned off! Send for help. Wait until the scene is safe.
- Don't move the person. There may be injuries from a fall, and the spine may be compromised.
- When it is safe to approach, attend to the ABCs and address "Shock" (see p. 200, 201).
- Treat burns where current entered or left the body (they may be on the soles of the feet).
- If a seizure is not caused by electric current, look for an alert bracelet and see if the patient carries any medication.
- Protect the seizing person from injury by moving furniture away.
- Do not force anything into the patient's mouth — you will be bitten.
- Expect the person to be sleepy afterward. Make them comfortable and provide privacy. If they can't be woken up after a few minutes, or if they have several seizures in a row, they need medical help.
- Try to identify a cause, such as fever or head injury, and treat that.

  DON'T leave the person alone for the next 24 hours. Electrocution patients may seem fine but become severely ill later.

  GET HELP for all encounters with live current and all undiagnosed seizures.

Poisoning

A person who has been poisoned may not know why they are sick. Poisons can be inhaled, swallowed, or absorbed through the skin. Swollen lips are a sign that the culprit was ingested or inhaled.

BEVERAGES

BELLINIS
Serves 4

4 peaches
1 split of sparkling wine

Peel peaches and puree all but one half. Divide between 4 champagne flutes and add chilled sparkling wine. Garnish with thin slices of remaining peach.

Difficulty

BEVERAGES

LAVENDER LEMONADE
Makes about 1½ quarts

½ cup sugar
6 cups water, divided
2 Tbsp fresh lavender buds
½ to ¾ cup freshly squeezed lemon juice

Bring the sugar and 2 cups of the water to a boil, add the lavender buds, cover, and remove from heat. Let the syrup steep for at least 30 minutes. Strain into a pitcher. Stir in ½ cup lemon juice and 4 cups water. Add more lemon juice to taste. Chill and serve.
Substitutions: Mint, lime juice
This drink is delicious made with mint syrup and garnished with fresh mint, but it should be consumed quickly on a hot day before it turns color.

Difficulty

- Attend to the ABCs and address "Shock" (see p. 200, 201).
- Call for transport and call your regional poison control center (www.calpoison.org/ offers information in several languages). Follow their instructions.
- Dilute the poison by getting the person to drink milk or water, if they are conscious.
- Try to identify the poison. Save a sample or any container it might have been in. Read warnings on the label and follow instructions.
- If the patient vomits, save some. If an unconscious person is vomiting, turn them on their side and clear their airway. Choking is a grave danger.

DON'T induce vomiting, unless ordered to do so by poison control and care is more than one hour away.
GET HELP for all instances of suspected poisoning.

Abdominal Pain

There are so many possible causes: indigestion, constipation, stomach flu, menstrual cramps, food poisoning, food or medication allergies, gas, lactose intolerance, ulcers, pelvic inflammation, hernia, gallstones, kidney stones, parasites, cancer, endometriosis, Crohn's, urinary trouble, reflux. If the patient shows any of the problems listed below, a doctor's help is needed as soon as possible.

- Nausea, fever, and several days of vomiting everything.
- Bloody stools (red or black or darker than usual).
- Trouble breathing.
- Vomiting red blood or "coffee grounds" (dried blood).
- Pregnancy or a late period.
- Abdomen tender to the touch (press firmly all over).
- Recent injury to the area or recent car wreck (i.e., seat belt injury).
- Pain for several days.
- Enlarged liver area (lower right abdomen) and yellow skin or eyes.

If the patient doesn't show the above problems:

- Offer "Comfort Measures" (see pp. 216-218) and Tylenol or other anti-inflammatories.
- Try to help the person find a comfortable position, usually sitting or lying on side with knees bent toward the torso.
- Offer a laxative if bowels have not moved in over 48 hours.

- Offer soothing teas and bland food. Milk often helps an upset stomach as much as an over-the-counter medication for indigestion.
- Monitor for changes.

    DON'T force a person to eat or drink.

    GET HELP if you have an reason to suspect severe illness, including such symptoms as pale skin from blood loss or signs of dehydration.

Infant Diarrhea

Because infants can die of dehydration quickly, never ignore diarrhea and try to find the cause. Fortunately, up to 95 percent of the cases of watery diarrhea can be treated without intravenous fluids. You must act early while the child is able to drink.

- Increase fluid intake. Give breast milk, pediatric electrolyte or sports drinks, fruit juice, coconut juice. For an oral rehydration solution, mix five cups boiled water, eight teaspoons sugar, and one teaspoon salt.
- Enforce strict handwashing standards for everyone in the household.
- Clean the child's clothing and bedding. Dry it in the sun or in a hot dryer.
- Use disinfectant on hard surfaces, especially where food is prepared and where people defecate.
- If the child is old enough for solid food, offer bananas, white rice, applesauce, and toasted white bread, or anything likely to cause constipation.

    DON'T ignore symptoms of dehydration, noted in the "Fever" section (see pp. 212-213).

    GET HELP before an infant becomes lethargic or unable to cry or feed.

Burns and Sunburns

Size and depth determine severity of burns. Get medical attention if any blistered burn is larger than the patient's hand or deep enough to expose tissue below skin layers (fascia, fat, muscle, bone). Be alert for signs of "Shock," "Infection," and "Hypothermia."

- Make sure burning has stopped. Remove patient from fire. If necessary, roll the patient in a blanket to exclude air. Put out smoldering clothing; use water, a fire extinguisher, or even dirt or sand to smother burning clothes, skin, or hair.
- Attend to the ABCs and address "Shock" (see p. 200, p. 201).
- Call for help. All serious burns should be seen by a doctor. Keep patient calm while waiting for the ambulance.

BEVERAGES

ISLA MUJERES SMOOTHIES

You don't have to live in Hawaii to have fresh pineapple on your table if commercial jet shipments become untenable. Since pineapple adapts exceptionally well to greenhouse production, it can be grown even in winter, even in Iceland — especially in Iceland, where abundant geothermal steam makes hydroponic gardening practical year-round.

Serves 2

½ cup silken tofu or soy yogurt
1¼ cup unsweetened pineapple juice
¼ cup coconut milk
2 ripe mangoes, peeled and seeded
4 Tbsp maple or other syrup
1 cup ice cubes
1 pineapple slice, for garnish

Blend all but last ingredient until smooth and creamy. Pour into two stemmed glasses and garnish each with half a pineapple slice.

Difficulty

BEVERAGES

GINGER COOLER

Serves 6 to 8

½ honeydew, cantaloupe, or other
sweet melon
Grated zest of 1 lemon, plus its
juice
Grated zest of 1 lime, plus its juice
Squeezed juice of 2 more lemons
1 tsp ginger root, peeled and finely
ground or minced
Pinch salt
½ cup honey
2 cups crushed ice
2 cups sparkling water or mineral
water

Dice melon and puree with lemon
and lime juices and zest, ginger
root, salt, and honey. Serve with
equal parts of crushed ice and
sparkling or mineral water.

Difficulty

- If medical care is not available, do not pull off clothing that is sticking to wounds. Cut clothing away if it is loose, and soak off any that sticks.
- Submerge minor burns in cold water. Cold compresses can be used, but there is danger of hypothermia if much skin is gone, so do not apply cold to large burned areas. Monitor the patient's temperature and wrap him or her in clean sheets and blankets if there is shivering.
- Extensive sunburns without blisters can be treated with topical analgesic creams like Solarcaine®. Aloe juice is soothing. Keep the person out of the sun and hydrate well until healed.
- If there are blisters, protect them from breaking. Use sterile dressings and antibiotic ointment if skin is not intact. Change dressings daily.
- Keeping burns very clean is extremely important. Protect burns with sterile gauze, taped lightly in place, or sterile sheets (inner surface of folded clean laundry). Keep patient, clothing, and bedding clean, and change sheets often. (Sheets and towels dried on high dryer heat will be sterile if folded while hot, or they can be wrapped in a brown paper bag and baked for two hours over a pan of water in a 200°F to 250°F oven.) Caregivers should wash their hands often and, if burns are serious, wear masks and sterile gowns or aprons.
- Treat the pain. See "Comfort Measures" below. DON'T apply grease or ointment except as noted.

GET HELP for any blistered burn larger than the palm of the person's hand, or any burn deeper than the top layers of skin.

Snakebite, Spider Bite, Allergic Reactions

- Attend to the ABCs and address "Shock" (see p. 200, 201). Call for help.
- If an allergic reaction is causing mouth or throat swelling or wheezing, the person needs medical attention immediately. Give antihistamines such as Benadryl if the person can swallow. See if anyone has an Epi Pen or asthma inhaler. Get to definitive care fast.
- Gently wash the bite with soap and water.
- Get a description of the snake or spider. While you attend to the patient, someone can try to kill or capture it for identification.
- Apply a cold, wet cloth over the bite. Don't use ice; it could damage tissue further.
- If you have a snakebite kit and medical care is distant, follow kit instructions.

- Offer "Comfort Measures" (see pp. 216-218).

DON'T apply a tourniquet. DON'T pack the bite area in ice. DON'T cut the wound with a knife or razor. DON'T use your mouth to suck out the venom. DON'T let the victim drink alcohol. DON'T delay the trip to the hospital.

GET HELP for all poisonous bites and all airway swelling or wheezing.

Fainting

Fainting is usually not serious unless a person suffers injuries from falling or from operating machinery, or has other health problems. A person who feels faint or lightheaded should sit down and put their head between their knees, or lie down with their feet up. If they do not soon feel well, take the following steps:

- Keep person lying down with feet elevated until recovery is complete. Protect the person from falls.
- Bathe face gently with cool water. Do not pour water over them.
- Sprinkling a few drops of ammonia on a cotton ball and placing it near the nose may speed recovery.
- Loosen tight clothing. Provide privacy. Be calm and reassuring.
- Attend to the ABCs and address "Shock" (see p. 200, p. 201).
- Seek the cause. Is the person ill, injured, in shock? Dehydrated? Hungry? Diabetic? Elderly? Too hot? Upset?
- Check to see if the pulse is strong and regular. If not, get help now.
- Older folks or people with heart trouble need to be seen by a doctor after a fainting episode.

DON'T leave the person alone.
GET HELP if their condition does not improve in a few minutes.

Heat Illness or Heat Stroke

Too much heat can be very serious. If it reaches the point where sweating stops, the person may die. People with any chronic illness are especially vulnerable. If people are in a hot environment, be alert for: dizziness or fainting; heavy sweating; muscle cramps; cold or clammy skin; headache; rapid heartbeat; nausea; confusion.

- Get the person out of the heat and into shade or air-conditioning.
- Call for help.
- Let the person sip cool water, juice, or a sports drink.

BEVERAGES

HOT LICORICE CIDER
Makes 2 quarts

8 quarter-sized slices fresh ginger
Four 3-inch-long cinnamon sticks
Pinch ground hot peppers (optional)
1 tsp whole cloves
½ tsp fennel seeds
2 quarts fresh apple cider
¼ cup anisette or other licorice-flavored liqueur

Place the ginger, cinnamon sticks, hot peppers, cloves, and fennel in a small strainer. Suspend the strainer over and in the cider as it warms on medium-low heat for about 30 minutes. Add liqueur. Do not boil.

Difficulty

BEVERAGES

HOT OR COLD COCOA MIX
Serves 6

1 cup cocoa
¼ cup sugar or equivalent sweetener
¼ tsp sea salt
4 cups nonfat dry milk or powdered soymilk

Combine ingredients and store in a tightly covered container. To use, gradually add 1 cup tepid water to ¼ cup mix for each serving, first making a smooth paste. Then heat or chill.

Difficulty
🐓🐓🐓🐓🐓

- Fan the person and sponge them with cool water.
- Attend to the ABCs and address "Shock" (see p. 200. p. 201).

The condition is severe if the person becomes unconscious or has rapid heartbeat; confusion or delirium; warm, dry skin; temperature higher than 104°F; severe headaches; seizure or muscle twitching.

- Send for immediate medical attention.
- Let the person rest, with feet elevated, in a cool dark place. Fan the patient. Loosen clothing.
- Apply cool, wet cloths, hose off, or sponge with rubbing alcohol.
- If the person is conscious, let them sip cool water, juice, or a sports drink.
- When the crisis is over, the person should rest for several days.

DON'T ignore early signs of heat stress, such as lightheadedness, cramps, and headache.

GET HELP if you think anyone has a heat-related illness.

Fever in Babies and Young Children (Under Three)

Fever in a child bears close watching. The degree of fever (temperature) may not have much relationship to the degree of illness.

- If a feverish child under three is alert, comfortable, drinking fluids, urinating every six to eight hours, and showing signs of improvement, offer plenty of liquids and ice pops and dress very lightly.
- If rectal temperature goes over 102°F, or if the child seems uncomfortable, you can give ibuprofen or Tylenol, following package instructions. Encourage the child to drink fluids and do quiet activities. Sports drinks and electrolyte drinks may help.
- You can give a sponge bath with lukewarm water — not cold, not alcohol.
- Be alert for signs of dehydration: fussiness; thirst; hunger; dark, strong-smelling urine; fewer than three diaper changes in 24 hours; crying with few tears; dry mouth; rapid heartbeat; cool arms or legs; sleepiness. For an oral rehydration solution, mix five cups boiled water, eight teaspoons sugar, and one teaspoon salt.
- Don't dress a feverish child warmly or cover with blankets.

DON'T give aspirin to anyone under age 20, or Aleve (Naproxyn Sodium) to anyone under 12.

GET HELP if fever persists, gets worse, or causes a seizure, or if there are any signs of dehydration.

Fever in Adults and Children

If a fever without other symptoms lasts three to four days, comes and goes, and gradually goes away, it is not a cause for concern. It is a way for your body to fight off illness. Try to treat the underlying ailment rather than the fever itself. Take in adequate food and plenty of fluids and see that you urinate normal amounts.

DON'T ignore a fever that persists for more than a few days or that causes other symptoms, such as dehydration or convulsions. A fever seizure is an emergency.

GET HELP if urination becomes dark and scanty or if a seizure occurs.

Hypothermia

The very young and very old are most at risk, but anyone exposed to low temperatures, indoors or out, is vulnerable. Signs to be alert for are shivering; cold, pale or blue-gray skin; apathy; poor judgment; unsteady gait or lack of balance; slurred speech; numb fingers; and difficulty functioning.

The person is at risk of death if the following late symptoms are present: cold torso, stiff muscles, slow pulse, shallow or slow breathing, weakness, sleepiness, confusion, unconsciousness. Someone who is extremely hypothermic may appear dead, so treat a person who is not warm to the touch unless there are injuries incompatible with life or signs of decomposition.

- Call for help. Hospitals have the safest rewarming methods. Rewarming can cause serious problems.
- If help will be delayed, start rewarming methods: Get the person to a warm, dry room. Remove all their clothing. Put them to bed under heavy covers. Get a rectal temperature if you can.
- Have two people strip off their clothing and get under the covers with the patient. Sandwich together in skin-to-skin contact and wrap tightly.
- Raise room temperature as high as you can with heater, stove, or fireplace.
- Apply hot-water bottles and heating pads to the patient's torso (not limbs.)

DON'T let embarrassment stop you from saving a life.
GET HELP for anyone with symptoms, and act fast.

Frostbite

Extremities like toes, ears, nose, and fingers are most vulnerable to exposure to cold, and frostbite can happen in minutes. Suspect cold trauma if the body part changes color, becomes hard, goes numb and then becomes painful, or does not return to normal when warmed. There may be swelling. Blisters or blood blisters may form after 6 to 24 hours.

- Protect the frozen area from further injury by moving the person to a warm environment and keeping the part warm and dry.
- Seek medical care.
- Do not rub; handle very gently.
- If the area is still hard and frozen, immerse it in warm, not hot, water (102°F to 108°F). Do not use a heat source like a hot-water bottle, heating pad, or stove.
- If the area is thawed and then refrozen, immerse in room-temperature water (70°F to 74°F).
- Discontinue warming as soon as the affected part flushes.
- Separate affected fingers or toes with dry sterile gauze and keep parts dry, clean, and warm when thawed.
- Attend to the ABCs and address "Shock" (see p. 200, p. 201).
- Treat for pain.

  DON'T forget that a person with frostbite may also have hypothermia; look for signs.

  GET HELP if you think someone might have frostbite; if you don't, they may lose the body part.

Emergency Childbirth

Most emergent deliveries take care of themselves without complication, and most mothers are prepared for the delivery. The rule is, when in doubt, do nothing. If you are expecting a home birth, check the Gentlebirth.org website for preparation tips (www.gentlebirth.org/Midwife/clntspls.html). If you find yourself assisting at such an event in an unexpected place:

- Call for help. Remain calm. Get an emergency operator on the phone to guide you through the process if you can.
- Encourage the mother to relax and breathe slowly and deeply through her contractions. Time them if you can. If she wants to push, suggest she pant, or only push gently if she must.
- Help her into a position, such as a squat, where gravity can assist her. A helper can kneel behind to support her. (Another helper can read these instructions to you.)
- If there is time, locate clean wraps for the baby (such as unread newspaper sections, clean towels) and a Space Blanket or sleeping bag you

can wrap mother and baby in afterward. It is important to keep the baby warm. A pile of clean towels and sheets will be handy.

- When the baby's head starts to emerge, support it with your hands so it doesn't pop out. Keep your hands outside the birth canal.

- Don't pull, but guide the baby out gently. It helps to have a clean towel ready because the baby will be slippery! Have your helper note the time.

- Stroke nostrils downward gently to expel fluid. If the baby does not start breathing within 30 seconds, stroke the soles of the feet, then rub the back. Wipe out any fluid or mucus in the mouth with a clean towel.

- If necessary, gently blow the air in your cheeks (not your lungs) into the baby, sealing your mouth over the baby's mouth and nose, stopping as soon as you see the chest rise. Repeat until the baby breathes on its own.

- Place the baby on the mother's skin, with head lower than body. Cover mom and baby with dry towels, coats, blankets, etc. Encourage mom to nurse right away and to keep the baby warm.

- Wait for the placenta to come out. Do not pull or cut the cord. Keep placenta higher than the baby. Wrap and save it for the doctor.

- If there will be no help arriving, you can tie off the cord six inches from the baby with clean soft string or strips of clean cloth. Tie the cord again six inches from the first tie toward the placenta. Cut between the ties.

- If mom is bleeding heavily, press down on her abdomen and massage her uterus firmly until the bleeding stops. Elevate the foot of her bed if you can. Cold packs on the area will help the pain.

- A competent helper should stay with the new mom and the baby as long as possible. Encourage the mom to rest and nurse, and make sure she has enough to eat and drink and will be able to stay warm.

DON'T panic. Birth is a natural process, and a rapid birth is likely to go well.

GET HELP at the earliest possible moment if childbirth is likely.

Water Rescue

You can help ... even if you can't swim. When someone is in trouble near a dock, a float, or the side of a pool, your number one priority is to stay dry. The rule is Reach, Throw, Row, Go, in that order, even if you are trained in lifesaving.

10-Codes	
10-1	Receiving Poorly
10-2	Receiving Well
10-3	Stop Transmitting
10-4	OK, Message Received
10-5	Relay Message
10-6	Busy, Stand By
10-7	Out of Service, Subject to Call
10-8	In Service, Subject to Call
10-9	Repeat Message
10-10	Transmission Completed, Standing by
10-12	Visitors Present
10-13	Advise Weather
10-14	Urgent Business
10-18	Anything For Us?
10-19	Nothing For You, Return to Base
10-20	My Location Is ____
10-21	Call by Landline
10-33	Emergency Traffic at this Station
10-34	Trouble at this Station, Help!
10-38	Ambulance Needed At ____
10-44	I Have A message For You
10-45	All Units Within Range Report
10-62	Unable to Copy, Use Landline
10-65	Waiting for Next Assignment
10-67	All Units Comply
10-70	Fire At ____
10-77	Negative Contact
10-93	Check My Frequency
10-99	Mission Completed, All Units Secure
10-100	5-Min. Break, Commonly Rest Room
10-200	Police Needed At ____

- Holler for help. Draw attention to the situation. Proceed with great caution because you are putting your life in danger. If the water is cold, the person will quickly lose the use of their hands and be unable to help. You'll have to get professional rescue involved, so make the call early.
- Lie down. Extend your upper body over the edge of the pool or dock. Make sure you have a firm foothold or have someone holding your belt or legs. Grasp the victim's wrists, clothing, or hair and draw them to safety.
- If they are too far away, extend a pole, towel, oar, shirt, or branch for them to grasp, and draw them to safety — don't let them pull you in. Beware fast currents and undertows.
- If the person is still too far away, use a buoy or any soft floating object. Attach it to a rope. Stand on one end of the rope, throw the float beyond the person, and slowly pull it into their grasp.
- You might be able to push a small boat, like a kayak or dinghy, or a floating item, like lumber, a surfboard, or a seat cushion, within the victim's reach. A panicked swimmer can capsize a small boat, so don't paddle out alone. And don't injure a panicky swimmer with an outboard motor.
- Once the person is out of the water, treat for ABCs, then "Shock," then "Hypothermia," and transport to medical care.

DON'T let the victim pull you in, or there may be two victims.

GET HELP for anyone who has experienced near-drowning, even if they feel well. They may develop breathing problems hours later.

Comfort Measures for Pain and Illness

There are many ways, besides administering painkilling drugs, to help someone who is ill or injured to feel better. These measures are even more important when standard medical care is not available or will be delayed. When hospitals and nursing homes are forced to close, severe illnesses and injuries must be treated at home. If a hospital is open but understaffed, it means you become the nurse.

Notice early changes. Be alert for subtle signals of discomfort like restlessness, personality change, and irritability. If you address them early, you may prevent more severe manifestations.

- Distraction is very effective. Put earphones on the patient and play music they like, or play a radio. Turn on the television or play a funny movie. Offer books, magazines, puzzles, games, cards, electronics, crafts, toys, musical instruments, conversation. Read a poem or a story aloud. Take dictation of letters. When one amusement loses effectiveness, try another.

- Company: Arrange for volunteers to stay at the bedside as much as possible, in shifts. Explain these measures to them.

- Temperature: Try warm and cold compresses, alternating them or applying whichever one the person likes. Heating pads? Too many blankets? Room too warm or cold? Too much of a draft?

- Position: More pillows? Raise the feet? Lie on stomach, back, or side? A person who is bedridden must be repositioned every two hours or their skin will break down. If you see reddened areas on heels or elsewhere, tape soft padding there to provide a cushion, massage the area, and check it often.

- Massage: You don't need to know any fancy moves — anyone can deliver a satisfying backrub or foot rub. Ask the patient what would feel good. Use a little olive oil or hand lotion.

- Personal care: Adjust the pillows and blankets, change sheets, help them wash their face and hands, apply lotion or cologne or powder, help with a change of nightgown or pajamas, give a pedicure or comb their hair, help with oral care. Think spa: Put slices of cucumber on their eyelids or a steamy towel on their face.

- Change the view: Move them to a couch near a window or to a different bed. Hang a different picture on the wall. Bring them snapshots of loved ones.

- Give control: Pay attention to requests. Visitors or privacy? Exercise or nap? Curtains open or closed? Let them control the environment and schedule as much as possible. Keep the space uncluttered, with medical devices and medicines out of sight.

- Spiritual care: Prayer works. Try progressive relaxation and visualization exercises too.

- Diet: Take special care with food and beverages. Use your nicest china, garnish food with color, offer favorite dishes. Bring special snacks, tea, and treats. Serve a glass of wine with dinner, or a beer.

- Children benefit from having a favorite stuffed animal or blanket for security. Adults don't mind having some well-loved familiar thing around too, like a special quilt for the bed.

- Be alert for the unpleasant aromas caused by many illnesses. Keep the room and the patient clean, and use candles and sachets and incense to mask bad odors.

   DON'T forget the patient will want periods of privacy. Leave a bell so they can summon you.

   GET HELP if there is a change for the worse in the person's condition.

Natural Cures

Certain well-known weeds are sources of modern medicines. Roots, leaves, and flowers of several species considered weeds in the United States are gathered, cured, and used in other countries. The early US American settlers learned from the indigenous peoples to use golden-seal as a curative for sore and inflamed eyes, as well as for sore mouth. The plant grows in patches in high open woods and was formerly found in great abundance in Ohio, Indiana, Kentucky, and West Virginia, but is now rare. Ginseng has also been hunted to near extinction in the wild.

Preparation: A decoction extracts the flavor by boiling in water. An infusion is steeped or soaked without boiling. Expressed juice has been pressed and squeezed out, often by wrapping the plant in cheesecloth and twisting hard. Pounding is done in a mortar and pestle or in a bowl with the handle of a knife or other hard object. Crushing is done with the side or back of a knife blade.

Many medicines can be found in fields and forests if you know what to look for. Identification guides are usually regional, for specific geographic areas, and are easy to find in libraries and used bookstores, as are herbals with extensive lists of plants and their therapeutic uses. The following are some common folk remedies of North America.

To Stop Bleeding

Dove's-foot/Crane's bill: Expressed juice
Giant puffball: Packed as poultice
Periwinkle: Expressed juice of leaves
Plantains: Pounded leaves as poultice
Self-heal: Expressed juice
Stork's-bill: Expressed juice of leaves
Woundwort: Expressed juice

Cleansing Rashes/Sores/Wounds

Note: Use these plants externally to bathe the skin or, where indicated, as a poultice. Apply two or three times a day.

Rapeseed

Burdock: Decoction of root; crushed raw root and salt for animal bites
Chamomile: Infusion of flowers as poultice
Chickweed: Expressed juice of leaves
Cleavers: Infusion of whole plant except roots
Comfrey: Decoction of root as poultice
Docks: Crushed leaves
Elder: Expressed juice of leaves
Elm: Infusion of bark
Horehound: Infusion of whole plant except root
Mallow: Decoction of leaves and flowers as poultice
Marsh mallow: Decoction of root; infusion of leaves and flowers as poultice
Nettle: Infusion of flowers and shoots
Oak: Decoction of bark
St. John's wort: Infusion of flowers and shoots
Sanicle: Infusion of whole plant except root
Scurvy grass: Crushed leaves
Shepherd's purse: Infusion of whole plant; root as poultice
Silverweed: Infusion of whole plant except root
Solomon's seal: Decoction of root as poultice
Sorrel: Crushed leaves
Tansy: Crushed leaves
Watercress: Expressed juice
Woundwort: Infusion of whole plant except roots
Yarrow: Infusion of whole plant except roots

Antiseptic

Note: These plants can be used externally or internally. They are particularly useful for wounds that have become infected.
Garlic: Expressed juice
Horseradish: Decoction of root
Mallow: Infusion of leaves and flowers
Marsh mallow: Decoction of root; infusion of flowers and leaves
Thyme: Infusion of leaves and flowers

Aches/Pains/Bruises/Stiffness

Note: Where indicated, use externally.
Balm: Infusion of leaves
Birch: Infusion of leaves

Flax

Borage: Infusion of whole plant except roots
Burdock: Decoction of root
Chamomile: Expressed juice of flowers applied to swelling
Chickweed: Infusion of whole plant except root
Comfrey: Decoction of root applied to swelling
Cowberry: Infusion of leaves and fruits
Dock: Crushed leaves applied to bruises
Dove's foot/Crane's-bill: Infusion of whole plant except roots applied to swellings
Elm: Infusion of bark
Figwort: Decoction of whole plant except root; use externally to draw bruises and blood clots
Garlic: Expressed juice applied to swelling
Remember especially for headache: Willow leaves and barks make a decoction containing salicin (a base for aspirin).

Fevers

These plants will induce perspiration to break a fever.
Chamomile: Infusion of leaves and flowers
Elder: Infusion of flowers and fruit
Elm: Decoction of bark
Feverfew: Infusion of whole plant except roots
Lime: Infusion of flowers

Colds/Sore Throats/Respiratory

Agrimony: Infusion of whole plant except roots
Angelica: Decoction of root
Bilberry: Infusion of leaves and fruits
Bistort: Infusion of whole plant except roots
Borage: Infusion of whole plant except roots
Burdock: Decoction of roots
Chamomile: Infusion of flowers; use as a gargle
Colt's foot: Infusion of leaves and flowers
Comfrey: Infusion of whole plant
Great mullein: Infusion of whole plant except roots; decoction of root as a gargle
Horehound: Infusion of whole plant except roots
Horseradish: Raw root
Lime: Infusion of flowers
Lungwort: Infusion of whole plant but roots
Mallow: Infusion of flowers and leaves

Chicory

Marsh mallow: Decoction of root; infusion of leaves and flowers
Mint: Infusion of whole plant but roots
Mountain avens: Infusion of whole plant; use as a gargle
Nettle: Infusion of leaves
Oak: Decoction of bark; use as a gargle
Plantain: Infusion of leaves and stems
Poplars: Infusion of leaves and buds
Rose: Decoction of hips
St. John's wort: Infusion of flowers and shoots
Sanicle: Infusion of whole plant but nut roots
Self-heal: Infusion of whole plant but roots; use as a gargle
Thyme: Infusion of leaves and flowers
Willow: Decoction of bark
Yarrow: Infusion of whole plant but roots; use as an inhalant

Settling Stomach

Balm: Infusion of leaves
Bilberry: Decoction of fruit
Bracken: Infusion of leaves
Dandelion: Decoction of whole plant
Horseradish: Infusion of root
Mint: Infusion of whole plant but roots with crushed charcoal
Sanicle: Infusion of roots
Solomon's seal: Decoction of roots
Yarrow: Infusion of leaves and flowers

Olive

Diarrhea

Note: Take two or three times daily till symptoms subside.
Bilberry: Decoction of fruit
Bistort: Infusion of whole plant but roots
Bramble: Infusion of leaves; decoction of fruit
Cowberry: Decoction of fruit
Elm: Infusion of bark
Great burnet: Infusion of leaves and shoots
Hazel: Infusion of leaves
Mint: Infusion of whole plant but roots
Mountain avens: Infusion of whole plants but roots
Oak: Decoction of bark
Periwinkle: Infusion of leaves; do not use for long periods

Plantain: Infusion of leaves and stems
Silverweed: Infusion of whole plant except roots

Constipation
Agrimony: Infusion of whole plant except roots
Barberry: Expressed juice of fruit
Cleavers: Infusion of whole plant except roots
Couch grass *(Elymus):* Decoction of root
Dandelion: Decoction of whole plant
Elder: Expressed juice of fruit
Feverfew: Infusion of leaves and flowers
Rose: Decoction of hips
Rowan: Expressed juice of fruit
Walnut: Decoction of bark

Hemorrhoids
Note: Apply externally two or three times a day.
Bilberry: Expressed juice of fruit
Chamomile: Infusion of leaves and flowers
Elm: Decoction of bark
Lesser celandine: Expressed juice of leaves
Oak: Decoction of bark
Plantain: Expressed juice
Poplar: Decoction of leaf buds
Silverweed: Infusion of whole plant except root
Solomon's seal: Decoction of root

Expelling Worms
Take internally.
Bracken: Infusion of root
Feverfew: Decoction of leaves and flowers
Figwort: Infusion of whole plant but roots
Tansy: Infusion of leaves and flowers; use sparingly in small amounts

Burns
Aloe: Make salve of the jelly
Comfrey: Express the juice from leaves to aid tissue regrowth (cuts/burns)

Appendix 2: Substitutions

Substitutions

You may find yourself in a situation where you are out of the herb specified in a recipe, or perhaps you just don't care for that specific herb. Whenever you substitute, the flavor will not be quite the same, so it is always a good idea to begin your substitution with half the specified recipe amount and then adjust to your own tastes.

Spices

Allspice	cinnamon; dash of nutmeg or mace; dash of cloves
Aniseed	fennel seed; anise extract
Cardamom	ginger
Chili powder	fine ground peppers (cayenne, jalapeño, serrano, habanero, or datyl) plus oregano and cumin
Cinnamon	nutmeg or allspice (use only ¼ of the amount)
Cloves	allspice; cinnamon; nutmeg
Cumin	chili powder
Ginger	allspice; cinnamon; mace; nutmeg
Mace	allspice; cinnamon; ginger; nutmeg
Nutmeg	cinnamon; ginger; mace
Saffron	dash of turmeric (for color) dissolved in milk

Herbs

Basil	oregano; thyme
Chervil	tarragon; parsley
Chive	green onion; onion; leek; shallot

Cilantro	parsley
Italian seasoning	blend of any of these: basil, oregano, sage, rosemary
Marjoram	basil; thyme; savory
Mint	basil; marjoram; rosemary
Oregano	thyme; basil
Parsley	chervil; cilantro
Poultry seasoning	sage plus a blend of any of these: thyme, marjoram, savory, black pepper, and rosemary
Red pepper	dash of bottled hot pepper sauce or other powdered pepper
Rosemary	thyme; tarragon; savory
Sage	poultry seasoning; savory; marjoram; rosemary
Savory	thyme; marjoram; sage
Tarragon	chervil; fennel seed; aniseed
Thyme	basil; marjoram; oregano; savory

Vegetables and Grains

Amaranth	millet; quinoa; buckwheat groats
Arame	hijiki; wakame; kombu; dulse
Artichoke	Jerusalem artichokes; salsify; burdock; hearts of palm
Arugula	watercress; tender spinach leaves plus dash of ground pepper; Belgian endive; escarole; young dandelion greens; young mustard greens; chicory; radicchio; Swiss chard
Asparagus	leeks; okra; fiddlehead fern; broccoli
Avocados	chayote squash; pureed raw peas; pureed cooked and chilled asparagus; artichoke hearts
Beet	carrot; slicing tomato (in salads)
Bermuda onion	Spanish onion; yellow onion; sweet onion; red onion
Black radish	rutabaga; turnip
Bok choy	Chinese broccoli; yau choy; Napa cabbage; broccoli; Swiss chard; celery; collard greens; beet greens
Boston lettuce	Bibb lettuce; lambs quarters; leaf lettuce; iceberg lettuce; celery leaves
Broccoli	broccoflower; cauliflower; broccoli rabe
Brown rice	converted rice; wild pecan rice; white rice
Brussels sprouts	broccoli flowerets
Bulgur	cracked wheat; couscous; quinoa; wheat berries
Burdock	salsify; asparagus; artichoke heart

Rosemary

Carrot	parsnips; jicama; daikon; celery; celeriac; turnip; kohlrabi; broccoli; rutabaga; cauliflower; salsify
Cassava	malanga; dasheen; potato
Cayenne	chile de arbol; Thai pepper; habanero; jalapeño; serrano; cascabel; pequin; tepin; holland; cherry pepper
Celeriac (celery root)	carrot; turnip; parsley root
Celery	carrots; fennel stalks; Chinese celery; bok choy; cardoon; jicama
Chayote	zucchini; kohlrabi; other summer squash; carrots; bell peppers
Chickpeas	great northern beans (for hummus); lima beans; black chickpeas
Collards	kale; kohlrabi leaves; bok choy; turnip greens; mustard greens
Corn	barley; garden peas
Cress	arugula; radish sprouts; tender spinach leaves; nasturtium leaves; young dandelion greens; endive; purslane
Cucumbers	zucchini; beets
Daikon	jicama; young turnip; black radish; pickled ginger; parsnips
Eggplants	zucchini; cocozelle; okra; portobello mushrooms
Eggs	flaxseed meal (Make meal by grinding flaxseed in a blender until it has the consistency of cornmeal. Use 2 Tbsp flaxseed meal plus ⅛ tsp aluminum-free baking powder plus 3 Tbsp water for each egg called for in a recipe.); cornstarch (substitute 1 Tbsp cornstarch plus 3 Tbsp water for each egg called for in a recipe); bananas (substitute ½ of a mashed ripe banana plus ¼ tsp aluminum-free baking powder for each egg); silken tofu (substitute ¼ cup tofu for each egg)
Endive	radicchio; arugula; watercress
Escarole	curly endive; radicchio; borage; mustard greens; arugula; spinach
Garden peas	edamame; fresh lima beans
Garlic	asafetida (powder); rocambole; shallots; onions garlic chives
Green beans	wax bean; Italian flat bean; dragon tongue bean; winged bean

Soya

Green cabbage	red cabbage; Napa cabbage; savoy cabbage
Green onion	spring onions; leeks; shallots; chives
Hominy	barley grits; dried beans; buckwheat grits; potatoes
Hominy grits	polenta meal; buckwheat grits; barley grits
Horseradish	wasabi; black radish
Iceberg lettuce	romaine lettuce; leaf lettuce
Kale	collard greens; rapini; Swiss chard; flowering kale; cabbage; Napa cabbage; kohlrabi leaves; mustard greens; spinach
Leeks	yellow onion; asparagus (as a side vegetable); ramps
Millet	quinoa; bulgur; couscous
Mushrooms	tempeh; eggplant; asparagus; bell peppers; zucchini
Mustard greens	gai choy; escarole; kale (less pungent); Swiss chard; spinach; radish greens
Nopale	okra; green beans; green peppers
Nuts	Grape-Nuts cereal; dried fruit; granola; rolled oats; chocolate chips
Olives	caper berries; cocktail onions; chopped sun-dried tomatoes; capers
Parmesan	Grana Padano; Romano; aged Asiago; sapsago; Swiss Sbrinz; Fontina; Monterey Jack; nutritional yeast; "soyco" grated parmesan (a soy-based cheese substitute); yeast flakes and ground almonds; oil-cured black olives (as a pizza topping); seasoned breadcrumbs
Potato	sweet potato; parnip; cassava; dasheen; malanga; yuca; jicama; lotus root; Jerusalem artichoke; rutabaga; cauliflower
Purslane	watercress; spinach; okra
Quinoa	couscous; rice; bulgur; millet; buckwheat groats; amaranth; teff
Radicchio	Belgian endive; escarole; chicory
Rhubarb	cranberries; quinces
Shallot	green onions (white part only); onions (1 small onion equals 3 shallots) plus dash of crushed garlic; red onion; green onions; garlic
Silken tofu	soft tofu; sour cream; mayonnaise; yogurt
Sorrel	spinach plus lemon zest; arugula
Soymilk	cow's milk; goat's milk; oat milk; rice milk; almond milk
Spinach	Chinese spinach; Swiss chard; beet greens; sorrel; kale; turnip greens; escarole

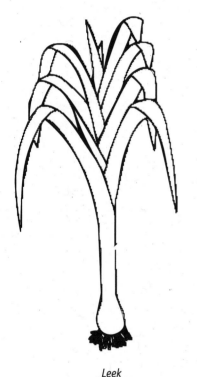

Leek

String beans	asparagus; broccoli; okra
Sugar peas	snow pea; asparagus; carrots
Sushi nori	soybean paper; purple laver
Sweet peppers	Holland bell peppers; Italian frying peppers; cubanelle; poblano pepper; Anaheim pepper; pimiento
Sweet potato	yams; boniato; mashed cooked pumpkin
Swiss chard	beet greens; spinach; turnip greens; bok choy; escarole; mustard greens
Swiss cheese	Emmentaler; Gruyere; Parmesan; Romano; nutritional yeast
Taro	malanga; parsnip; sweet potato; yam; new potatoes
Tempeh	tofu; hamburger; TVP; seitan
Tomatillos	green tomatoes plus dash of lemon juice; plum tomatoes plus dash of lemon juice; cape gooseberries
Tomatoes	roasted red peppers; tomatillos; mangos; papayas
Turnip greens	dandelion greens; mustard greens; kale; collard greens; Swiss chard; spinach
Vidalia	Spanish onion plus 1 Tbsp sugar; Bermuda onion (plus sugar); red onion; bulbs of green onions
Wakame	sea lettuce; dulse; arame
Water chestnut	jicama; Jerusalem artichokes; lotus roots
Wheat flakes	triticale flakes; rolled oats
Zucchini	cocozelle; yellow squash; chayote squash; eggplant; cucuzza; carrots; pumpkin

Leavens

Baking powder	(1Tbsp)Combine ⅝ tsp cream of tartar plus ¼ tsp baking soda. Combine two parts cream of tartar plus one part baking soda plus one part cornstarch. Decrease another liquid in the recipe by ½ cup and add ¼ tsp baking soda to dry ingredients and ½ cup buttermilk or yogurt or sour milk to wet ingredients. Decrease another liquid in the recipe by ½ cup and add ¼ tsp baking soda to dry ingredients and ¼ cup molasses to wet ingredients. Decrease another liquid in the recipe by 2 Tbsp and add 1 tsp baker's ammonia.
Salt	citrus zest; pepper; herbs; soy sauce; hatcho miso (especially in hearty soups and stews; 1 tsp sea salt or kosher salt equals 2 Tbsp hatcho miso); salt substitute; kelp powder; marinades

Oils and butters

Baking fat	applesauce; pureed prunes; apple butter; fruit-based fat substitutes; ricotta cheese; bananas (mashed); nutritional yeast; omit or reduce
Frying fat	clarified butter; olive oil; vegetable oil; beer and wine (for sautéing — use 3 Tbsp of flat beer or wine for every Tbsp of butter called for in recipe)

Sweeteners

Cane sugar	honey; brown sugar; maple syrup; sugar; rice syrup; barley malt syrup; molasses; fruit juice; fructose
Palm sugar	Mix 1 cup dark brown sugar plus 2 tsp molasses; jaggery; piloncillo; brown sugar; maple sugar; date sugar

Nutritionists recommend that we cut down on saturated fats and cholesterol.

Fats ranked in descending order of saturated fat content are: coconut oil, butter, palm oil, animal fat, cottonseed oil, vegetable shortening, margarine, soybean oil, olive oil, peanut oil, corn oil, sunflower oil, safflower oil, canola oil.

Fats with cholesterol: butter, animal fat.

Nutritional Yeast

This nutritional supplement has a pleasant nutty-cheesy flavor and is packed with protein and B vitamins. It comes in flakes or powder and is popular for cheese substitutes, gravies, and many other dishes. Nutritional yeast is very similar to brewer's yeast, which is also used as a nutritional supplement and is made from the same strain of yeast. The difference is that brewer's yeast is a by-product of beer production and retains some of the bitter flavor of hops. Don't confuse nutritional yeast, which is deactivated, with active forms of yeast, like the kinds bakers, brewers, and winemakers use. If you eat them, active yeasts will continue to grow in your intestine, robbing your body of valuable nutrients.

Appendix 3: Acronyms

AC: Alternating current
AIDS: Acquired immunodeficiency syndrome
ASPO: Association for the Study of Peak Oil
AvAlc: Aviation alcohol
AvGas: Aviation gasoline
B-57:   A heavy US bomber aircraft
BCE: Before current era
BTU: British Thermal Unit, a common measure of energy content
CB: Citizens band radio frequency
CD-ROM: Compact disk read-only memory, a data storage medium
CE: Current era (past 2000 years)
CH_3:   Methane
CIA: US Central Intelligence Agency
CO_2:   Carbon dioxide
CPR: Cardio-pulmonary respiration, a resuscitation technique
DC: Direct current
DDT: Dichloro-diphenyl-trichloroethane, an insecticide
DME: Dimethyl ether
DNA: Deoxyribonucleic acid, the genetic code carrier molecule
DVD: Digital video disk
EIA: US Energy Information Agency
EtOH: Ethanol
GEN: Global Ecovillage Network
GMO: Genetically modified organism

GNR: Geno-, nano-, robo- technologies
H_2:   Hydrogen
H_2O: Water
HEPA: High efficiency particle arresting or high efficiency particulate air
HIV: Human immunodeficiency virus
HPDE: High-density polyethylene
IPCC: Intergovernmental Panel on Climate Change
LED: Light emitting diode
LETS: Local exchange trading system
MeOH: Methanol
MISI.   Management Information Services Inc.
MTV: A popular music-oriented television network
NASA: US National Aeronautic and Space Administration
NASCAR: National Association for Stock Car Auto Racing
NBC: Nuclear, biological, and chemical
NCACS: National Coalition of Alternative Community Schools
NVC: Nonviolent communication
OPEC: Organization of Petroleum Exporting Countries
PV: Photovoltaic
RME: Rapeseed methyl ester
RV: Recreation vehicle
SAIC: Science Applications International Corporation
SHARE: Self-Help Association for a Regional Economy
SUV: Sport/utility vehicle
TiVo: A popular brand of digital video recorder
Tu-154:   A heavy Soviet bomber aircraft
VCR: Video color recorder

Index

About the Author

lbert K. Bates is a retired public interest attorney and author of several books on energy, environment, and history. He is a co-founder of the Ecovillage Network of the Americas and the Global Ecovillage Network. During his 26-year career as an attorney, he argued environmental and civil rights cases before the US Supreme Court and drafted a number of legislative acts while publishing Natural Rights, a quarterly newsletter on deep ecology. His books Shutdown: Nuclear Power on Trial (1979) and Climate in Crisis: The Greenhouse Effect and What You Can Do (1990, with foreword by Al Gore) provided early insight into two of the greatest dangers now confronting the world. An inveterate inventor, he holds a number of design patents and was designer of concentrating photovoltaic arrays and solar-hybrid automobiles displayed at the 1982 World's Fair. He has been director of the Global Village Institute for Appropriate Technology since 1984 and of the Ecovillage Training Center at The Farm community in Summertown, Tennessee, since 1994, where he has taught natural building, sustainable agriculture, and appropriate technology to students from more than 50 nations.

Justine Kurkland

If you have enjoyed *The Post-Petroleum Survival Guide and Cookbook*
you might also enjoy other

BOOKS TO BUILD A NEW SOCIETY

Our books provide positive solutions for people who want
to make a difference. We specialize in:

**Environment and Justice • Conscientious Commerce • Sustainable Living
Ecological Design and Planning • Natural Building & Appropriate Technology
New Forestry • Educational and Parenting Resources • Nonviolence
Progressive Leadership • Resistance and Community**

New Society Publishers

ENVIRONMENTAL BENEFITS STATEMENT

New Society Publishers has chosen to produce this book on recycled paper made with
100% post consumer waste, processed chlorine free, and old growth free.

For every 5,000 books printed, New Society saves the following resources:[1]

35	Trees
3,160	Pounds of Solid Waste
3,477	Gallons of Water
4,536	Kilowatt Hours of Electricity
5,745	Pounds of Greenhouse Gases
25	Pounds of HAPs, VOCs, and AOX Combined
9	Cubic Yards of Landfill Space

[1]Environmental benefits are calculated based on research done by the Environmental Defense Fund and
other members of the Paper Task Force who study the environmental impacts of the paper industry.

For a full list of NSP's titles, please call **1-800-567-6772** *or check out our website at:*

www.newsociety.com

NEW SOCIETY PUBLISHERS